THE
J.E.D.I.
LEADER'S
PLAYBOOK

THE
J.E.D.I.
LEADER'S
PLAYBOOK

THE INSIDER'S GUIDE TO ERADICATING INJUSTICES, ELIMINATING INEQUITIES, EXPANDING DIVERSITY, AND ENHANCING INCLUSION

Omar L. Harris

PUBLISHED BY: Intent Books

Copyright© 2023 by Omar Luqmaan-Harris

The J.E.D.I. Leader's Playbook: The Insider's Guide to Eradicating Injustices, Eliminating Inequities, Expanding Diversity, and Enhancing Inclusion.

Omar L. Harris asserts the moral right to be identified as the author of this work.

All rights reserved. No part of this publication may be reproduced, stored, or transmitted in any form or by any means—electronic, mechanical, photocopying, recording, scanning, or otherwise—without written permission from the publisher. It is illegal to copy this book, post it to a website, or distribute it by any other means without permission.

Omar L. Harris has no responsibility for the persistence or accuracy of URLs for external or third-party Internet websites referred to in this publication and does not guarantee that any content on such websites is, or will remain, accurate or appropriate.

Designations used by companies to distinguish their products are often claimed as trademarks. All brand names and product names used in this book and on its cover are trade names, service marks, trademarks, and registered trademarks of their respective owners. The publishers and the book are not associated with any product or vendor mentioned in this book. None of the companies referenced within the book have endorsed the book.

Lucasfilm LTD has neither endorsed nor approved the book or the author.

First published by Intent Books 2023

ISBN: 9798862054576

Library of Congress cataloging-in-publication data is available.

First edition

Cover design: Michael Rehder

Design: Gwen Gades

OTHER PUBLISHED WORKS BY OMAR L. HARRIS

One Blood (under pseudonym Qwantu Amaru)

From Authors to Entrepreneurs (with co-authors Stephanie Casher and James W. Lewis)

Leader Board: The DNA of High-Performance Teams

The Servant Leader's Manifesto

Be a J.E.D.I. Leader Not a Boss: Leadership in the Era of Corporate Social Justice, Equity, Diversity, and Inclusion

Hire the Right W.H.O.M.

Leading Change: The 4 Keys

EPISODE II: THE J.E.D.I. LEADER'S PLAYBOOK

RIGHT HERE AND NOW IN THE MILKY WAY GALAXY...

THE IDEALS OF JUSTICE, EQUITY, DIVERSITY, AND INCLUSION (J.E.D.I.) ARE UNDER SIEGE. A CLIMATE OF RESISTANCE, FUELED BY IGNORANCE AND FEAR, IS SPREADING. EVEN SENIOR EXECUTIVES, ONCE CHAMPIONS OF THE CAUSE, HAVE BECOME DISTANT. THE NARRATIVE IN BOARDROOMS HAS SHIFTED FROM EQUITY TO BUDGET CUTS, LEAVING J.E.D.I. PRACTITIONERS FEELING BELEAGUERED AND BURNED OUT. HOPE IS DWINDLING.

ENTER A GAME-CHANGER: THE J.E.D.I. LEADER'S PLAYBOOK. FAR FROM A MERE GUIDE, THIS PLAYBOOK IS A REVOLUTIONARY TOOLKIT FOR REINVIGORATING FALTERING J.E.D.I. INITIATIVES. DEVELOPED BY VISIONARIES WHO SEE J.E.D.I. AS A CULTURE AND A MOVEMENT, NOT JUST A PROGRAM, THE PLAYBOOK OFFERS TRANSFORMATIVE FRAMEWORKS AND ACTIONABLE INSIGHTS TO EMPOWER EVERYONE, FROM THE ENTRY-LEVEL TO THE C-SUITE, TO BECOME AGENTS OF MEANINGFUL CHANGE.

ADDRESSING THE GAPS IN CONVENTIONAL APPROACHES, THE PLAYBOOK GOES BEYOND SURFACE-LEVEL SOLUTIONS. IT DISARMS SKEPTICS, REKINDLES EXECUTIVE SUPPORT, AND PROVIDES A ROBUST STRATEGY TO COMBAT

BURNOUT. THE PLAYBOOK LAYS OUT A BLUEPRINT FOR SHIFTING THE PARADIGM: FROM RESISTING DARKNESS TO SPREADING ENLIGHTENMENT, FROM CONFLICT TO UNITY.

EQUIPPED WITH THIS PLAYBOOK, A NEW GENERATION OF J.E.D.I. LEADERS EMERGES. THEY'RE NOT JUST THE HEROES IN STORIES, BUT REAL PEOPLE—MARGINALIZED VOICES GAINING PROMINENCE, ALLIES BECOMING CHAMPIONS, EXECUTIVES REDISCOVERING THEIR COMMITMENT TO AN EQUITABLE AND INCLUSIVE CULTURE. THE TIDE IS TURNING; ORGANIZATIONS ARE WAKING UP TO THE IRREFUTABLE IMPACT OF J.E.D.I. LEADERSHIP.

THIS JOURNEY IS FAR FROM OVER, BUT NOW THERE'S A GUIDING LIGHT. THE J.E.D.I. LEADER'S PLAYBOOK IS MORE THAN A RESOURCE; IT'S A BEACON ILLUMINATING THE PATH TO A GALAXY WHERE JUSTICE, EQUITY, DIVERSITY, AND INCLUSION ARE LIVED REALITIES, NOT JUST BUZZWORDS.

SO, THE SAGA CONTINUES, FUELED BY THE PLAYBOOK AND LED BY J.E.D.I. LEADERS WHO KNOW THAT THEY CARRY THE TORCH FOR A NEW DAWN. IN A GALAXY NOT SO FAR AWAY, CHANGE ISN'T JUST A POSSIBILITY; IT'S A GUARANTEE. AND IT STARTS WITH EACH OF US.

Dedicated to those doing *the work*—
yesterday, today, and tomorrow.

"It's not who I am underneath, but what I do, that defines me."
- *Batman Begins*

CONTENTS

OTHER PUBLISHED WORKS BY OMAR L. HARRIS · 5

FOREWORD: BE LIKE DAVID · 17

INTRODUCTION · 21

The "J" Really Matters — 23
Where Is the Progress? — 24
Opposing Forces — 27
Accelerating Advancement — 29
My Story — 30
What's New in this (Play) Book? — 33

PART I: DISCOVERY AND DEFINITION

1

THE *WHY* OF THE J.E.D.I. LEADER · 39

The Code — 39
What's Your J.E.D.I. **Why**? — 40

2

DEFINITIONS AND DATA · 44

Optimist or Pessimist? — 44
Fanatic Discipline — 46
Productive Paranoia — 47
Empirical Creativity — 48
Stakeholder Capitalism — 49
Justice — 54

Equity -- 57
Diversity --- 60
Inclusion --- 63
Unpacking Justice, Equity, Diversity, and Inclusion ---------- 66
A Path to J.E.D.I. Leadership ---------------------------------- 67
Enabling J.E.D.I. Work --- 68

3
KARATE VERSUS JUDO • 71

Karate --- 71
Judo -- 72
Harnessing Momentum -- 79
Understanding, Agreement, and Alignment -------------------- 84

4
THE FOUR ARGUMENTS FOR CHANGE • 87

The Change Curve -- 95
Leading Change --- 97

5
BELIEFS, BIASES, AND BEHAVIORS • 101

The Shadow of the Leader -- 101
Johari's Window --- 102
The Origins of Belief --- 104
Making the Unconscious *Conscious* ------------------------ 105
The Power of Incentives --- 107
Valuing How It Gets Done Versus What Gets Done --------- 108

6
PRINCIPLES, PRIORITIES, PROCESSES, AND PRACTICES • 112

Principles: Leading with Purpose ---------- 113
Priorities: Alignment Between *Why* and *What* ---------- 115
Processes: How Work Gets Done (On Paper) ---------- 116
Practices: What Work Actually Gets Done ---------- 117
Impacting the Four P's ---------- 120

7
ESTABLISHING GOALS, PRIORITIES, AND CAPABILITIES • 124

Wildly Important Goals (WIGs) ---------- 125
Setting Priorities ---------- 130

PART II: DEVELOPMENT AND DELIVERY

8
DRIVING ADOPTION • 137

Another Hat ---------- 137
J.E.D.I. SWOT ---------- 138
Where to Play and How to Win ---------- 143
Selling J.E.D.I. ---------- 153
Measuring Adoption ---------- 156

9
RESTORATION • 159

The J.E.D.I. Restoration System™ ------------------------------ 160

10
RENEWAL • 170

Physical Renewal and the Power of Sleep---------------------- 174
Emotional Renewal and Maintaining Outside Interests --- 177
Mental Renewal and the Impact of Meditation --------------- 178
Spiritual Renewal and Work Life Integration----------------- 180

11
EXTERNALIZING IMPACTS • 183

Maximizing Managerial Effectiveness -------------------------- 185
Representing the Reality of Customers ------------------------ 188
Elevating the Communities Where We Operate -------------- 191
Restoring the Environment--------------------------------------- 197
Achieving the Highest Standards of Internal Governance
200
Harnessing the Toolkit -- 204

PART III: DISCIPLINE AND DETERMINATION

12
KEEPING SCORE • 209

Elements of a Compelling Scoreboard-------------------------- 211

The Cadence of Accountability --------- 217

13
EMBRACING TRADE-OFFS • 220

Paradoxical Thinking --------- 221
Seeking Win-Wins Over Zero-Sums --------- 223
Influence Without Authority --------- 226

14
MAINTAINING MOMENTUM AND COMMITMENT • 231

Expanding Self-Awareness --------- 231
Accelerating Personal Agility --------- 235
Claiming Agency --------- 237

15
SUMMARY • 239

What's Your J.E.D.I Why? --------- 240
Judo Versus Karate --------- 242
Leading Change --------- 244
Three B's and Four P's --------- 247
Establishing Goals, Priorities, and Capabilities --------- 250
Driving Adoption --------- 253
Externalizing Impacts --------- 261
Keeping Score --------- 264
Embracing Trade-Offs --------- 266
Maintaining Momentum and Commitment --------- 268

RESOURCES • 271

ACKNOWLEDGEMENTS • 283

REFERENCES • 286

ABOUT THE AUTHOR • 299

EXCERPT FROM *LEADING CHANGE: THE 4 KEYS* • *301*

FOREWORD: BE LIKE DAVID

**It's the powerful versus the powerless.
It's David versus Goliath.**

It's an uphill battle.

These are descriptions I've heard from fellow DEI practitioners attempting to shift business culture toward enhanced inclusion for all. A general feeling of engagement tinged with hopelessness. The issue with this mindset is that while on one hand it seems to recognize the reality of the situation, it misses the opportunity inherent in the perception of the power gap between those in privilege and those fighting for seats at the table. Yes, David was less physically mighty than Goliath, but he had a few very crucial advantages which led him to volunteer for the challenge in the first place.

In his book of the same name,[1] Malcolm Gladwell turns the tables on how we view the events of that historic day between a gigantic infantry soldier and a shepherd. Goliath, the Philistine's mightiest warrior descended into the ravine—a no-man's land in the stalemate between the Cretan army of battle tested combatants and the encampment of Israelites they meant to conquer—and made his challenge to the other side, shouting, "Choose you a man and let him come down to me! If he prevail in battle against me and strike me down, we shall be slaves to you. But if I prevail and strike him down, you will be slaves to us and serve us."[2]

David was a shepherd boy who had brought food to the Israelite soldiers and heard the call to action. When no one else stepped forward, David, who claimed to have overcome more challenging opponents than the likes of the 6 ft. 9 giant, stepped forward with his speed, guile, and deadly slingshot to defend his people. Goliath expected single hand-to-hand combat, but David had no such plans. He could tell by the fact that Goliath had to be escorted by a consort into the ravine that his opponent's vision was impaired, that his lumbering size made him slow, and that David had the element of surprise: his trusty slingshot.

Goliath was thus completely unprepared for David's approach to the challenge before him. David ran toward him, swinging and then releasing his projectile with enough force at that distance to penetrate Goliath's skull and kill him. Had he missed, the tables might have turned; but he didn't, and the rest is history.

So, it's time for us to be like David. Be like David in his courage. Be like David in his belief and self-assurance. Be like David in his strategic acumen and unique skillset.

Be Like David

J.E.D.I. leaders are not as powerless and/or outmatched as we may seem based on the outsized task of carrying transformation like David holding his rocks. If we were, there would really be no point of writing yet another book on this subject and further saturating the literary landscape. So, at the outset of this book, let's lay down our skepticism and imagine the possibility that we already have everything we need to make the change happen. And on top of that, we have the extreme benefit of being on the side of doing what's right for others—which creates an inertia unlike any other force.

This playbook is designed to remind us of the power and distinct advantages we possess as practitioners operating in this space. We are far from overwhelmed. We are primed for success, and we have the might of right on our side. Please keep that in mind every day as you're doing the good work and progressing through this resource.

Now, let's get started!

INTRODUCTION

Search on LinkedIn for Diversity, Equity, and Inclusion functions, google DEI, or look up the term on Amazon books and what you will find is something physicist Brian Nord dubbed as "the equity-diversity-inclusion industrial complex."[3] What he means by this term is that both prior to and after the murder of George Floyd in 2020, the demand for action led to a widespread search for expertise to lead in the moment. But the intention and the effort that ensued was as misplaced as calling the fire department after a house has already burned to the ground. This is partly due to the litany of progressive and unchecked injustices done to disenfranchised people, from the brave women who instigated the #metoo movement to the courageous organization of Black Lives Matter[4,5]—and, soon after, the killings that sparked the spirited initiation of the #stopAsianhate protests.[6]

These calls for corporate action were so reactive as to be rendered nearly futile.

Still, necessity is the mother of invention, and great innovation springs forth from constraints. A litany of diversity, equity, and inclusion professionals and experts began to spring forth from every corner of society to fulfill the burgeoning demand. Despite the broad-based pledges of action and clear need for change, these professionals soon found themselves restricted to the box of delivering rah-rah speeches, training on unconscious biases, and forming and facilitating employee resource groups or ERGs. Not to say that this work isn't important, but to continue our burned-down house analogy: the significantly restricted space for diversity, equity, and inclusion work in the public and private sector is akin to the dirt spread over the site of a fire so that the rebuilding can begin.

Unlike other established functions, such as human resources, marketing, finance, and legal, there was no universal playbook—or even a standard job description for diversity, equity, and inclusion professionals to occupy. This is because this nuanced and often complicated function requires significant breadth and depth seldom seen in typical subject matter expertise roles. Which other functions require not only expert vision and strategy-setting, risk assessment and management ability, change management chops, and internal and external communications talent; but also surveying and analysis, market research, technological acumen, project and visual performance management, tactical plan-building skill, public relations expertise, training and facilitation, and more? Hence the lack of clarity regarding even the name of the position. Is it DEI, DEIB, DEIJ, D&I, DIB, or some other combination of the term's diversity, equity, inclusion, belonging, and justice?

The fact is that functional expertise must be related to clear outcomes. In marketing, the desired outcome of the function is brand loyalty; in finance, the required result is leveraged profitability; and in human resources, the job centers on productivity per capita. When we cannot even agree on the basic outcomes we expect of diversity, equity, and inclusion professionals (as demonstrated by the alphabet soup of our acronyms), how can we possibly do the necessary work we've been employed to do?

That's why this book exists—to codify the why, how, and what of this work so that *anyone* reading these pages possesses the clarity as well as the toolbox to impact change. As Patrick Lencioni writes in *The Four Obsessions of An Extraordinary Executive*,[7] "clarity is not merely about choosing the right words to describe a company's mission, strategy, or values; it is about agreeing on the fundamental concepts that drive it." So, for clarity's sake, embracing J.E.D.I. as the functional acronym, the why, and the desired output of the work allows us to understand, agree on, and align on how we must proceed moving forward.

The "J" Really Matters

In the months since I published *Be a J.E.D.I. Leader, Not a Boss: Leadership in the Era of Corporate Social Justice, Equity, Diversity, and Inclusion*,[8] the question I've received more than any other is, "Why the 'J?'"—as in, "What does Justice have to do with diversity, equity, and inclusion (DEI) work?" The answer is quite straightforward. If an organization has effectively addressed the concerns linked to DEI, all this good progress can be undermined and/or derailed by persistent injustices within the culture. Which leads us to defining exactly what justice is as it relates to an organization.

Justice fundamentally relates to enforcement of the values an entity deems crucial. When people, practices, and/or priorities are allowed to persistently violate the covenant of an organization's principles, then those values inevitably collapse. Justice is the security blanket—as well as the clearly marked boundary—that lets everyone know that within a given organization, what we believe, say, and do is highly congruent. Justice is having and adhering to a disciplinary matrix that applies to everyone operating in the system in a measure proportionate to their potential violations. Justice maintains order and trust in the operation as a whole; it's what solidifies and makes all the lofty values talk concrete.

Only once an organization has learned to defend its stated values can it begin to consider externalizing these principles beyond its walls. If Patagonia, for instance, pays for *sexual harassment insurance* for misbehaving executives versus systematically eliminating these bad actors from the company,[9] no amount of social or environmental justice measures will matter. The employees will know that Patagonia doesn't care for their safety—and once employees check out, how can a company deliver on their goals and commitments? Safety comes from a collective acknowledgement of shared boundaries without exception. Too often, the rules that apply to lesser-paid employees are completely ignored and disregarded by their higher-paid counterparts.

DEI without the enforcement of Justice is a house of cards waiting for a strong wind to collapse all the good will, good work, and good intentions of the organization. If a company cannot enforce its own rules and regulations, how can it be expected to stick to long-term commitments related to social justice issues? Ignore or diminish the justice component at your own peril.

Where Is the Progress?

It is because of this lack of justice work that, despite the best intentions of many organizations, true progress has been slow to come by. In my previous book— published in June 2021—there were only three Black Fortune 500 CEOs. As of this writing (in October 2023), *there are now eight,*[10] which is a new high. Still, not a cause for celebration.

According to the *2023 Women CEOs in America report,*[11]

since May 2022, "For the first time, women lead over 10% of Fortune 500 companies. The S&P 500 went from thirty-two women last year to forty-one in 2023, an increase of 30%. The Russell 3000 showed an especially encouraging increase in women CEOs, going from 186 in 2022 to 204 in the first half of 2023, an increase of 18 or 9.68%. For private companies with revenues over $1 billion dollars, there are 79 women CEOs."

The pandemic brought greater visibility to the concept of living wages and the CEO pay ratio, or the amount CEOs make versus their lowest paid employees. *Just Capital* states that "the top priority for companies should be to pay their workers a fair, living wage—covering local needs for food, housing, and medical care, and adjusting for cost-of-living increases."[12] As tracked by *AFLCIO*,[13] the average S&P 500 company's CEO-to-worker pay ratio was 272-to-1 (down from 324-to-1) in 2022. This is an area of persistent injustice because, as AFLCIO states, "company pay ratio data is important. It shows which companies are investing in their workforce to create high-wage jobs."

The *gender pay gap persists*,[14] with women still bringing home just $89 for each $100 that men do. The only win in this space is the rise of *pay equity audits*,[15] which many companies have or are undergoing in order to address this issue. Unfortunately, addressing it means acknowledging that there are important gender differences and choices that contribute to this area of continued inequity—and that means there are no silver bullet solutions. Many women take on more burden outside of work, accept less overtime, and have less flexibility to work weekends than their male counterparts. Understanding, empathy, and structure are as important to solving this situation as audits and raises.

The Great Resignation has given rise to ***Quiet Quitting*** in the months and years since the pandemic upended our lives.[16,17] Nearly forty-three million American workers voluntarily quit their jobs between January 2021 and April 2022. Fifty percent of the US workforce is considering quitting their jobs,[18] there is significant labor market demand for workers, and there is a war of attrition between employers and employees as offices begin to reopen and expectations for in-person interactions increase. This disconnect between executive desires and employee demands is leading to one of *the largest sustained productivity downturns in recent memory.*[19] Attempts to expand diversity amidst such headwinds is akin to spitting in the wind.

Employee Resource Groups (ERGs) are status quo in many leading companies,[20] but inclusion initiatives are not moving the needle. ERGs and affinity groups have been around for decades and have shifted through many forms and norms; but because they are mostly volunteer driven, underfunded, and not prioritized by senior leaders, their efforts to enhance inclusion and belonging are being beaten back by other organizational pressures. How can a celebration for Indian Independence, for example, take precedent over organizational fallout from a poor second quarter?

Slow-moving statistics such as these can lead to a degree of disillusionment— but that is because of over-emphasis on lag measures of improvement. A lag measure is the ultimate outcome expected of an initiative, such as a new house build completion. If we look instead at lead measures of improvement, there has been notable progress in a few key areas. Lead measures would focus our attention on key metrics that indicate that the house build is advancing as per plan, such as hours worked per day on the house build, material orders delivered on time, and number of inspection incidents uncovered.

The 2022 Racial Equity Tracker tracks such lead measures across six specific dimensions of racial equity:[21]

- Antidiscrimination Policies
- Pay Equity
- Racial/Ethnic Diversity Data
- Education and Training Programs
- Response to Mass Incarceration
- Community Investments

The latest report states: "Because 92 percent of Americans overall (up from 79 percent last year) and 95 percent of Black Americans believe it is important for companies to promote racial diversity and equity in the workplace, the demand for action on corporate commitments has only increased—especially considering that 68 percent of Americans, and 87 percent of Black Americans, agree companies have more work to do." Thus, there has been marginal progress in workforce diversity data disclosure, board diversity data disclosure, racial/ethnic pay equity analysis disclosure, and disclosure of pay ratios by race/ethnicity. Without disclosure, there can be no effective analysis and benchmarking which would create the momentum to set targets and achieve them.

Opposing Forces

Since the watershed events of 2020, there has been a growing backlash against so-called antiracist movements in the US. The opposition has come in the forms of legal, political, and even parental blowback to efforts to increase diversity and inclusion in America. Books have been banned, courses that instruct on critical race theory at the university level have been defunded, and the Supreme Court has abolished gains from women's rights and affirmative action dating back to the 1960s. It is truly a polarizing time to be engaged in the work of advocating for systemic change.

As it relates to this current state of affairs, Ibram X. Kendi, author of *How to Be an Antiracist*,[22] said: "The momentum was just crushed by a pretty well-organized force and movement of people who are seeking to conserve racism. Who've tried to change the problem from racism to antiracism. And who've tried to change the problem from police violence to the people speaking out against police violence."[23]

This was always to be expected. The science of change management dictates that any needed transformation will be met with denial and anger. The objective of those leading change must be to anticipate and meet the past-based thinking, negative inertia, skepticism, and pessimism with the concerted force of momentum, optimism, and excitement fueled by a vision of the future where everyone benefits from progress.

The Change Curve

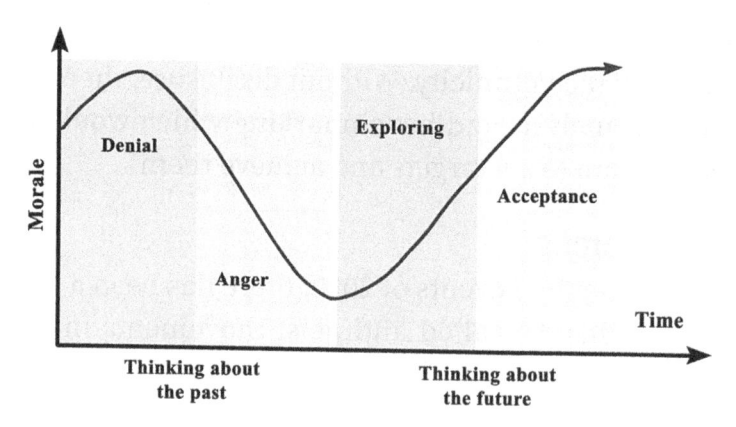

Morale (y-axis) vs *Time* (x-axis)

Denial — Anger — Exploring — Acceptance

Thinking about the past | Thinking about the future

What we have been missing is a shared collective approach to this momentous change that all practitioners buy in to and have a stake in making a reality. If we continue to go at this as lone wolves with similar but not equal approaches, we will continue to suffer stops and starts—which is why a big part of this work has to contemplate coalition building in addition to change leadership.

Accelerating Advancement

Understanding the current state is essential to effectively designing a desired state of justice, equity, diversity, and inclusion in our organizations. The intent of this book is to provide the tools to conduct a successful organizational self-assessment across a variety of dimensions, prioritize areas for improvement, develop necessary capabilities, and track and communicate implementation progress to key stakeholders. Importantly, this is not a book (just) for DEI professionals. In fact, this is not a DEI book at all. This is about the modernization of leadership in order to achieve *the lofty goals of stakeholder capitalism* issued by the companies of The Business Roundtable back in 2019.[24]

Those goals were for companies to make a shift away from *shareholder* capitalism, which is the pursuit of profitability as the central corporate goal, and toward *stakeholder* capitalism, which is all about providing more outcomes for more stakeholders—employees, customers, communities, the environment, and shareholders. In this regard, the very essence of how companies are being led must be reengineered. Hierarchies must be inverted. Bossdom must be condemned. Employee experience must be prioritized.

Stakeholder capitalism must live in the heart of every person connected to the mission of the organization. This only happens when leadership from the top to bottom is aligned on why this shift must happen now, how this needed change will be achieved and sustained, and what practically will be different from before. That's why *every leader* needs to become a J.E.D.I. leader—a leader who advances the causes of stakeholder capitalism by influencing positive employee experience first, in order to manifest the desired outcomes for the other stakeholders.

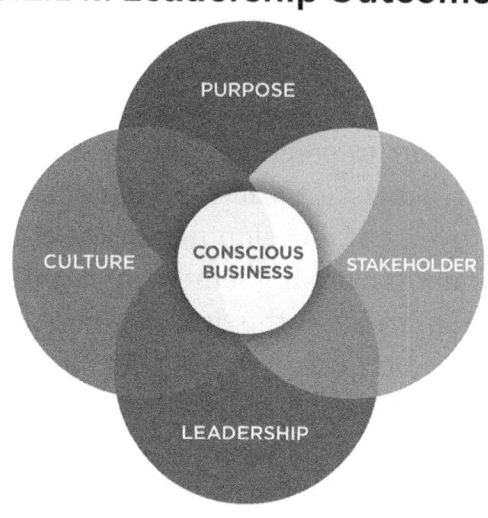

J.E.D.I. Leadership Outcomes

Diagram: Four overlapping circles labeled PURPOSE, CULTURE, STAKEHOLDER, and LEADERSHIP, with CONSCIOUS BUSINESS at the center.

When we modernize leadership, we create the truly elevated outcomes of belonging, esteem, altruism, and abundance.

My Story

I am not an academician or a theoretician. My education (and passion and expertise) stem directly from working in some of the largest pharmaceutical companies in the world over twenty-plus years, on four continents, and as one of the few Black professionals in my field, industry, and level. My focus during my career was elevating alignment to organizational purpose by enhancing conditions for those in my employ. Early on, I knew that there had to be a better way to achieve financial goals than adhering to an outdated corporate hierarchy that created a pervading sense of scarcity of opportunity, development, and agency due to the toxicity inherent in a model designed to serve executives' whims—often at the expense of employee needs.

By embracing servant leadership principles and positive psychology as my principal tools, I was able to carve a path of success built on the empowerment, enablement, and support of those doing the work. But I knew I needed to amplify the message to like-minded leaders seeking a better way to lead in modern times, so I wrote and published *Leader Board: The DNA of High-Performance Teams* and *The Servant Leader's Manifesto* in 2019 and 2020.[25,26]

Then George Floyd was murdered by a police officer in Minneapolis, and everything changed.

The call to action was unambiguous, and the platform was ablaze. Still, what I was seeing in the wake of this unique moment was nearly exclusively performative (ala inspirational speeches), misapplied (unconscious bias training), or vindictive (shaming white male executives as racists). As DEI strategist and consultant Lily Zheng states in a 2022 ***Harvard Business Review article:***[27] "the actual efficacy of an uncomfortably large proportion of our 'flagship' services, talking points, and interventions—unconscious bias training, racial sensitivity workshops, the 'business case for diversity,' résumé anonymization, and the like—is lower than many practitioners make it out to be."

Having worked in the corporate sphere for so long and led change initiatives of significant port around the world, I had acquired the tools to move these Titanic-esque enterprises into the future. I knew I needed to provide those tools broadly to my colleagues seeking to do the same as it related to eradicating injustices, eliminating inequities, expanding diversity, and enhancing inclusion.

In order to more fully connect the why of our work, I linked the thesis of Be a J.E.D.I. Leader, Not a Boss: Leadership in the Era of Corporate Social Justice, Equity, Diversity, and Inclusion to providing the keys to delivering on the *promise of stakeholder capitalism*[28]—something nearly two hundred top CEOs agreed was necessary for corporations to embrace. Going beyond a business case, this book positioned J.E.D.I. action as equally essential as environmental social governance (ESG), compliance, digital transformation, and corporate social responsibility (CSR) have become to modern business operations.

Since publishing Be a J.E.D.I. Leader, Not a Boss in June 2021, I have been in the trenches working side by side with fellow practitioners as we collectively push these boulders up steep hills. I've experienced significant successes with the approaches outlined in this playbook, but most of these highs came with the cost of a rigorous (and, at times, torturous) learning curve. My goal has never been to reinvent the wheel, but to take established and proven insider practices and simply apply them to new circumstances, fail fast, iterate, and scale. Along the journey, I have learned a lot of what works, what doesn't, and what's next in this crusade for a better world.

That's why I am in this fight. To empower every manager, senior leader, DEI worker, and executive with the tools to modernize business so that we can deliver on this significant value of providing more benefits for more stakeholders: employees, customers, communities, the environment, and shareholders. This book and the work that I do in this space are unique, not only because of my insider's vantage point of having operated as a VP-level executive in corporations around the world, or because of my specific expertise in servant leadership and positive psychology, but also because it is driven by proven strategies to deliver on change initiatives of which J.E.D.I. may be the most crucial of our time.

What's New in this (Play) Book?

A playbook is a framework for action. It is a document with clarity at its very essence. But it also contains proprietary, codified information on exactly how an entity plans to achieve success. This content is detailed in the format of plays, or sequences of coordinated effort, that are specifically designed to achieve desired outcomes.

Taking a page from design thinking, the sections in this playbook are allocated to provide practical tools necessary to doing this important work of embedding justice, equity, diversity, and inclusion into the DNA of our teams, divisions, functions, and organizations.

The J.E.D.I. Leader's Playbook

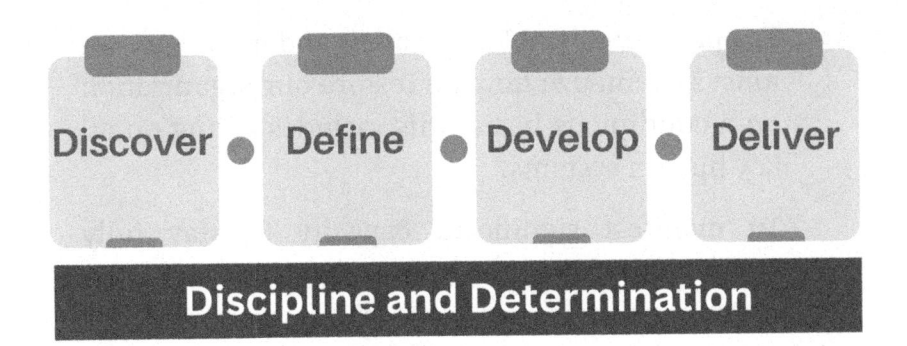

Discover • Define • Develop • Deliver

Discipline and Determination

Part I: Discovery and Definition

- Rather than beginning with company mission, we start with the Why of the J.E.D.I. Leader, as it is clarity in the why that will drive the how and what of the job.

- Before we get into setting goals, we must increase our awareness of key definitions and data, decide whether to employ karate or judo in our efforts to influence, calibrate the four arguments for change, examine beliefs, biases, and behaviors and the incentives that drive them, and delve into our organization's principles, priorities, processes, and practices to identify problems that need to be addressed.

- Next, we clarify our goals and key priorities that will allow us to complete our design.

Part II: Development and Delivery

- Long before we get into training on diversity, equity, and inclusion concepts, we must contemplate our strategy and design experiences that will shift our culture from limited awareness to broad-based adoption.

- To operationalize J.E.D.I. efforts and initiatives, we must systematize how we restore our organization on a continuous basis—this includes acting on all key human systems.

- To manifest significant capacity to stay fully committed and connected to our missions, we must learn strategies to continuously renew our energy stores.

- Instead of only contemplating community engagement, we seek to externalize for the benefit of employees, customers, communities, the environment, and shareholders.

Part III: Discipline and Determination

- Delivery is not the endgame for internal and external stakeholders; it is merely the beginning of a cycle of measurement, problem solving, and continuous improvement all collected on a compelling scoreboard.

- The path to progress is mired with potholes and barriers. This is where possessing the power of trade-offs in the form of paradoxical thinking, win-win solutions, and leveraging influence without authority can be essential.

- In addition to regular renewal, we must also maintain our momentum and commitment to our purpose by remaining continuously inspired through increasing our self-awareness, accelerating personal agility, and claiming our agency.

This playbook is chock full of leading edge thinking and resources but also can serve as a jumping off point for collective reflection, data gathering, and debate about the appropriate course of action for your business situation. Just as every company had to make the painful shift into a digital economy, so shall every company have to embrace this crucial work. The ground of the old business model is quickly crumbling underneath us, and we are facing a crisis of shift or perish.

Shift or Perish

But shifting doesn't have to be completely painful, and this playbook aims to illustrate a process that anyone in any entity can begin undertaking to move to safer more sustainable ground.

With that said—let's discover the *why* of the J.E.D.I. Leader.

PART I: DISCOVERY AND DEFINITION

1

THE *WHY* OF THE J.E.D.I. LEADER

The Code

J.E.D.I. leaders live by a certain code. Much like the Knights of the Round Table of Arthurian legend concerned themselves with maintaining order, justice, and civility, so must J.E.D.I. leaders work diligently to serve and support their employees, customers, communities, environment, and shareholders. It is an honor and a tremendous burden to take on this mantle, because J.E.D.I. leaders cannot ignore inequity, incivility, inconsideration, instability, and/or injustice in their midst. It is their obligation to stand up and be the consistent voice of the people and positive change, even if it is unpopular or unrequested.

Modern-Day Knights

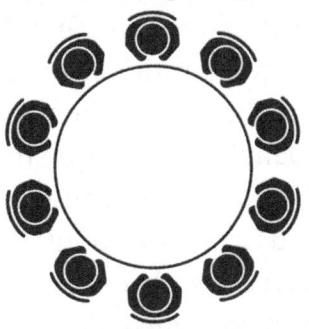

Just like in any superhero movie, once fantastic new powers are discovered, they must be developed, and then ultimately applied for the good of the people. Along the way, hard lessons are learned, difficult choices are made, and values are cemented. Not that J.E.D.I. leaders have a hero complex. On the contrary, their duty to serve stems from a deep understanding and respect for the position of leadership and the implications of its negative application on others. Because of this, there is a consistent commitment to wield the force of J.E.D.I. leadership always in service of removing barriers to productivity and progress.

What's Your J.E.D.I. *Why*?

It is difficult to sustain the efforts necessary to truly impact an organization's culture without a clear J.E.D.I. *why*. Answering this question for ourselves requires us to consider the benefits of eradicating injustices, eliminating inequities, expanding diversity, and enhancing inclusion on a personal level. What do we stand to gain by operating in a system where the rules and boundaries apply to everyone and are equally reinforced, where policies and practices ensure equitable treatment across the board, where we get to work with the best and brightest and most diverse people, and where we feel a sense of belonging and know that our voice matters to the ongoing success of our company? What do we stand to lose by being an advocate for this type of culture?

Remember, this is about a culture that will enable the proliferation of more benefits for more stakeholders. As such, each of us must move away from the archaic idea of shareholder capitalism and the toxic fallout of this system in favor of the far more progressive idea of improving outcomes for employees, customers, communities, and the environment. Leaning into one or more of these stakeholder groups can be a gateway for mindset transformation.

- To be a true employee experience advocate means our why is linked to internal improvements and restoration across the J.E.D.I. spectrum.

- To be inspired by customer excellence is to understand that the better we treat our employees, the better they can deliver for this crucial stakeholder.

- If community improvement and sustainability is our passion, then having employees with the capacity and willingness for social responsibility is the key lever.

- If environmental regeneration is important to us, then having strong balance between principles, priorities, processes, and practices—all of which require enhanced understanding, agreement, and alignment across our organizations—is fundamental.

Basically, people are at the center of this needed change. As modern leaders who lead with empathy, will, and humility versus power-based ego, we can find our why in the everyday needs, concerns, motivations, and development of those in our employ. Our J.E.D.I. why manifests the inspiration, capacity, and resilience we need to show up and restore conditions across the spectrum of justice, equity, diversity, and inclusion for our people first—and then for the organization as a whole, and eventually for those key external stakeholders without whom there can be no business.

For many people engaged in this work, it comes down to a desire to fight, to declare that not only are we not racists, sexists, heterosexists, classists, ageists, or ableists—which are the ambiguous, passive, wishy-washy, and finger pointing excuses given by those who don't want to be judged—we are actively anti. To be anti (against racism, sexism, heterosexism, classism, ageism, and ableism) is to leverage our principles, activism, resilience, and accountability in the fight against these injustices. For many (if not most) of us in this space, we are toiling day after day to convert those in the not camp into the anti-camp; but this playbook is going to introduce a new way of thinking.

Anti Versus Not

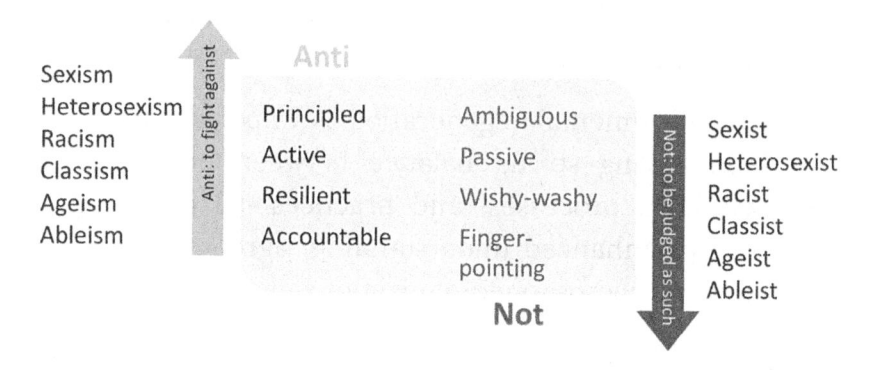

	Anti		
Sexism	Principled	Ambiguous	Sexist
Heterosexism	Active	Passive	Heterosexist
Racism	Resilient	Wishy-washy	Racist
Classism	Accountable	Finger-pointing	Classist
Ageism			Ageist
Ableism			Ableist
		Not	

(Left arrow: Anti: to fight against. Right arrow: Not: to be judged as such)

The simple fact is, there are major issues inherent in the anti approach to our work. The moment we declare ourselves anti, we create a line in the sand opposite many of the very stakeholders we need to embrace our causes. These individuals may not possess the fire in the belly and/or the rationale for supporting these causes that we do. We need to help others help themselves by offering something they can get behind. Something to be for, not against.

This playbook advocates for J.E.D.I. leaders to shift our emphasis from being *against* (racism, sexism, heterosexism, classism, ageism, and ableism) to being *for* fairness, opportunity, innovation, and productivity. When we work for a higher purpose that most people can accept, we inspire, empower, enable, and sustain our work. This pivot is not stating that anti is inherently wrong or bad. It is merely stating that anti is limiting, and we instead need to be as expansive and inclusive as possible to see our missions through.

For Versus Anti

	For		
Fairness	Inspired	Principled	Sexism
Opportunity	Empowering	Active	Heterosexism
Innovation	Enabling	Resilient	Racism
Productivity	Sustainable	Accountable	Classism
			Ageism
			Ableism

For: to embrace a cause
Anti: to fight against
Anti

Once we turn this corner, we can begin to reframe J.E.D.I. as such:

- **Justice:** ensuring fairness and consistency.
- **Equity:** providing opportunity for fuller participation.
- **Diversity:** transforming difference into innovation.
- **Inclusion:** being engagement- and productivity-focused.

These are whys that move the needle—not just for the advocates, allies, and activists among us, but for everyone. And when everyone embraces our why, the work can progress at pace.

Now that we better understand the *why* of J.E.D.I. leadership, it's time to align on some key definitions and data that support the work.

2

DEFINITIONS AND DATA

It is essential that when we discuss eradicating injustices, eliminating inequities, expanding diversity, and enhancing inclusion that we have an aligned basis for this discourse. This chapter will serve as the foundation for the rest of the book. This data and these definitions may shift over time—but let us meet this information with the intention for which it was included: to establish a common language and understanding for the work to come.

Optimist or Pessimist?

Right off the top of this playbook, it is important to assess our mental state related to this struggle for greater justice, equity, diversity, and inclusion. Some of us approach the struggle as optimists, while others are naturally more pessimistic. Why does this matter? Because to be glass half-full or half-empty is fundamentally a choice, and choosing optimism is crucial to the success of our endeavors.

Optimists believe that their actions make a difference in defining outcomes, whereas pessimists believe they have little to no control over their fate. When an optimist is confronted by adversity, they acknowledge it—"a thing happened"—without judging it. They calibrate their belief by stating, "It is possible to overcome/improve/move forward from this thing that happened." And they believe the consequence of the event is that everything will turn out fine in the end and they will learn and grow from it. Pessimists place a negative judgment on the adversity—"a *bad* thing happened." They follow this judgment up with a belief that nothing they do will have any impact on this bad thing that happened. Therefore, the consequence of this judgment and belief is that they feel sure more bad things will keep happening, so they had better just accept it.

This approach is known as the ABCs, which stands for *adversity, belief, and consequences*. Adversity is ever-present; automatically judging it as negative begins to manifest a destiny of crippling pessimism. What we believe and tell ourselves about adversity is crucial; it can be an obstacle to be overcome or a soul-crushing barrier. Finally, in terms of consequences—acting or remaining passive both create destinies. When we maintain a growth mindset regardless of what happens, we learn and develop far faster than when we simply accept fate.

The ABCs of Optimism

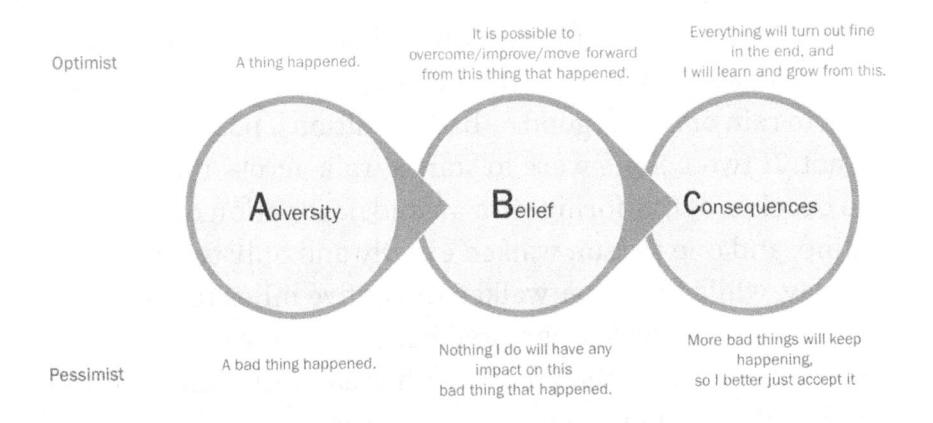

	Adversity	**B**elief	**C**onsequences
Optimist	A thing happened.	It is possible to overcome/improve/move forward from this thing that happened.	Everything will turn out fine in the end, and I will learn and grow from this.
Pessimist	A bad thing happened.	Nothing I do will have any impact on this bad thing that happened.	More bad things will keep happening, so I better just accept it

We start at this juncture because much of the current data can be interpreted as bad, leading us to believe that progress is impossible and that things will never change. If you purchased this book, it is because you are dedicated to making positive change happen. No matter how bleak the data, we never lose faith in our collective ability to overcome, improve, move forward, and advance.

One of my favorite optimistic resources is *Great by Choice: Uncertainty, Chaos, and Luck—Why Some Thrive Despite Them All*,[29] by Jim Collins and Morten T. Hansen. The model conveyed in the book plus the outcomes evidenced by the approach can be quite informative to our work as J.E.D.I. leaders. Proactivity, positivity, and optimism combine in a rubric which starts with Level 5 Ambition—or a big, hairy, audacious goal (BHAG). Eradicating injustices, eliminating inequities, expanding diversity, and enhancing inclusion within a two-to-three-year time frame is such a BHAG. Achieving Level 5 Ambition requires Fanatic Discipline, Productive Paranoia, and Empirical Creativity.

Fanatic Discipline

The example used in the book is called "twenty-mile marching."[30] This is the idea of setting a progress milestone that you stick to rain or shine, good or bad conditions, positive outlook or not. If two people were to start a walk across the US from the beaches of California with an end destination of the tip of Maine, and one person walked exactly and only twenty miles per day, while the other walked thirty-five miles the first day, rested for a day, and progressed based on their mood and external conditions— the person with greater discipline gets to their destination far quicker. It isn't even close.

This informs our J.E.D.I. work, because often setting clear goals and gaining broad-based alignment can be the most difficult part of the job. Holding executives' feet to the fire for outcomes is a tremendous challenge—but until we know where we are going, it is impossible to structure our march. Dr. Martin Luther King demonstrated this on *the second (successful) march* to Selma.[31] With the goal in mind, he and his supporters did not stop until the goal they had visualized was realized—despite significant adversity.

This is where the lead and lag measures approach can be extremely helpful. When we set lead measures, we acquire far greater control over our ability to navigate toward desired outcomes. If we focus on a justice goal such as increasing living wages for all employees, it may be much harder to see the forest for the trees, much less stay on our path. If we break the living wages goal down into lead measures, such as analyzing executive pay ratio by the end of Q1, conducting focus groups with a representative cross section of employees by end of Q2, identifying financial impact and productivity increase required to justify wage and benefits increases by end of Q3, and presenting findings to key stakeholders by end of Q4, our march will be far more successful—and visible to everyone.

Productive Paranoia[32]

It's easy to be paranoid and anxious in periods of extreme difficulty. It is far more productive to be paranoid when seas are calm. In this way—the most effective individuals and organizations never stop asking the question—are we proactively identifying and addressing risks before they overcome us? It is this process of anticipating and building contingencies that keeps the most successful of us going when others get stopped in their tracks because they didn't consider what could go wrong. As J.E.D.I. practitioners, we do not have this luxury; our mission is too crucial.

The book recommends writing and continually updating a "kill list" outlining all the things that could derail progress, from internally generated friendly fire to external possibilities. This is what the National Security Council was doing when it crafted the *pandemic playbook* back in December 2016[33]—taking stock of all the available information and compiling a step-by-step action plan that future administrations could simply dust off and activate in the event of such an emergency. That the next administration didn't use it at all is an indictment of the leaders of that time. It would have saved tremendous time and effort that went into reinventing what had already been crafted.

When I speak to organizations and DEI leaders, productive paranoia is often alive and well. It just takes the form of intense pessimism and lack of will to act because of the factors outlined in the kill list. My job is often to put this resource in the appropriate context and encourage leaders to take the next step, which is "Okay, these barriers exist; what now? How do we build contingency plans for each of these what-if scenarios? Is each of them equally likely? How can we better prioritize this list? In this way, we move away from doom and gloom to ensure we have a plan of action if such adversity occurs. Knowing you have a backup plan goes a long way in keeping efforts alive.

Empirical Creativity[34]

With clarity of goals and contingencies comes the opportunity for creativity. But there is a right way and a wrong way to approach ideation. The right way is an evidence-based agile method to innovate. The wrong way is to take huge swings that exhaust resources and the will to continue.

With the example of two pirate ships doing battle, the book illustrates the concept of empirical (or evidence-based) creativity with an idea called "bullets, then cannonballs."[35] The captain of one ship goes to his heaviest artillery and begins blasting cannon balls at his enemy—all of which land in the ocean. The other captain, however, goes to the deck of his ship and, equipped with a handgun, shoots arching bullets at the other ship until he hits it consistently. He then communicates the trajectory to his cannon team, who in turn fire a succession of artillery right on target, sinking their opposition's ship.

Much of J.E.D.I. work in the corporate sphere feels new, and each company therefore tries to invent and reinvent the best way to tackle the challenges inherent in this effort. However, there are tons of empirical examples of effective change initiatives that can be applied far more precisely than the broad swings (and misses) many companies are attempting. Digital transformation is one area rife with replicable examples. Compliance is another, and environmental and social governance are yet others.

Rather than shoot cannon balls, most of which will miss the target, starting and building on success in other areas where change has taken root in the organization can provide a blueprint that can be washed, rinsed, and repeated for J.E.D.I. work. And, as quick wins are especially critical in our sphere, why not emulate what's working?

Stakeholder Capitalism

In 2019, a collection of some of the top US companies known as The Business Roundtable met and agreed to update the purpose of corporations. They had previously met in 1997 to define shareholder capitalism, or the idea that corporations primarily existed to increase profits for shareholders. In the intervening years, trends related to digitization, greater social and environmental awareness, calls for transparency, and better consumer protections led to the reevaluation of this purpose statement.

The shared statement reads, "While each of our individual companies serves its own corporate purpose, we share a fundamental commitment to all of our stakeholders."[36] We commit to:

- **Customer Value:** We're here to uphold the legacy of American companies by always striving to exceed customer expectations and delivering unmatched value.

- **Employee Investment:** Our employees are our foundation. We not only offer fair compensation and vital benefits but also invest in their ongoing development through robust training and education. We champion a diverse, inclusive, and respectful environment where every individual is valued.

- **Ethical Supplier Relations:** It's crucial to be ethical and fair partners to all our contributing companies, whether big or small. We are committed to working cooperatively to achieve our shared goals.

- **Community Support:** Our communities are our homes. We honor and respect the individuals within them and are committed to sustainable practices to protect our environment and enrich our communities.

- **Shareholder Value:** We are devoted to creating enduring value for our shareholders, acknowledging their vital role in providing the capital that fuels our growth, innovation, and investment. Transparency and active engagement with our shareholders are key to our mutual success.

In the wake of their announcement, entities such as *Just Capital* and *PolicyLink,* to name a few, decided to measure companies' alignment to these stakeholders. Just Capital creates and regularly revises a ranking system which can be leveraged as a sort of measuring stick for the modern enterprise. In their *latest ranking:*[37]

- Workers are weighted 39 percent, and the primary issues being measured (in order of importance) are the degree to which companies pay a fair living wage, protect worker health and safety, provide benefits and work-life balance, cultivate a diverse, inclusive workplace, and invest in workforce training. The 2021 top five companies for workers based on these criteria are Nvidia Corp, Salesforce.com Inc., Biogen Inc., Goldman Sachs Group Inc., and Cisco Systems Inc.

- Communities are weighted 20 percent, and the main issues are the degree to which companies create jobs in the US, respect human rights in the supply chain, contribute to community development, and give back to local communities. The 2021 top five companies doing good community work are Bank of America Corporation, PepsiCo Inc., Alphabet Inc., Amazon.com Inc., and The Walt Disney Company.

- Shareholders are weighted 19 percent, and the focus areas are the degree to which companies prioritize accountability to all stakeholders, act ethically at the leadership level, and generate returns for investors. The 2021 top five companies with this stakeholder focus are Intel Corp, Newmont Corporation, AT&T Inc., Altria Group Inc., and PayPal Holdings Inc.

- Customers are weighted 11 percent, and the targeted areas are the degree to which companies protect customer privacy, treat customers fairly, communicate transparently, and make beneficial products. The 2021 top five companies focused on customers are HP Inc., Adobe Inc., Intel Corp, Apple Inc., and Best Buy Co. Inc.

- Environment is weighted 10 percent, and the principal analysis focused on the degree to which companies develop and support sustainable products, minimize pollution, help combat climate change, and use resources efficiently. The 2021 top five companies linked to environmental progress are VMware Inc., Microsoft Corporation, Intuit Inc., Apple Inc., and Moody's Corp.

It is interesting that the only company to show up in the top five in multiple stakeholder categories is Apple—in both the customer and environmental groups. What this tells us is that every company has significant work to do across multiple stakeholder groups, that companies can learn from each other, and that we are nowhere close to our desired destination. Stakeholder capitalism is therefore an important definition to commit to memory because it creates the burning platform for change. If the leading companies in the US and the world have adopted this mission, what is the justification for others not to do so?

It is also compelling that Just Capital's top five companies across all stakeholders—Alphabet, Intel, Microsoft, Salesforce.com, and Bank of America—are enjoying tremendous financial success in terms of market capitalization and year-over-year growth. What this tells us is that financial success and social good do not have to be mutually exclusive. When employees, customers, communities, and the environment achieve positive outcomes, so do shareholders—which is something Paul Polman, former CEO of Unilever stated when he said, "Leaders of tomorrow need to be purpose-driven...need to feel comfortable with the level of transparency...need to be able to work in partnership...need to be systemic thinkers to be able to handle this complexity...but above all, need to be human beings."[38]

Justice, Equity, Diversity, and Inclusion (J.E.D.I.)

This acronym may have different origin points, but one is certainly Marcelo Bonta—an environmental activist and conservation biologist by training who created the *J.E.D.I. Heart organization*,[39] dedicated to "supporting the ever-growing number of J.E.D.I. change agents in the environmental movement, especially those shaking up the pervasive white-dominant culture and co-creating a racial and ethnic J.E.D.I. culture." The *J.E.D.I. collaborative*,[40] founded by Aparna Rajagopal, Ava Holliday, Carlotta Mast, Lara Dickinson, MaryAnne Howland, and Sheryl O'Loughlin, and inspired by Marcelo's efforts, has taken the work forward in a powerful way by offering Pathways to Action, four training programs intended for natural products industry companies.

To Marcelo Bonta, "J.E.D.I. is a term that encapsulates the foundational, internal, and external work that needs to happen on an individual and organizational level to create a movement that effectively speaks to, listens to, invites, and validates people from all races and ethnicities."

Taking that idea forward, our definition of J.E.D.I. contemplates Bonta's and the J.E.D.I. collaborative's concepts, crystallizing the definition as follows:

- **Justice:** The work of identifying and righting past wrongs, eradicating unjust policies and procedures, and preventing future prejudices from denying everyone the right to live with full dignity.

- **Equity:** The work of acknowledging privilege gaps and eliminating biases from key systems to enable access to opportunities and better standards of living and being for all.

- **Diversity:** The work of appreciating and capitalizing on the differences between people to drive innovation and consistent high performance.

- **Inclusion:** The work of accepting and embracing all identities by amplifying voices, seeking perspectives, and supporting different styles of living and being.

As with any concept, it is important that we put these letters into our own words and nomenclature for higher understanding, agreement, and alignment. To assist in this effort, the following sections will further break down each term and offer compelling data related to each.

Justice

Maximizing justice requires confronting the brutal fact that injustices happen every day in every business. It is an inconvenient truth of commerce today that bad things still happen to good people and that—despite our elaborately written and conveyed intentions related to policies, procedures, and practices—many bad actors go unpunished in our ecosystems.

The Institute for Women's Policy Research report: *Paying Today and Tomorrow: Charting the Financial Costs of Workplace Sexual Harassment* states that "up to 85 percent of women will experience workplace sexual harassment over the course of their careers."[41] This is an outlandish and extremely alarming statistic that illustrates the flimsiness of our standard operating procedures. It is a fact that these policies designed to prevent workplace harassment are not working, and it's costing all of us. The direct costs of sexual harassment are reduced earnings from cutbacks in shifts; lost promotions and lost bonuses; job loss and unemployment; lost benefits; increased medical fees and copays; and costs of retraining and education for re-entry into the workforce.

Some of the knock-on/consequential costs are an adverse impact on personal finances, reduced wealth and delayed asset purchases, and housing and retirement insecurity. Finally, intangible costs relate to physical health problems, psychological trauma, and harm to relationships. Not to mention the burgeoning industry of employee employment practices liability (EPLI) insurance, which protects employers in the event of losing harassment lawsuits. Is there any greater injustice than companies protecting their bottom lines versus ensuring an environment where women can work unscathed?

In 2020, Gallup produced a longitudinal analysis of the percentage of Americans who cited race or racism as the most important problem facing the US.[42] Unsurprisingly, over 50 percent of Americans agreed with this statement in 1965 near the peak of the Civil Rights Movement. That percentage dropped as low as 2 percent in the mid-1980s and has climbed back to as high as 19 percent in 2020 during the season of social justice protests linked to the murders of George Floyd, Ahmaud Arbery, and Breonna Taylor. Which leads us to inquire: when society has a racial injustice problem, do companies also have this problem? As race permeates employment, consumption, and societal productivity, the answer is a resounding *yes*.

Persistent racial injustices against African Americans, for example, has created significant economic disparities in employment, home and business ownership, economic and healthcare security, and consumerism. In a collaboration between the *McKinsey Institute for Black Economic Mobility and the McKinsey Global Institute* titled *The economic state of Black America: What is and what could be*,[43] this disparity becomes crystal clear. According to the report, published mid-2021, 43 percent of African American workers are in jobs that pay less than $30K annually; African Americans have a life expectancy that's three and a half years lower (this was pre-pandemic); median African American family wealth is $24K versus $188K median white family wealth); 2.7 million African Americans live in areas that lack multiple vital services; and African American business owners are 2.4 times more likely to be denied financing than white owners. The report states that "dismantling the barriers that have kept Black Americans from fully participating in the US economy could unleash a tremendous wave of growth, dynamism, and productivity".

When companies create more opportunities for disenfranchised groups, train and develop them, pay them livable wages, retain them, promote them, and increase their value, they directly contribute to closing these sorts of gaps. Injustice in all its forms must be rooted out and eradicated proactively and persistently. Only then can the conditions of equity, diversity, and inclusion be fully realized.

Embracing our *for* approach, we can flip this definition into the work of ensuring fairness and consistency throughout our organizations as a core principle via the following:

- **Clear Policies:** We make fairness and consistency our backbone by implementing clear and comprehensive policies. They guide our actions and are the same for everyone—no exceptions.

- **Objective Performance Assessment:** Performance evaluations are transparent and objective. We all know what's expected, and rewards are based on merit.

- **Accountability for All:** Everyone is held to the same standard of accountability, no matter the role. We monitor adherence to our values and act swiftly to correct any deviations.

- **Employee Well-Being:** We look out for each other, addressing challenges and needs proactively to maintain a healthy and balanced work life for everyone.

- **Ethical External Relations:** Our dealings with customers and suppliers are transparent, ethical, and respectful. These relationships are integral to our sustained success.

By living these principles, we solidify a culture of fairness and consistency that boosts satisfaction, increases productivity, and strengthens our organizational reputation.

Equity

Maximized equity means that privilege has been rebalanced and there are no discernible differences between how people are treated with regards to opportunity to participate, perform, and progress. Improving equity requires the recognition and reconciliation of privilege to enhance participation. Importantly, equity and equality are not the same. Equality says that everyone has the right to participate regardless of actual opportunity. Equity focuses on leveling the playing field so that the right to participate becomes truly possible.

Despite the facts that significantly more White, Black, and Hispanic women ages 18–24 (as a percentage of their ethnic population) are enrolled in college—45 percent of White women in this age bracket versus 39 percent of White men for example—the median weekly earnings of White men remain 20 percent higher than all other groups, and White men still make up the vast majority of Fortune 500 CEOs. This begs the question: are White males just better? Or, has the system of employment been disproportionately tilted in their favor due to centuries of privilege?

We must begin to wrestle with this question. McKinsey and Co's 2022 *Women in the Workplace* report illustrates that while White men and White women are fairly close in terms of absolute figures in entry level positions (36 percent to 31 percent, respectively), 61 percent of the C-suite is occupied by White men versus only 21% for White women.[44] These numbers are staggeringly low for men and women of color, as they make up 17 percent of entry-level positions but only 13 percent and 5 percent of C-suite positions, respectively. These figures are a clear reflection of the inequity that still persists in corporate spheres. The report also conveys that for every hundred men who are promoted, only eighty-seven women are promoted.

To wrangle with equity requires transparency in terms of data. According to the 2022 EEO-1 report from the Department of Labor,[45] 10.5 percent of Fortune 500 companies shared data on the race and gender of their employees. This is an increase from 4 percent in 2018, but it is still a relatively low percentage of companies. Calls for pay equity audits have begun to assist in the reconciliation of gender pay equity— but there are far more underlying issues to be addressed in addition to correcting compensation. This is why so many organizations have opted into racial and gender bias training initiatives since the #metoo and #blacklivesmatter movements entered the zeitgeist. They falsely believed they could train away privilege.

During the Civil Rights Movement, African Americans

fought for equality—the right to vote, the right to be treated the same as other ethnicities, the right to fully participate in society. The opposition understood then, as they do now, that equity and equality are not the same. By leveraging gerrymandering and voter restriction laws, they have made the equal right to vote far more difficult for African Americans than for other races. Leveraging economic bias or "placeism," they have barred African Americans from fully participating in wealth creation activities such as real estate, home ownership, business creation, savings, and investing. When a man of mixed race ascended to the Presidency of the United States, they questioned his very citizenship.

None of these issues can be mitigated simply via more training. Only a full re-rendering of principle, priority, process, and practice can achieve true parity when it comes to enhancement of privilege for everyone.

Shifting to the *for* approach, we enhance our definition of equity by clarifying the intention of providing opportunity for fuller participation. To truly redefine equity, we must go beyond mere words and concepts; we breathe life into it by unlocking more doors and creating broader paths for participation. It's about weaving a tapestry in which every thread, every color, every texture has its unique place and significance through:

- **Amplifying access:** We don't just open doors—we invite in. We create more seats at the table, ensuring every voice is heard and every idea is valued. By doing so, we build a foundation where opportunity isn't a privilege, but a right that's accessible to all.

- **"Inclusifying" Growth:** Growth isn't unilateral—it's a collective journey. We foster environments where everyone has the tools, resources, and support to climb, to reach, and to aspire. It's about nurturing potential and fueling aspirations, allowing each one to rise and expand.

- **Empowering Environments:** We cultivate spaces where empowerment isn't just encouraged—it's embedded. Everyone is endowed with the confidence and platform to lead, to influence, and to make impactful decisions. This empowers every individual to be an active participant in shaping our shared destiny.

- **Purposeful Action:** We make intentional, purpose-driven strides to level the playing fields, obliterate barriers, and dismantle the structures that hinder full participation.

- **Continuous Learning:** We're all students on this journey. We embrace learning as a continuous, evolving process, diving deep into the rich reservoir of diverse knowledge and insights. This constant evolution of understanding enhances our collective wisdom and drives equitable progress.

In essence, enhancing our definition of equity means breathing opportunity into every aspect of our organizational fabric. It's about fostering a harmonious symphony of collective progress and mutual growth.

Diversity

Unfortunately, diversity is seen more as a public relations issue than as a performance driver, despite significant data to the contrary. The business case for diversity is stronger than ever. For diverse companies, the likelihood of outperforming industry peers on profitability has increased over time, while the penalties are getting steeper for those lacking diversity. According to McKinsey & Company's 2022 Diversity Wins report,[46] companies in the top quartile for gender diversity on executive teams were 25 percent more likely to have financial returns above their national industry medians than companies in the bottom quartile. This is an increase from the 11 percent difference that was found in the company's 2020 report. This advantage increased even further for companies with both gender and ethnic diversity—companies in the top quartile for ethnic and racial diversity on executive teams were 36 percent more likely to have financial returns above their national industry medians than companies in the bottom quartile. This is a significant increase from the 19 percent difference that was found in the company's 2020 report.

Furthermore, executive teams made up of more than 30 percent women are more likely to outperform those with fewer or no women by a substantial factor— in fact, 48 percent more than executive teams with fewer than ten women.[47] But just as with equity, the most popular diversity program interventions— mandatory training, job tests, and grievance systems—make firms less diverse because managers resist strong-arming. A Harvard Business Review article entitled "Why Diversity Programs Fail" states: "The positive effects of diversity training rarely last beyond a day or two, and a number of studies suggest that it can activate bias or spark a backlash. Nonetheless, nearly half of midsize companies use it, as do nearly all the Fortune 500."[48]

Here is an interesting conundrum. Publicly traded companies are primarily valued on financial performance indicators such as revenue growth, expense management, profitability, and returns to shareholders—all of which hold innovation as a key component. The data indicates that the most innovative companies also score the highest in terms of gender and ethnic diversity. And yet, there is extreme resistance to initiatives that expand diversity. How do we explain this rationally?

No one can claim ignorance to these data in 2023. What is the root cause for this continued apathy in the face of overwhelming evidence? Some might point to the *-isms*, such as racism and/or sexism, but the answer is far simpler: change is hard, and fundamental transformation is harder still. When people resist evolving despite this evolution clearly being in their favor, we can surmise that the fight mechanism (as in "fight or flight") has kicked in. The people in charge are not necessarily bad, but their willing stagnation points to a fear of an unknown destination—a future where they may need to relinquish control or discard well-worn paradigms to achieve.

To genuinely escalate buy-in to diversity, it's not about merely acknowledging differences, but about converting these varied experiences, perspectives, and skills into groundbreaking innovation. It's a dynamic journey of embracing diversity as our greatest asset in forging new paths and creating unprecedented solutions by these approaches:

- **Transformative Thinking:** We blend the diverse tapestry of thoughts and ideas into a powerful concoction of transformative thinking. This convergence of multiple perspectives serves as a fertile ground where innovative ideas are sown, nurtured, and bloomed, pushing boundaries and challenging norms.

- **Cultivating Strengths-Based Leadership and Culture:** Leadership here is not merely a position but a collective responsibility of enabling the highest degrees of engagement and productivity by fostering an environment of trust, compassion, stability, and hope. By placing the emphasis on uncovering, developing, and harnessing individual and collective talent into consistent, reliable strengths, we not only innovate—but we do so in an irreplicable fashion.

- **Collaborative Ecosystems:** We build ecosystems characterized by collective intelligence. By fostering collaboration across varied experiences and backgrounds, we're generating a synergy where the sum is greater than its individual parts. This harmonious fusion of diverse insights is our incubator for revolutionary ideas and strategies.

- **Celebrating Difference:** Differences are not just accepted; they are celebrated. By valuing and honoring every unique element within our mosaic, we are fueling a culture where difference is the catalyst for creativity and the architect of innovation.

By actively transforming differences into innovation, we are not just endorsing diversity; we are living it, breathing it, and embedding it into the very core of our organizational DNA. It's this dynamic interplay of diversity and innovation that is sculpting our journey and illuminating our paths.

Inclusion

Companies spend billions of dollars on advanced digital tools but don't leverage the voices within their midst that not only understand the company's offerings and goals better than the average consumer, but also represent the unique perspectives and values of these key constituencies. Inclusion is about being heard, valued, and supported. It's not only the seat at the table, but the willing eyes, ears, hearts, and minds of those in the room. Enhancing inclusion has both behavioral and systemic enablers.

Behavioral enablers include peer and leadership mindsets of openness, community, growth, and sustainability—as well as behaviors such as growth opportunity, feedback, and open and honest communication. Systemic enablers of inclusion relate to structures such as promotion opportunities and recruiting processes; rituals and norms including coaching and performance development conversations and safe spaces with supervisors; and purpose, strategy, and aspiration with clarity of DEI mission and goals and company values.

In a Bain and Company Inclusive Organizations Survey from 2021,[49] gender and racial inclusion is felt by respondents to be more behaviorally enhanced than systemically. It's not enough to have the right structures in place if people don't adhere to them or are not held accountable for violations. Of seventy-two behavioral enablers evaluated across eighteen populations spanning seven countries, growth opportunity and transparent feedback were seen as the most effective enablers of inclusion by far, with open and honest communication a nearby second. Therefore, it is correct to surmise that inclusion lies in the manager/employee relationship as well as the executive-to-employee dynamic.

Managers who create psychological safety and are growth- and development-oriented enhance inclusion. Executives who speak clearly and honestly about the state of the business and are open to a two-way exchange with employees about their needs do the same. Therefore, inclusion comes down to the orientation toward employees and the company's ability to enhance the overall experience for them.

Inclusion reaches its zenith of impact when it goes hand in hand with heightened employee engagement and productivity. It's about creating an ecosystem where inclusivity is the catalyst, sparking heightened involvement and optimal output from every member of the team through the following:

- **Energizing Atmosphere:** We are sculpting an environment where inclusivity is the heartbeat, pulsating energy and vigor throughout the organization. This invigorated atmosphere is the terrain where engagement flourishes, and productivity scales new heights, fostering a culture of mutual growth and collective achievement.

- **Continuous Dialogue and Feedback:** Inclusion is nourished by ongoing conversation and constructive feedback. We maintain open channels of communication where ideas are exchanged freely and feedback is embraced, paving the way for continual improvement and refined strategies, keeping the engagement alive and productivity soaring.

- **Celebrating Every Achievement:** We rejoice in every accomplishment, big or small, recognizing and celebrating the collective efforts and individual contributions. This culture of acknowledgment and appreciation fortifies engagement and motivates continuous pursuit of excellence.

- **Proactive Wellbeing Support:** Inclusion means caring for each other. We are proactive in supporting the well-being of every individual, ensuring a balanced and fulfilling work environment that nurtures both the professional and personal facets of life.

By intertwining inclusion with elevated levels of engagement and productivity, we're not just building a modern organization; we're crafting a holistic ecosystem where every individual is a pivotal contributor, and every contribution is a step toward our shared vision and collective success.

Unpacking Justice, Equity, Diversity, and Inclusion

Now that we have increased understanding of key definitions and data, we must start to ascertain the current state of our team, function, division, and company related to each. The exercise here is to review the definitions linked to each term and assign a current state of either no progress, some progress, or significant progress. This way, we understand our starting point.

Justice Assessment

JUSTICE	NO PROGRESS	SOME PROGRESS	SIGNIFICANT PROGRESS
Identifying and righting current and past wrongs			
Eradicating unjust practices			
Preventing prejudices from denying everyone the right to live with full dignity			

Equity Assessment

EQUITY	NO PROGRESS	SOME PROGRESS	SIGNIFICANT PROGRESS
Acknowledging privilege gaps			
Eliminating biases from key systems			
Enabling access to opportunities and better standards of living and being for all			

Diversity Assessment

DIVERSITY	NO PROGRESS	SOME PROGRESS	SIGNIFICANT PROGRESS
Appreciating and capitalizing on the differences between people			
Driving innovation			
Delivering consistent high performance			

Inclusion Assessment

INCLUSION	NO PROGRESS	SOME PROGRESS	SIGNIFICANT PROGRESS
Accepting and embracing all identities			
Amplifying voices and seeking perspectives			
Supporting different styles of living and being			

A Path to J.E.D.I. Leadership

It is crucial to recognize that J.E.D.I. work is inside out—meaning that we fix our own house before trying to solve the ills of society. That means we start with the most important stakeholder: employees. When conditions are right for them, all other stakeholders will be served in time. To be a J.E.D.I. leader, therefore, is to be actively engaged in addressing internal injustices, inequities, biases, and exclusion. It signifies creating, implementing, and monitoring new operating procedures that drive increased employee belonging, engagement, and productivity.

Employee value increases as we move from traditional management, antiquated leadership standards and practices, and prioritization of only shareholders and begin embracing stakeholder capitalism, servant leadership, and positive psychology. This shift enables us to emphasize high performance coaching and empathy, will, and humility while de-emphasizing ego. All of this is in the service of establishing new leadership standards, prioritizing employee experience, and maximizing managerial effectiveness.

We must continuously ask ourselves the following:

1. To what degree are employees living a full and dignified life within this organization? How do we know that?

2. To what extent do employees in this organization have access to the same opportunities? How can we prove that?

3. To what degree are we valuing and, more importantly, capitalizing on the differences between us? What do our results show?

4. To what extent are we centering, valuing, and amplifying the voices, perspectives, and styles of those employees who experience more barriers based on their identities? What are these employees telling us?

Enabling J.E.D.I. Work

Imagine an ecosystem that begins with clarity of purpose and ends with advocacy. It works something like this: We work to align the organization on how the organization's operations impact employees, customers, communities, and the environment—positively and negatively. Our executives then not only galvanize the organization, but they also actively serve and support those doing the crucial work of moving the organization forward. We achieve agreement on goals by defining meaningful targets that can be set and committed to by the organization related to eradicating injustices, eliminating inequities, expanding diversity, and enhancing inclusion. We concretize the from: to for the period in question. We detail the metrics that will be reviewed and with what frequency, and we ascertain how problems will be solved and how decisions will be made and documented.

With this done, we ensure that we have the right people in the right jobs and that they are empowered to act. Organizations serious about making sustainable change treat J.E.D.I. work with the same level of commitment as they do ethics, compliance, governance, and corporate social responsibility—all in terms of human resources, budgets, and prioritization. In this way, these teams can start tackling our principles, priorities, processes, and practices; uncover and realign our collective beliefs, biases, and behaviors; and take the organization on the journey from awareness to advocacy.

Enabling J.E.D.I. Work

Clarity of Purpose: Everyone aligned on how the organization's work impacts employees, customers, communities, and the environment – positively and negatively		
Tone from the Top: Executive leadership not only galvanizes the organization, but they also actively *serve and support* those doing the crucial work of moving the organization forward.	**Agreement on Goals:** What are meaningful targets that can be set and committed to by the organization related to eradicating injustices, eliminating inequities, expanding diversity, and enhancing inclusion? What is the desired *from:to* for the period in question? What are the metrics that will be reviewed with what frequency? How will problems be solved and decisions be made?	**Right people in the right jobs and empowered to act:** Organizations serious about making sustainable change treat J.E.D.I. work with the same level of commitment as they do ethics, compliance, governance, and corporate social responsibility.
Principles, Processes, Priorities, and Practices		
Uncovering and Realigning Beliefs, Biases, and Behaviors		
Awareness, Acceptance, Appreciation, Alignment, Activation, Advocacy		

We must also understand that there are significant challenges of implementing J.E.D.I., linked to each of our areas of focus. For justice to be defended, we must truly understand the issues comprehensively and act responsibly. With equity, we must reconcile short-term impacts on employee costs and establish relevant benchmarks to achieve or exceed. Expanding diversity involves not only overcorrecting in terms of pure numbers, but also ensuring the necessary development programs are in place to effectively manage and leverage the workforce. Enhancing inclusion, we must ensure that employees truly support and are aligned with the new degree of heterogeneity and are appropriately trained in terms of relating to different groups.

None of this is easy—and if this chapter already has us overwhelmed, imagine the thousands of DEI practitioners working in silos to shift organizational culture forward. Nobody said building the Burj Khalifa would be easy—but isn't the result worth the effort?

With this in mind, let's move on to the next area of our playbook: karate versus judo.

Worth the Effort

3

KARATE VERSUS JUDO

Whether we are starting out on our J.E.D.I. journeys or already well established in the trenches, it is important to remember that strategy—or the way we choose to pursue our objectives—matters. When it comes to making strategic choices, there are multiple paths to pursue, some with more resistance than others. This is where karate versus judo comes in.

Karate

Karate (which means "open hand") is the martial art of hand-to-hand combat. It is often violent and brutal and requires combatants to identify weaknesses in their opponents and attack mercilessly until they yield. For the purposes of this text, karate can also be defined as confronting the challenges and obstacles inherent in J.E.D.I. work head-on, anticipating resistance, and using energy, skill, and persistence to ultimately wear down the opposition so that we get to make progress. We see the karate approach in mandated diversity training, antiracism lectures, and employee protests. Karate is confrontational by design, which means that parties on all sides will take their fair share of punishment in the fight for greater justice, equity, diversity, and inclusion.

Judo

Judo (which means "the gentle way") is the martial art of leveraging an opponent's inertia and movements against them. It requires a deep understanding of kinetic energy and keen observation of where the opponent is naturally going anyway and then hastening them to that fate. In the context of J.E.D.I. work, judo is present in leveraging known areas of opportunity to attach initiatives that will enhance progress. Recent areas of broad-based prioritization, investment, and focus include digital and data transformation; environmental, social, and governance (ESG) reporting requirements; and internal audit processes.

To further illustrate how the choice of karate versus judo (or, more importantly, how to know when to employ each), I present the stories of Mason and Kenya—two DEI heads for their respective companies.

Mason's Story

Inspired by the social justice protests of 2020, Mason desperately wanted to get involved in changing the status quo at his financial services company. He was a senior HR business partner at the time, and when the word came down the line that his company was creating its first Diversity, Equity, and Inclusion department, he saw his chance to do the work he was so passionate about (and to get a huge promotion in both pay and visibility). After applying and interviewing, he eventually got the job and was named his company's Chief Diversity Officer despite having no previous experience in the role (the CEO had confided in him during the final interview that they just needed someone to represent the organization to show their public support for social justice and Black Lives Matter). Mason knew quite a few of his more "diverse" peers had applied, as well, but they didn't have the visibility with senior management that he did.

Still, he hoped to leverage their collective passion to make a difference. He started researching best practices and contacting thought leaders in academia and other organizations to see how they were approaching their work. He thumbed through *How to Be an Antiracist*,[50] *White Fragility*,[51] *The Conversation*,[52] and *It's Time to Talk About Race at Work* to get his bearings.[53] The learning curve bumped up against internal pressures to act, and so Mason decided to issue new diversity hiring targets for the organization. He wanted to double the number of African Americans in entry-level positions and accelerate the pipeline for women leaders into managerial positions.

At his first company Town Hall, he was asked by a White male colleague exactly how these targets were going to be achieved and if this meant some sort of affirmative action was being instituted inside the company and whether it was legal. He answered that the company had a societal responsibility to embrace all ethnicities and that it was time for White men, especially, to recognize their role in oppressing these other identities for their own gain. This interaction inspired him to also launch a mandatory unconscious bias training initiative for which he paid an outside consultant (a friend from college) a handsome sum.

With most of his budget and political capital exhausted, Mason decided to engage the company's existing employee resource groups (ERGs) as an additional volunteer labor force. He set them to work designing endomarketing campaigns mostly focused on raising awareness during Black History Month, Women's Month, Pride Month, and other relevant months. When the ERG leaders complained about a lack of compensation for their extra effort, Mason reminded them of the Civil Rights struggle and how everyone had to pitch in to make a difference.

Meanwhile, on his watch, two cases came to light. A high-level woman executive made a claim of sexual harassment against a C-Suite member, and an African American male manager resigned over microaggressions and a toxic work environment. The CEO expected action from Mason that would protect the company against additional liability. Mason said the company needed to launch a full-scale Antiracism and Antiharassment initiative he coined AA. The CEO was violently opposed to both because he didn't want to be tagged as leading a racist and sexist company. Mason backed down and circulated some articles via email to raise awareness of the company's Speak Up hotline and how to leverage it.

Mason also was a master of the employee engagement survey—using it to force managers (middle, not senior, of course) to adopt his change initiatives, holding it over people's heads, and using it as evidence of progress, however small, linked to managers who never needed the change initiatives in the first place because they were already doing the right things.

With this approach, it was unsurprising that several constituencies were rather unhappy with Mason's efforts. White men were protesting being blamed for the sins of slave owners, ERG participants were tired of being used as free labor, the C-Suite was unhappy with employees leveraging Speak Up lines to put them under scrutiny, and the CEO was passing his ire regarding investor disappointment due to poor financial performance on to Mason. Taking fire from all sides, Mason decided that greener pastures would be better and left his employer to take his hard-won experience on the road as an external consultant.

Kenya's Story

Kenya had been working in DEI since the Trayvon Martin tragedy. Prior to that, she'd been a highflier in marketing for her consumer goods company. But back in those days, they didn't call the function DEI; it was called Corporate Social Responsibility, managed in tandem by the HR and PR functions. Kenya wasn't a big fan of HR/PR work, but she'd gotten into this space because she knew she could leverage her marketing and messaging talent to make a difference. She'd had a few wins, such as establishing the first single-identity spaces and ERGs in her company's history, and she'd had to fight tooth and nail to make those happen.

Kenya hailed from Minnesota, and the murder of George Floyd, which happened near where she'd grown up, deeply impacted her. She took time off to participate in the Black Lives Matter protests that sprung up in the wake of the terrible event. After hearing that her company was initiating a search for a Chief Diversity Officer, she knew this was her moment to leverage the inertia of the zeitgeist to really make a difference. Besides, she had been doing the work for seven years at this point and had a portfolio of wins, learnings, and relationships to offer during the recruitment process.

Her first act as CDO was to ask for an hour at the upcoming senior leadership team offsite meeting to align the executive team on what they wanted to accomplish with DEI. When it became apparent that the CEO was merely seeking to virtue signal and had no idea what she expected from the function, Kenya knew she would have difficulty moving things forward without first establishing a baseline of understanding from the top of the house. Because every day there was continued fallout around the country, she was able to easily tee up DEI topics with her mentor, the Head of HR, and began using her as a mouthpiece and go-between with the CEO (they played tennis together weekly).

Before long, the CEO was literally parroting her words and ideas in front of not just the senior executive team, but during Town Halls, as well. This was the burning platform Kenya had been waiting for, and she didn't plan to let it go to waste. Because Kenya knew that diversity (especially increasing the amount of women in leadership) was a hot-button issue for her CEO, she started her DEI efforts there—creating a three-pronged plan to augment women leadership by 1) developing the first fully funded training program for women leaders within the company; 2) tasking strategic recruiters with building a bench of the most talented women in and outside of the consumer goods industry; and 3) establishing a talent pipeline, seminar track, and paid internship program with two all-women HBCUs (Spelman and Bennett College) as well as two Ivy league women's schools (Smith and Wellesley College). This approach guaranteed that they would have more than enough qualified woman leaders, both now and in the foreseeable future.

Because the feedback from the first cohort of the women leader's training program was universally positive, and her CEO could see the benefits (having spoken to the group herself), Kenya was then able to construct a more robust agenda that contemplated gender and ethnic pay equity, enhanced health and wellness benefits for single mothers, identity celebrations, and a robust disciplinary matrix against sexual harassment. Still, she knew that it would be a while before she could declare victory by any stretch—so she made her smartest decision yet.

Understanding that her company was deeply committed to emerging environmental, social, and governance standards, Kenya made the data-driven argument that DEI should be linked to ESG and funded and resourced accordingly. She needed the capabilities that these other areas possessed to truly enhance her impact, and rather than recreate the wheel, she proposed resource and knowledge sharing and collaboration. This shift was approved during the budgeting cycle for the next fiscal year, and Kenya couldn't wait to keep the momentum going.

Reflections

If some of us are feeling a certain kind of way about these two cases, that's to be expected. They were written to elicit a reaction. At this point, some might be thinking, "Mason's story is outlandish, and Kenya's is way too convenient." We will reflect and examine each case in turn to see just how outlandish or convenient they are. Importantly, the race/gender of the characters in these cases matters far less than their why for doing the work and their approach. To this end, neither's race is ever mentioned. With that in mind, let's examine each person's process.

Mason and Kenya each used a judo approach to land their coveted positions. They did so by capitalizing on existing momentum within their respective enterprises to apply for and eventually achieve new roles. But this is where their approaches diverge.

Mason goes on the attack (karate) by immediately issuing diversity hiring targets, alienating a key constituency within the company (White men), mandating training initiatives, and implementing other broad-based programs before understanding where everyone stood in relation to this significant change. As issues begin to snowball within his company, he doubles down on the attack with the antiracism and antiharassment program—well-intentioned, sure, but tone deaf. And lastly, he uses employee engagement surveys as a hammer to bludgeon resistance against his programs. When all that fails, he is left without political capital or employee trust and/or good will to continue his efforts, and he must exit.

This is what many employees experienced in the wake of the social justice protests of 2020—broad-based public declarations of support and allyship, construction of new functions, and a burning platform to shift the culture. This launched an industry of antibias, antiracist, and diversity training programs and made the careers of quite a few Masons and external consultant Masons ready to capitalize on newly opened wallets. The reason why this wave of so-called awareness instruction was not as successful as initiators desired was that it created a significant backlash (counterattack) from people in positions of authority throughout the organization. The other explanation for the lack of traction gained via the karate approach was that, to many employees, it felt punitive and even tone deaf, thus leading to people digging in their heels and applying the "in one ear and out the other" approach to the process.

Kenya, on the other hand, perhaps due to her broader experience in the field and her having won and lost her share of battles, decided to piggyback all her initiatives on areas of lesser resistance within her sphere of influence. The only thing she fights for is an hour on a senior leadership team agenda—and she comes with a clear ask: to hear from senior executives on what they understand about DEI work. When she detects that pushing too hard will only backfire, she uses her mentor's relationship (judo) to begin educating her CEO via someone she trusts. And once the CEO is on board, she uses this new mandate (judo) to set attainable but extremely aligned targets that will make an immediate shift in how the organization develops, promotes, and attracts future women to the company. With wins under her belt, she expands her asks, increases her influence, and ultimately continues driving toward impacting the company in a fundamental way.

Harnessing Momentum

In the landmark book From Good to Great,[54] several conditions are required for organizations to truly excel and break away from their competitor set. These conditions are designed to create significant positive momentum and inertia. They are divided into the distinct areas of "disciplined people, disciplined thought, and disciplined action," respectively. The key principles within disciplined people were named "Level 5 Leadership" and "First Who, Then What."[55,56] Within disciplined thought came the principles of "Confronting the Brutal Facts"[57] and "Developing a Hedgehog Concept."[58] And disciplined action came down to "The Flywheel."[59] Although the topic of the book was about financial performance, these principles also apply to a myriad of areas within business, including cultural transformation.

Let's review each in turn to see their applicability and relevance to J.E.D.I. work.

Level 5 Leadership

Level 5 J.E.D.I. leaders are those who don't make the work personal, despite their closeness to what's happening in society at large. They accept the enormity of the challenge with humility, will, and empathy, which enables and empowers them to assume nothing, influence action, and connect with all constituencies who are going on the journey with them. They establish audacious but attainable and (more importantly) measurable targets broken down into short-, medium-, and long-term shifts. They lead with a sense of purpose bigger than themselves and invite everyone to connect in their own way to this shared purpose and mission.

First Who, Then What

The Chief Diversity Officer role is still relatively new to the corporate hierarchy; as such, the requirements, expectations, resourcing, and support were being invented in real time. Those working in this space prior to 2020 were largely marginalized and minimized within their roles and bounced around from employer to employer seeking leaders who "got it" and were serious about doing this work and doing it right. Complying with the First Who, Then What principle of getting the right people on the bus before deciding on a direction has proven to be very challenging. As many of these roles came with visibility to the C-suite, they required someone who had already climbed high in the organization and could effectively engage with the executive wing.

These leaders also needed to be experts in change initiatives, well-connected within their individual companies and within the broader DEI industry, massively influential, patient, and hopefully diverse in their own right. And therein would lie the rub. There weren't many of these people traversing corporate halls at the moment of crisis. So senior leaders did what they almost never do and plucked high-energy, camera-ready talents for the job and gave them an almost impossible task to change the entire company culture.

Get the right people on the bus, and then decide where to go.

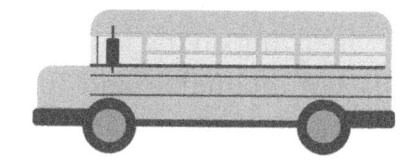

Confronting the Brutal Facts

In the words of the From Good to Great authors, "productive change begins when you confront the brutal facts. Every

THE J.E.D.I. LEADER'S PLAYBOOK

good-to-great company embraced what we came to call 'The Stockdale Paradox'—maintaining unwavering faith that we can and will prevail in the end, regardless of the difficulties, and at the same time, have the discipline to confront the most brutal facts of the current reality, whatever they might be." This is the step that most companies failed to lean into when announcing their broad-based DEI initiatives. One of the most brutal of brutal facts was that for many companies, merely accessing data on employee diversity was going to be quite the chore, as HR systems were not set up to capture demographic data. How, then, to achieve diversity targets when the actual current state is unknown?

This is where effective issue identification and root cause diagnosis are key tools. At the beginning of any change initiative, it is essential to quantify the extent of the problem as well as to get a sense of the why to develop the right solution for the problem at hand. In the 1990s movie Armageddon,[60] for instance, a severe meteor shower leads NASA to realize that there is an asteroid the size of Texas on a collision course for Earth in eighteen days and that shooting nukes at it will not deter its path. Only once they realize these sobering facts can they draw up the plan to send expert drillers to space to insert the nukes in time to split the asteroid in half and avoid an extinction-level event.

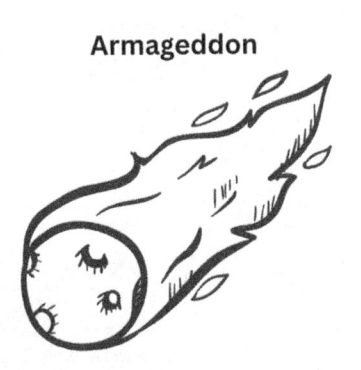

Developing a Hedgehog Concept

The Hedgehog concept is derived from a fable about a fox and a hedgehog—the fox being crafty and cunning, trying many ways to get at the hedgehog's belly but being deterred by a single, but 100 percent effective defense system (the spines of the hedgehog)—and the insight that the best companies don't constantly shift tactics but instead lean into what makes them truly unique. Companies can develop their own Hedgehog concept by combining the answers to three insightful questions that give rise to greater purpose and focus if done correctly. The three inquiries are:

1. What are we wildly passionate about?
2. What can we be the best in the world at? and
3. What drives our economic engine?

The intersection of these three answers is a guiding principle that can be followed for years.

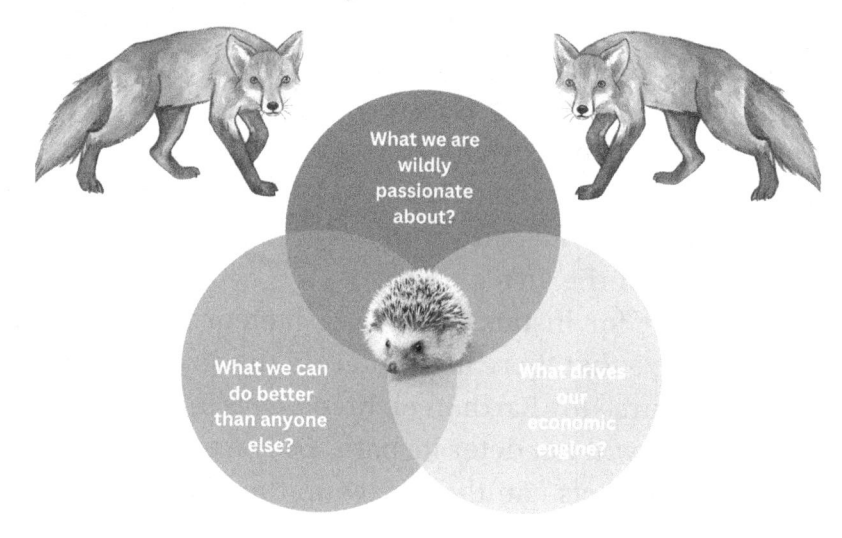

Very few organizations have yet to crystallize their why for pursuing J.E.D.I. change in this manner. In the chapter about four arguments for change, we will revisit how the Hedgehog Concept is foundational to getting executives on board with J.E.D.I. work.

In essence, we might be wildly passionate about expanding diversity and inclusion for our employees, but how can we be the best in the world at it (and is that even our objective?), and how does it drive our economic engine? This is why so many DEI programs are flagging and losing momentum in 2023—lack of a sharp focus that cuts through the day-to-day whirlwind and connects every employee. For the purposes of J.E.D.I., the questions need to be revised as follows:

- How does eradicating injustices, eliminating inequities, expanding diversity, and enhancing inclusion fuel our collective passion?
- In what ways does this drive us to be even better than we already may be?
- In which areas does our economic engine require a J.E.D.I. tune-up in order to deliver on goals in the short, medium, and long term?

At the intersection of these responses, we will find the clarity that we need to drive our J.E.D.I. initiatives for the long-term and link and embed this work into the core principles, priorities, processes, and practices of the organization.

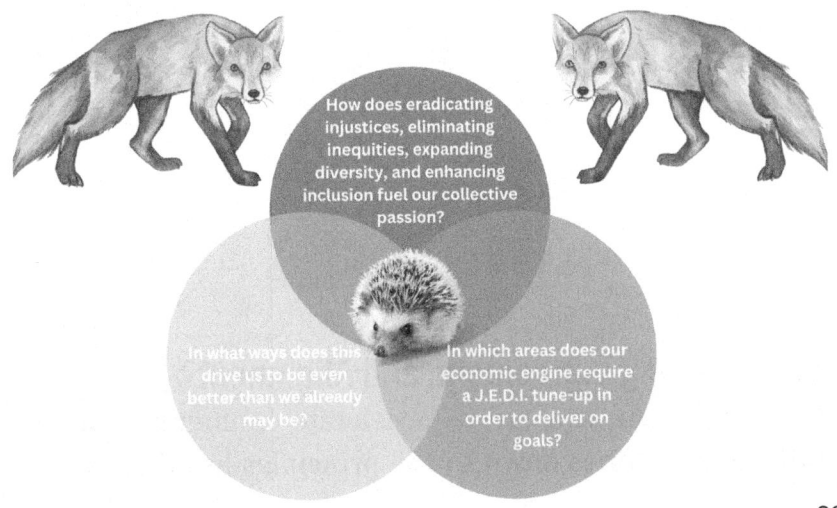

The Flywheel

The previous principles generate energy and momentum within a company. But change does not truly take root until the moment the resistance against progress reduces and the ease with which we can affect outcomes dramatically increases. This is the principle of the flywheel at work. There is no one magic bullet or single initiative that will magically manifest the results we want. Only by remaining truly committed to the journey, day by day, KPI by KPI, and person by person can we loosen the levers of control and make the leaps forward that we desire.

As the authors state, "No matter how dramatic the end result, good-to-great transformations never happen in one fell swoop. In building a great company or social sector enterprise, there is no single defining action, no grand program, no one killer innovation, no solitary lucky break, no miracle moment. Rather, the process resembles relentlessly pushing a giant, heavy flywheel, turn upon turn, building momentum until a point of breakthrough, and beyond."

The Flywheel

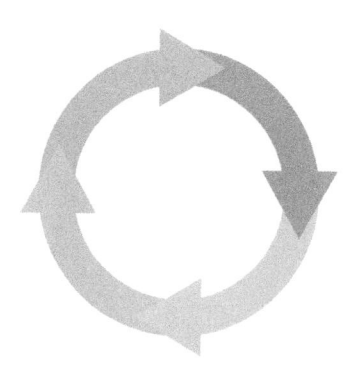

Understanding, Agreement, and Alignment

Leveraging judo strategy to accelerate momentum in our J.E.D.I. work comes down to the principles listed above and applying them to achieve the three confirmations required to drive any initiative forward: understanding, agreement, and alignment (or UAA). This is why level 5 leadership is so important—level 5 leaders naturally seek to understand before acting. The more we understand the issues and opportunities at hand, the easier it is to agree and then to achieve the broad-based alignment necessary to move the organization forward.

When we have the right people on the bus before we decide where we are going (first who, then what), we have the capability in place to achieve UAA much faster. If no one on a team has ever been a victim of privilege, then how can you help everyone understand that it is in no one's interest within a company committed to a cause to allow toxic privileges to persist? When we have enthusiasm for the work but lack experience in doing it, then we will fall victim to certain burnout, as good will only lasts for so long.

Confronting the brutal facts draws a direct line to UAA. It enhances understanding at a root-cause level so that when we agree on a plan of action, we know why we are agreeing, and it therefore becomes far more straightforward to align on roles, responsibilities, and timelines. If we are acting on superficial problems, then full understanding will be deterred, and we will burn through agreements and lose accountability that is necessary to achieving our objectives.

Linking J.E.D.I. work to our core organizational purpose via The Hedgehog Concept enlightens everyone as to how going on this journey will truly make our company stand out in a good way and provide the benefits to gaining agreement and alignment. Too many DEI initiatives feel disconnected from the broader purpose of the company (other than morally), and therefore many constituents find it easy to poke holes in the resources and time being invested in this activity versus others. When this happens, it is only a matter of time before the program spirals into oblivion.

Finally, communicating at the outset of the J.E.D.I. journey that there is no magic bullet and that this is collective, comprehensive, and committed work from all parties will ensure that people understand exactly the scope of what is expected. With clarity of scope, it becomes simpler to gain agreement and alignment on the objectives and key results for a given period. Using the flywheel analogy is a great way of describing the process and will keep everyone honest and aligned and focused in moving forward consistently, day by day, until the job is done.

The check for whether we are employing karate- or judo-based strategy in delivering on our objectives is therefore the degree of understanding we create, the agreement we gain, and the alignment we collect as we move into action. With karate, every step will be a battle—for every bit of momentum we gain, there are an equal or increasing number of setbacks—which was depicted in Mason's story. Judo, by contrast, will feel iterative—understanding will deepen, agreement will widen, and alignment will sharpen. Using the *Good to Great* principles checklist will allow us to calibrate and recalibrate our strategies to be more judo-oriented than karate-oriented, which will keep us moving forward.

Strategy, however, is only one tool in our playbook. We also have the power of argument, which we will delve into next.

4

THE FOUR ARGUMENTS FOR CHANGE

It should come as no surprise that one of the core competencies of successful J.E.D.I. leadership is the ability to manage change. Once we define our strategies (utilizing the judo approach), we need to convince stakeholders to align with our initiatives. There have been many attempts at accelerating this process—from the so-called business case for DEI to other empirical and data-driven arguments for broad-based adoption—and yet many organizations remain on the fence about the need to wade into these waters. Once we achieve alignment and begin taking targeted action, it is also crucial to anticipate what sort of reaction to expect from the organization.

In this chapter, we will discuss how to make the arguments for and then successfully lead the change.

Change is Hard

As we have previously discussed, the most successful organizations are those that know what they do singularly well (The Hedgehog Concept) and stick to it with relentless, maniacal discipline. That does not mean they are immune to change, however. External and internal volatility, uncertainty, complexity, and ambiguity affect everyone in different measures. As the practice of business management has evolved from the industrial revolution (the age of labor) to today's technological era (the age of digitization and automation), few companies have survived, many have been born and perished, and many more have barely held on.

As former Apple evangelist Guy Kawasaki has been fond of saying, the company that creates a paradigm rarely jumps the curve to the next innovation. The examples he gives are that of the early ice companies being replaced by refrigerator manufacturers and Kodak being supplanted by smart phones. Current technological giants such as Amazon, Google, and Apple must contend with an entirely virtual ecosystem of someone else (Meta's) design. Even for the best companies, anticipating, adapting, and surviving major change is tremendously difficult.

Therefore, we should not hang our heads as J.E.D.I. practitioners. We knew the work of changing hearts, minds, software, and hardware was going to be difficult coming in the door. It's always hard. Still, demographic trends point to the fact that *by 2043* (or even sooner),[61] America will be a majority black and brown nation. The composition of the American workforce is already the most diverse in history, and this heterogeneity is only increasing. The need for J.E.D.I. leadership is therefore a necessity, not some woke dream.

The Four Arguments for J.E.D.I. Change

Amongst ourselves, we lament the need to even argue for change at all. It is obvious to us. Global employee engagement is at historic lows, managerial effectiveness is waning in traditional hierarchies, and productivity is grinding to a halt. Employees are resigning in droves and quiet quitting. Something's got to give. And yet we still must convince senior executives, making in some instances thousands of times more than the average employee, that their precious terrain is under assault.

> **We live in an age of information, yet finding the truth seems harder than ever before.**

Initially, these same executives demanded empirical data proving that diverse organizations were more effective than non-diverse ones—and still, when presented with unimpeachable facts by giant names in consultancy such as McKinsey & Co. and Bain, many executives still balked at making the necessary moves forward. Many asked, "What are they waiting for?" Then the summer of social justice protests shook more executives out of their stupor, and they began to lumber headlong into the future of work.

Three years after that mandate, some executives are beginning to pump the breaks on DEI spending and commitments to stakeholder capitalism, claiming the need to shore up the basics after taking on damage due to the global pandemic. This stop and start, take two steps forward and five steps backward phenomenon should not be surprising. It comes back to the concept of UAA we discussed in the previous chapter. If one doesn't really understand why they are being forced to move, it is extremely unlikely that they will agree with the actions needed to do so, and even less likely that they will provide their full alignment.

This is why the four arguments for change are fundamental not only to increase understanding, but also to gain the agreement and alignment necessary to galvanize the organization to commit to and embrace the change. The concept here is that the companies who have embraced J.E.D.I. work have done so because they've fundamentally bought into either all four of these arguments (moral, peer-pressure, innovation, risk-mitigation) or bits of each. Importantly, each of these arguments hinges on judo strategy—these things are already happening, there is already momentum in these directions, investment being made, priorities being aligned—so it's merely a matter of calibrating where your organization is on each of these areas.

The Moral Argument

Many DEI practitioners falsely believed that this argument—changing because it's the right thing to do—would be all they needed to inspire activation. This idealism was quickly squashed by deflection or business practicalities and priorities. Executives evaded, stating that may be the case on an aggregate level, but certainly not here! In terms of business priorities, how does a company invest in doing the right thing when its business model is built on selling anything it can monetize? This is where the judo approach is fundamental.

When making the moral argument, it is essential to ground the discussion in empirical facts relevant to your specific business situation. The general facts are as follows:

- Workforce composition and participation is at its most diverse in history. *What is it in our business?*
- Yet senior management positions are overwhelmingly held by White, cisgender males. *To what degree is this the case for our business?*
- Employees deserve to see representation at all levels of the organization. *How can you prove that this is an issue for our business?*
- This creates the environment of psychological safety and support needed to fully engage these different types of employees. *How can we bolster this statement with internal data?*

Without homegrown data, we will likely be engaging in hand-to-hand combat (karate) using broad-based facts versus someone else's beliefs or opinions. Not a recipe for success.

The Peer Pressure Argument

Many companies jumped on the change bandwagon because they saw others doing it and didn't want to be left behind. This is the essence of the peer-pressure argument: changing because everyone else is doing it. This was the case for sexual harassment training in the 1990s, compliance adoption in the early 2000s, and digital transformation in the 2010s. A few companies on the vanguard of shifting business culture led the way, and everyone else shortly followed.

Still, most executives would prefer to be in the front versus in the passenger's seat, and therefore this argument lacks appeal. Just as there are some people who have never seen Lost,[62] Breaking Bad,[63] Harry Potter,[64] or Game of Thrones,[65] there will be executives who note the stampede toward a new normal and decide to stand pat. They require additional rationale, such as the following:

- Competitors are more attractive to a more diverse group of talents. *Which competitors are winning the talent war currently?*
- Companies that don't follow the trend will fall behind in terms of public perception and reputation. *How is our company being perceived?*
- But companies found guilty of merely "performative" DEI are the most negatively affected. *What are the examples not to follow?*
- Starting slow and building momentum (without big public statements) is the way to enter this space à la Good to Great. *Which companies are doing this the best, and what can we learn from them?*

Ultimately, peer pressure wins over many executives, but we may not have that kind of time. Hence the next areas of argument: innovation and risk-mitigation.

The Innovation Argument

We can usually count on the competitive nature and ambition of executives (judo). They didn't achieve their lofty posts by being complacent or possessing an attitude of playing just to play the game. They play to win. As such, we can harness their ambition, leveraging the innovation argument—changing because it will enhance our ability to remain competitive.

While this may seem very similar to peer pressure, the internal motivator for change is to be a leader—to win, not just to follow—hence the appeal. When backed up with the following facts, this argument can begin to move the needle with those excellence-oriented executives.

- Diverse organizations have been proven to be more successful than non-diverse ones. *What are the sorts of targets we should be aiming for, and what's the delta from our current state?*

- Capitalizing on diversity requires efforts to enhance gender and ethnic representation. *Where are we doing well, and where are we lagging internally?*

- Teams able to maximize diversity of collective strengths are far more profitable and sustainable. *What are the best-practice approaches to make this a reality?*

- Diverse teams increase understanding of a variety of markets and psychographics, leading to potential competitive advantages. *What sorts of opportunities will open to us once we fully embrace this approach?*

By positioning this change as necessary to beating the competition, we stoke the fires of ambition while simultaneously educating on the specific areas of change needed.

The Risk-Mitigation Argument

When morality, peer-pressure, and innovation don't get the juices of change flowing, it's time to bring out the big guns. The risk-mitigation argument—that of changing because there is significant reputational and financial risk to not doing so—is quite compelling because it aligns well with the job description of most executives: achieve the numbers while mitigating risks and managing reputation (judo). And when backed up by the following facts, it can jolt even the most complacent executive into action.

- Innovation risk leads to potential business stagnation and lack of competitiveness. *What are current examples of companies falling behind due to lack of adoption, and what has happened to them (and their executives)?*

- Inaction against injustices can lead to financial risks (lawsuits, fines, etc.). *What is the current degree of risk in this company, and how much could we potentially reduce the likelihood and/or impact of such occurrences?*

- Unaddressed inequities lead to higher potential employee attrition rates. *What are our current attrition rates relative to our industry and others? What are exit interviews telling us about the reasons why people are exiting? Where are they going after they leave us?*

- Reputational risk can lead to significant issues across stakeholders. *What kind of recent reputational*

> hits have we taken, what has been their impact, and what is the tangible benefit of enhancing reputation in this way?

Executives like keeping their paychecks coming. The best way to do so is to take risk mitigation seriously. As such, embracing J.E.D.I. turns out to be in their best interest—not just something nice to do, but something fundamental to how they will be measured.

A Single Combined Argument

When we put key elements from all four arguments into a single rationale, we can truly move the needle with stakeholders. That rationale might look and sound something like the following:

> *The leading companies (peer pressure) have embraced J.E.D.I. as a compelling business success strategy (innovation). The data demonstrates that these leading companies (peer pressure) have a double-digit financial advantage (peer pressure/innovation/risk mitigation) over lagging companies, and they are achieving this advantage by driving greater gender and ethnic diversity (moral/innovation), which are both required for a successful J.E.D.I. approach. Leaning into J.E.D.I., however, requires thinking of this more as consistent with ESG, Compliance, and Ethics (risk mitigation) efforts than merely an HR-led initiative or good PR (moral). Fully pursuing J.E.D.I. will not only keep us in step with the times (moral), but it will also make us a stronger employer and competitor and more attractive to investors and current and future customers (innovation).*

Importantly, the more we can link the need for change to existing initiatives, beliefs, and/or priorities (judo), the easier it is to get the patient to swallow this pill that ultimately is for their own good. But achieving buy-in is only half the battle. Leading change at an enterprise level is no cakewalk under the easiest of circumstances— which is why we must endeavor to dramatically upskill our change management capabilities.

Now that we better understand the four arguments for change, there are two keys to managing change: anticipating the emotional reaction to change, and driving high alignment and energy behind making the change a reality. Change is truly daunting, but thankfully, we don't have to recreate the wheel. Two models will be our guide to these keys. Let's deal with the emotional aspect first: the change curve.

The Change Curve

It is important to understand that when we initiate change, we also instigate an emotional response from those impacted by the change. This emotional response is literally embedded in our DNA, put there during the days of intense fear and scarcity of our ancestors. Back in those days, change could literally mean death. Launching a change initiative, therefore, creates the fight or flight response in others.

Based on her research into death and those it leaves behind, in her book On Death and Dying: What the Dying Have to Teach Doctors, Nurses, Clergy and Their Own Families,[66] Elisabeth Kübler-Ross introduced the change curve, or Kübler Ross' Change Curve Model, in 1969. It depicts seven stages of grief: shock, denial, frustration, depression, experimentation, decisions, and integration. Over the years, organizational psychologists and change management gurus have adopted this model for business, as they have seen significant overlap.

The Change Curve

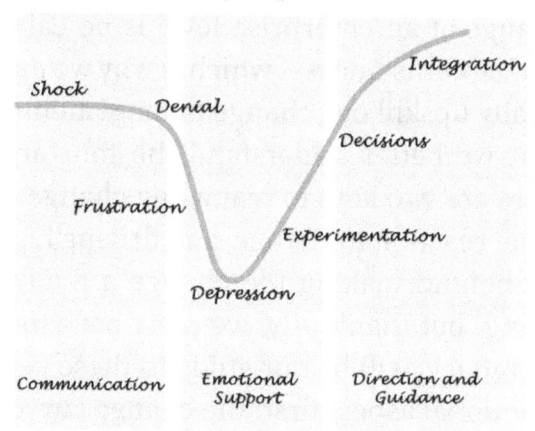

```
                                    Integration
   Shock
        Denial
                        Decisions

      Frustration
                      Experimentation

              Depression


  Communication    Emotional      Direction and
                   Support          Guidance
```

Visualize a graph with the X-axis depicting productivity and engagement and the y-axis measuring time – the curve starts at the status quo level of engagement with shock/denial, descends to its low point at depression, and then exceeds the previous status quo once integration is achieved. The primary question is how quickly we can navigate these stages without getting caught up in one or more of them for too long. But first, we need to delve into the stages themselves and understand what to expect.

- The shock/denial stage is characterized by defensiveness and a dramatic resistance to changing the status quo.
- Frustration (and even anger) at being forced to do something different is the next reaction.
- Next, demoralization sets in, in the form of depression.
- With the right direction and guidance, most people ultimately come to terms with the change as the

new normal; once they accept this, productivity and engagement rebound.

Knowing the likely emotional reaction to change can allow us to not only anticipate but also counter the natural resistance. We mitigate shock and denial by engaging our key stakeholders in designing the change. When we open up avenues for venting about the change and taking in feedback, we can reduce anger. If we set up the proper incentives in the system related to the change, we can transform depression into excitement, and then acceptance becomes a matter of course.

It is when we ignore the change curve because we are moving too fast or are too driven by our own desires that we meet maximum resistance, which can kill the initiative altogether. Once we accept that this change curve is inevitable, we can skillfully lead change.

Leading Change

John P. Kotter first introduced a novel model for change management (The Kotter Eight-Step Change Model) in his 1996 publication Leading Change and updated it in the 2014 title Accelerate. Despite the age of the model,[67,68] it is as relevant today as it has ever been—and it is up to us, change agents, to learn how to wield it for maximum impact. It is not the tool, but the application of the tool, that truly matters.

Kotter's Eight-Step Change Model is a process for helping organizations implement change by mobilizing their employees to adopt and implement the new change quickly and effectively. In other words, Kotter's model is a way for organizations to make big changes by getting their employees on board and helping them to work together to make those changes happen. Many of Kotter's steps are strongly linked to the expected emotional reactions from the Kübler-Ross change curve, but this model goes above and beyond merely managing emotions. The eight steps in the Kotter Change Model are as follows:

- Establish a Sense of Urgency: Clearly communicate the need and reasoning behind any proposed changes to employees, and work to secure buy-in from at least 75 percent of management in order to lead effective change.

- Assemble a Guiding Team: Identify change leaders and delegate tasks to experienced individuals, educating them about the reasons for the change to increase support and buy-in from various functions.

- Develop a Strategic Vision: Create a change management plan that outlines project milestones and deliverables, as well as a clear vision to help balance various aspects of change implementation, and set realistic timelines.

- Communicate the Change: Organizations often prioritize logistics over communication, but effective change management communication is crucial for success. Make sure the change is understood and supported by employees.

- Remove Obstacles: Avoid top-down change imposition, and instead identify and remove any factors that may hinder success. Utilize available resources to overcome obstacles without disrupting other business areas.

- Celebrate Short-Term Wins: Implementing change can be a long and difficult process, so it's important to recognize and celebrate small successes along the way to keep employees motivated.

- Make Change Ongoing: Change initiatives require ongoing effort to fully adopt and make it a habit. Set SMART goals and continuously evaluate progress to ensure long-term success.

- Incorporate Change into Org Culture: Change initiatives require behavioral changes, so it's important to offer continuous employee training and make the change a part of the organization's culture and processes. Without ongoing support, employees may fall back into old practices.

As you can see, it is woefully insufficient to gain understanding, agreement, and alignment from the top of the house without the ability to anticipate the change curve and then effectively lead the change. And as many DEI practitioners are not change management professionals by trade, but instead educators, disruptors, and influencers, this is where many good intentions have failed. Remembering that the most effective change initiatives address a clear problem is crucial—and the problem in this instance is that companies failing to adopt J.E.D.I. change are falling behind morally, lagging their peers, failing to innovate, and increasing their risk exposure.

Not to mention the money being left on the table:

- *Citigroup estimates* the US economy would see a $5 trillion boost over the next five years if the US were to tackle key areas of discrimination against African Americans.[69] What about company revenues?

- *Closing the gender pay gap* could add $512 billion to

the GDP—not to mention how this current inequity impacts everything from healthcare and higher education to international trade and the middle class.[70] What about the engagement boost from woman employees?

- *Companies with above-average total diversity,*[71] measured as the average of six dimensions of diversity (migration, industry, career path, gender, education, age), had both 19 percentage points higher innovation revenues and 9 percentage points higher EBITDA margins, on average. How useful would this increase be to ongoing business operations?

- *Workplace belonging leads to a 56% increase in job performance.*[72] Employee disengagement costs companies dearly every year—up to $550 billion a year. How can our companies afford to allow this to persist?

Because I recognize the crucial need for J.E.D.I. leaders to become change management experts, I've also written my own comprehensive book on change leadership, published in June 2023, called Leading Change: The 4 Keys (Context, Confidence, Construction, and Culture) There is a preview at the end of this book; I hope you find it a helpful resource.[73]

In addition to lack of a clear imperative for change, the other reason our initiatives are suffering is linked to failing to act on the beliefs, biases, and behaviors across the various internal stakeholder groups, which is the next area of our focus.

5

BELIEFS, BIASES, AND BEHAVIORS

The Shadow of the Leader

What comes to mind when you hear the phrase Shadow of the Leader?[74] In essence, the phrase translates to mean what people say about you when you are out of the room. A leader's reputation, legacy, influence, and impact are constantly under scrutiny. What many people in positions of authority fail to realize is the degree to which everything employees experience is filtered through the leader's values, beliefs, focus, outlook, stress level, emotional intelligence, and self-awareness.

This realization becomes especially crucial when we begin to understand that very few people possess a high level of self-awareness. Most leaders have no idea how positively or negatively they are affecting those around them. Studies suggest that only 10–15 percent of people are truly self-aware.[75] There are three primary reasons for this:

- There are two types of self-awareness: extrinsic and intrinsic. Extrinsic self-awareness is what others know about us. Intrinsic self-awareness is what we know about ourselves. These two elements of self-awareness are rarely had at the same relative level at the same time.

- There is a paradoxical relationship between success and self-awareness. The most successful people are often the least self-aware because they stick to an image of self that serves them and often surround themselves with people who reinforce this self-image and perception.

- There is a fallacy that introspection can fill in the blanks of self-awareness. There are areas where no amount of reflection will complete the picture. This is because we all possess natural blind spots in terms of our ability to truly see ourselves, as well as in experiences we just haven't yet had. It's difficult to predict how we will behave in a circumstance we've never encountered.

Johari's Window

Invented in 1955 by American psychologists Joseph Luft and Harry Ingham,[76] the Johari Window model (a play on both men's first names) provides deep insight into how we can gain greater self-awareness. The model is a four-box matrix where on the left we assess what others know about us, and on the top we contrast that with what we know about ourselves. This creates four blocks of self-awareness: the area known to us and to others (the open area), the area known to us but not to others (the hidden area), the area unknown to us and to others (the unknown area), and the area known to others but not to us (the Johari Window).

The Johari Window

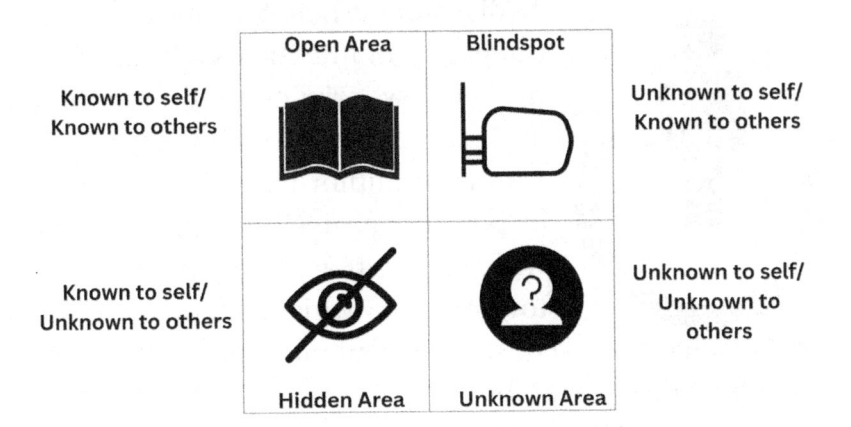

	Open Area	Blindspot	
Known to self/ Known to others	📖	💡	Unknown to self/ Known to others
Known to self/ Unknown to others	👁‍🗨	❓	Unknown to self/ Unknown to others
	Hidden Area	Unknown Area	

The open area serves as our public brand; this is how we choose to represent ourselves to others and is likely how we think of ourselves. The hidden area is full of vulnerabilities, traumas, and experiences we would rather not share—and our situational recognition of the impacts of these hidden aspects may or may not be very high and/or accurate. The unknown area can only truly be filled in by continuous learning and new experiences—which is why so few people access this valuable knowledge, because they stick to familiar routines. Finally, The Johari Window requires transparency from others to complete the picture. This is the area where the leader's shadow truly lies.

When leaders are unwilling to look at themselves and their possibly unintended impacts on those around them, it becomes exceptionally challenging to shift their beliefs one way or the other. Therefore, one of the tools of choice for DEI practitioners is the employee survey. Unfortunately, the way these surveys are conducted rarely provides truly insightful information for senior leaders on their own conduct and the effects on their organizations. So, how do we help leaders reflect on their beliefs, biases, and behaviors—and what overall influence does doing so have on moving our J.E.D.I. work forward?

OMAR L. HARRIS

The Origins of Belief

To disentangle belief, we must deal with the powerful influences of nature, nurture, access, privilege, culture, society, and experience (ours, and that of others who have authority, real or perceived, or power over us). The reason we start with belief is that it is the primary input toward bias—which, in turn, informs how we behave both consciously and unconsciously. In purely psychological terminology, belief is the state of mind in which we accept something to be true or real, regardless of whether there is evidence to support it. Beliefs can be based on our own personal experiences, the experiences of others, or on what we have been taught. They can be rational or irrational, conscious or unconscious.

In the book *The Believing Brain: From Ghosts and Gods to Politics and Conspiracies—How We Construct Beliefs and Reinforce Them as Truths*,[77] psychology professor Michael Shermer says that we form our beliefs first and then look for evidence in support of them afterward. He goes on to state: "As a 'belief engine,' the brain is always seeking to find meaning in the information that pours into it. Once it has constructed a belief, it rationalizes it with explanations, almost always after the event. The brain thus becomes invested in the beliefs and reinforces them by looking for supporting evidence while blinding itself to anything contrary... Basically, "what we believe determines our reality, not the other way around."

This means that beliefs and the act of believing are far from rational occurrences—and, as such, signifies the challenge inherent in changing and challenging beliefs (karate). Humans have the unique capacity to believe in things unseen or intangible. In fact, our entire society hinges on such beliefs. Belief transformed paper into currency and regular humans into monarchs. What we accept becomes our reality, and our reality has tremendous influence over our biases and behaviors. Remember, we used to believe that disease was a result of four humours, and we used leeches to bleed out the sickness.

Making the Unconscious *Conscious*

We've established that most of us lack sufficient self-awareness, and that our beliefs—especially those stemming from an irrational basis—can be very hard to impact. Therefore, it should come as no surprise that we are unaware of and/or mistaken about the nature of many of our thoughts and feelings. This leads us to the study of implicit bias and its ability to influence our attitudes toward others.

In his books *Blink* and *Talking to Strangers*,[78,79] Malcolm Gladwell deals with bias in two different perspectives: our bias toward what he calls *thin slicing* or making quick judgments, and our bias to default to truth (or what we believe to be true), meaning we usually assume honesty. This relates to J.E.D.I. work because, in both instances, the processing behind fast decision-making and biases are not happening consciously. Recognizing that the battle for belief and bias rests in raising awareness is key to doing this work effectively.

Implicit or unconscious bias is a nearly automatic process of overgeneralization that can lead to discrimination even when people feel they are being fair. In this way, our biases are often more predictive of our actions than our conscious values are. There is a wealth of evidence that implicit bias is real. It can manifest in people perceiving harmless objects as weapons in the hands of Black men, having a negative reaction to abstract images paired with Black faces, and having faster reaction times to identifying negative words when paired with Black faces compared to White faces. This evidence is not limited to any one specific study or test, but rather is supported by a significant amount of research.

When implicit bias leads to injustice, augments inequity, prioritizes sameness, and inhibits inclusion, it is in our path and therefore must be dealt with accordingly. But to go into the work assuming that our leaders are implicitly biased against different groups is a flawed approach and likely to create a blowback from the very group we need to align to make progress. Following the school of thought that slavery led to capitalism, which created much of the White male privilege and supremacy that many non-White males experience, and that the only way to shift the culture is to force recognition of this belief system on these same privileged individuals is to lose the thread.

Yes, some degree of historical recognition is crucial to moving forward. If we can't acknowledge the basis for current disparity and treatment of marginalized groups, how can we take steps to ensure that history doesn't repeat itself? However, many people, not only those in positions of authority, aren't behaving the way they are because of slavery, Jim Crow, racism, or other extreme toxic systems of oppression. They are doing so because there have been no true repercussions for their actions— no justice for the aggrieved. Whether we attribute this to White privilege or merely a lack of proper enforcement is a personal decision for each J.E.D.I. practitioner. Just remember, everyone possesses implicit bias to some degree. What happens when the biases of the marginalized are driving the behaviors of the very people trying to create more positivity for actors in the system?

Eliminating bias is a slow process of reverse engineering.

Reverse Engineering Bias

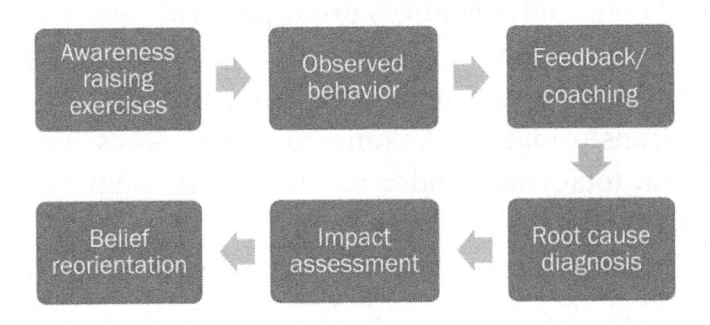

Awareness raising exercises → Observed behavior → Feedback/coaching → Root cause diagnosis → Impact assessment → Belief reorientation

It starts with raising awareness of how beliefs and biases manifest in the first place. The next stage is to link bias with any observed behaviors, thus increasing self-awareness. Through feedback and coaching, we can help leaders and teams identify root causes linked to beliefs and biases—especially when we are able to tangibly quantify negative impacts of these beliefs and biases. The hope is that by the end of this process, we have achieved a degree of belief reorientation.

But hope, as we know, is not a strategy.

The Power of Incentives

While there is some merit in training implicit or unconscious bias, the data reflects a limited impact on behavioral change. Ultimately, what we should care about most of all is how people are treated within the systems. We are not responsible for brainwashing anyone or changing anyone's core belief system. We are tasked with improving the internal environment so that all employees can have lives full of dignity, opportunity, acceptance, and belonging.

Fortunately, there is an existing system that prevails in most businesses that can be leveraged (judo) as a behavioral change driver. Incentives are pervasive and powerful behavioral motivators—so much so that when we change incentives, we change actions. According to a McKinsey & Co article,[80] "Financial incentives are a powerful tool for executives to motivate employees during transformation efforts. Companies that implemented financial incentives tied directly to transformation outcomes achieved almost a fivefold increase in total shareholder returns (TSR) compared with companies without similar programs."

Yes, financial incentives work; but cultural incentives do, as well. What gets valued ultimately gets done. When we investigate the incentives driving negative practices in the company, this is where we find the bullseye to act. Importantly, adjusting incentives requires data and analytics that indicate the danger of continuing the current course and the opportunity unlocked by pursuing new cultural motivators.

When we enter an organization, we bring with us our beliefs, biases, and behaviors—which may or not be aligned with the values of the entity we are joining. Let's imagine, for example, we work for a company that values servant leadership; people development; justice, equity, diversity, and inclusion; high-performance team leadership; communication, collaboration, innovation, agility; training, transparency, and one set of rules that apply to all. Now, consider that these values are strictly enforced and incentivized via reward and recognition and career development selections. Wouldn't this system be very likely to produce outliers for removal, aligned behavior, and a modern business culture equipped for the goals of stakeholder capitalism?

Valuing How It Gets Done Versus What Gets Done

In the business world, we rarely take the time for reflection. Things are coming at us too fast, and our obsession with progress and the more mentality keep us from truly examining root cause to really dig beneath the surface and understand why things are happening the way they are happening. Still, rather than confront executives with their potentially toxic beliefs, biases, and behaviors (karate), it is far more effective to find methods to help them reflect on their own.

Asking people to read the following questions and truly consider their responses can be a good starting point:

- What have been the privileges I have experienced in my own life and career?
- To what degree is the role of this business to be a force for good in society?
- To what degree do I value bossing (hierarchy) versus leadership (serving)?
- What is the value of diversity to me and this business?
- What is the role of inclusion in the success of this business?
- How might my beliefs (related to the above questions) create unconscious biases in my relationships and decision-making?
- How have these unconscious biases manifested in my behaviors related to issues of justice, equity, diversity, and inclusion within my [company, division, department, function, team, etc.]?
- To what degree do I value what gets done over how it gets done?

The answers we receive to this short questionnaire are very revealing and will let us know the degree of resistance we should expect going into our J.E.D.I. work. In the spirit of judo, wherever we assess there is positive momentum, that should be our starting point. For example, if most executives agree that the role of this business is to be a force for good in society, we can probe there to uncover exactly in what areas they see the business making a difference and start projects that align with that vision. Or, if we hear the right things related to diversity and inclusion, we can leverage this sentiment to fuel our initial proposals in this regard.

The key here is not to judge but to explore. This is a safe space for us to reconcile and wrangle with the hidden, unknown, and areas known to others but not to ourselves that show up in the open area as potential cavities corroding our desired effect. We help the executives in charge peer into their own Johari Windows relative to justice, equity, diversity, and inclusion and invite them to evaluate the role of current incentives in the system that are likely leading to most of the issues we need to address —much more so than unconscious biases. When we make it known that we can have the greatest positive impact on behaviors by shifting incentives, we make this a procedural area versus a personal indictment.

An exercise we can conduct in this regard is to have groups respond to the following four questions:

1. What desirable behaviors are being incentivized in this culture?

2. What undesirable behaviors are being incentivized in this culture?

3. What is the cost/risk of allowing the undesirable elements to fester and grow?

4. What are some ways to reengineer incentives so undesirable elements cannot survive?

In this way, we co-design the new incentives (judo) and gain greater awareness and alignment into what needs to change. With alignment that we need to take a hard look at these incentives, we can now move forward to working on the four P's (principles, priorities, processes, and practices) that drive companies forward while also, in many instances, manifesting toxicity.

6

PRINCIPLES, PRIORITIES, PROCESSES, AND PRACTICES

A company's practices are governed far more by what senior executives value and focus on than what we'd like to admit. Just as the direction of the country shifts with each President, so does a company ebb and flow depending on who is in charge. This is why we must understand the strengths and disconnects of the four driving elements of a company's culture.

Three Bs to Four Ps

Executive Influence
- Beliefs
- Biases
- Behaviors

Organizational Culture
- Principles (only as stable as leadership)
- Processes (always in flux)
- Priorities (always shifting)
- Practices (always changing)

Principles are the set of cultural guidelines including vision, mission, and values designed to align and govern how people behave within a given system—these usually change very rarely once established. Priorities are written to drive focus into the system and are need-based, and therefore easier to influence than principles. Processes are how things are supposed to get done, and they're easier to adjust and address than priorities. They need to be re-evaluated to the extent that changes are needed in these key hows. Practices indicate how things are actually done in the system; this is the area where most problems are identified for action, even though executive values and priorities usually have the most influence over practices.

To be effective J.E.D.I. leaders, therefore, we must increase our knowledge of these four P's, their current state, gaps, and issues. Then we must use our findings to drive our initiatives forward with everyone on the same page.

Principles: Leading with Purpose

Almost every organization possesses a written reason for being, or a statement of what it does and how it operates. As Simon Sinek points out in his book, Start with Why,[81] far fewer can articulate why they do what they do—which can lead to a lack of internal and external alignment and, ultimately, a lack of differentiation in the markets in which they operate. In the spirit of judo, we can leverage company principles as the first port of call of our work. Getting the context into how the principles were developed, who was involved, and the degree to which these principles are producing the desired outcomes for the business is where we start our journey into the four P's.

Earlier, we reviewed the concept of *Level 5 Leadership*. Level 5 Leaders are those who lead via principles and not their personality or ego. When the very executives in charge of running an organization are not even adhering to the guiding principles of the business, there is no change initiative that will survive beyond an initial spark. It is essential that we assess the degree to which our executives are willing to walk the talk of organizational principles. Where they are clearly unwilling, the best suggestion is to work with them to craft a set of new principles that are more reflective of what they truly value; otherwise, the dissonance will likely destroy any efforts to progress.

If we are working with leaders who truly adhere to the principles of the organization, the work here is to demonstrate the degree to which these principles are driving the desired practices on the ground. There are a variety of tools at our disposal, from organizational surveys to the process of GEMBA—going and seeing for ourselves—and sometimes, we need to use multiple approaches to get a clear picture. This is not going to result in quick wins, which is why aligning on the four arguments for change and doing the incentive work from the previous chapters is recommended prior to taking this major step. In this stage, we are acting as detectives with a hunch that something is not right downstream, and we are obsessed with finding out the truth.

GEMBA

But before we progress in this direction, we need to assess the degree of alignment between principles and priorities.

Priorities: Alignment Between *Why* and *What*

The most common disconnect to detect is a misalignment between organizational principles and priorities, or what over why. This disconnect is understandable, because principles are aspirational, and priorities are often a combination of proactive measures and reactive needs. Priorities are not only driven by the acute needs of the business but also by external pressures, internal crises, and progress against the never-ending mission of business sustainability and growth. It is when priorities begin to lose focus on this mission in favor of the acute needs and external pressures that organizational alignment toward the overall mission begins to erode.

In a high-performance organization, however, there is nearly always a clear line of sight between the stated priorities and the overall principles of the entity—the why and the what. One of the primary goals of J.E.D.I. leadership for these organizations, therefore, is to work with senior management to ensure clarity in terms of communication and also in terms of human systems. This is what Patrick Lencioni describes as the Four Obsessions of the Extraordinary Executive:[82] 1) building a high-performance leadership team, 2) creating clarity, 3) overcommunicating clarity, and 4) embedding clarity in human systems. Human systems translate into processes such as hiring, reward and recognition, promotion, compliance, and customer excellence (to name a few).

For other companies, the work lies solely in helping senior management articulate a clear why for the business that goes beyond the profit motive (so it connects with everyone in the organization) and then working with them to revise priorities and to make this clarity as sharp as possible. Therefore, one of our first responsibilities is to assess which type of organization we are working for—high-performance, or low-clarity.

High-Performance or Low-Clarity

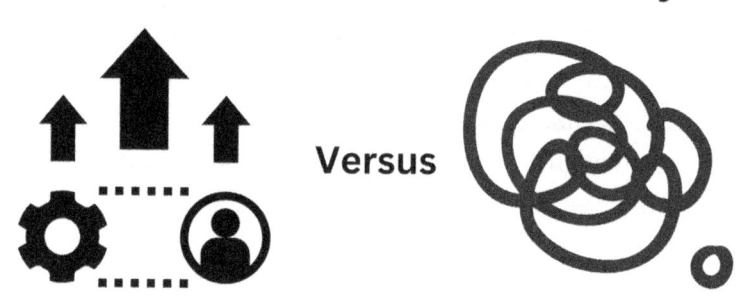

Versus

Processes: How Work Gets Done (On Paper)

A company's culture is codified into the DNA of the organization via key processes which spell out how each function performs its specific job for the organization. Both principles and priorities have an impact on processes, which is why misalignments between these two crucial areas can lead to significant confusion and gaps in processes. Although processes are usually designed as instruction manuals that take guess work out of the system, rarely do process owners understand the degree of compliance and adherence to these processes without some sort of audit function evaluating the strengths and weaknesses of the system.

Many of the opportunities inherent in J.E.D.I. leadership lie in the systematic evaluation of key processes related to human systems—recruiting, hiring, onboarding, training and development, reward and recognition, talent management, compensation, and incentives, to mention a few common areas that most organizations have documented via standard operating procedures (SOPs). This is why we state that J.E.D.I. leadership can begin right where someone finds themselves within the company structure, whether a new joiner, a first-line manager, a functional leader, a divisional head, or a senior executive. Simply by taking it upon ourselves to examine processes through the lenses of justice, equity, diversity, and inclusion, we can begin to identify issues or system weaknesses; delve into root cause to create corrective and preventative actions; strengthen our disciplinary matrix; design new operating procedures; communicate and train on these areas; and ensure robust monitoring of what we expect.

We call this J.E.D.I. process *restoration*—as in, restoring the processes to the proper state where injustices are eradicated, inequities are eliminated, diversity is expanded, and inclusion is enhanced. If these goals are not codified into the human systems of the company via new operating procedures, then it becomes very challenging to implement them into actual practices.

Practices: What Work Actually Gets Done

In the world of internal and external audit, the risk that a company's internal controls won't detect or prevent mistakes is known as control risk. The greatest control risk root causes, on average, are linked to hiring, process clarity, training, and management monitoring. When we hire poorly (such as not conducting thorough background checks, or selecting individuals with a track record of fraud), we permit potentially toxic individuals to enter into our systems. When processes are overly cumbersome, don't use plain language, or seem irrelevant or out of touch with on-the-ground realities, we create barriers to understanding, agreement, and alignment. When we don't thoroughly train on processes and procedures (whether they are well crafted or not), we create gaps in application that can lead to major violations. Finally, when we don't have a management monitoring system in place (or it lacks sufficient robustness), problems fall through the cracks.

Merely having a policy in place is not sufficient to improve upon or prevent negative occurrences.

If the audit system is the company's hardware, then the biases, beliefs, and behaviors of the employees are the software. And as we discussed in the previous chapter, the fastest way to influence behaviors is through incentive reevaluation. As humans, we mostly operate within established boundaries of societal or group norms, and what gets valued often gets done. When we have the right processes in place but still see individuals consistently acting in violation of these processes, either we have hired fundamentally "bad" folks, or—more likely—their behavior is being driven by a shadow incentive system.

In June of 2021,[83] Ernst and Young (EY), a multinational professional services network, was subject to a case brought forth by the Securities and Exchange Commission (SEC) due to alleged widespread cheating by its audit professionals on CPA exams and subsequent withholding of misconduct evidence during the SEC's investigation. The SEC charged EY for violations that occurred over several years, where numerous EY professionals engaged in cheating on the ethics component of their mandatory CPA exams and in other professional education courses essential for maintaining CPA licenses.

Be on the Lookout for Red Flags

THE J.E.D.I. LEADER'S PLAYBOOK

EY was accused of and admitted to failing to convey accurate information regarding cheating issues to the SEC's Enforcement Division during the ongoing investigation into the suspected misconduct within the firm. Despite being aware of potential cheating and conducting an internal investigation confirming the same, EY did not amend its submission to the SEC. The discussions about the cheating incidents reached senior lawyers and members of the firm's management, and yet EY still chose not to cooperate with the SEC's investigation and continued to provide misleading submissions.

As a result of the misconduct and the subsequent disclosure failures and lack of cooperation, EY was hit with a substantial penalty of $100 million. This penalty was imposed after the admission of the professionals to cheating and the firm's failure to report correct information about the unethical practices to the SEC, thereby violating principles of ethical integrity and professional conduct.

To remediate its deficiencies, and as part of the sanction, EY is mandated to adopt extensive corrective measures, including the engagement of two independent consultants. One of the consultants will be tasked with reviewing and providing recommendations on EY's ethical and integrity-related policies and procedures. The other consultant will examine EY's disclosure failures and the roles of any EY employees in contributing to the firm's continued provision for misleading information to the SEC.

In summary, this case against EY highlighted significant lapses in professional ethics and integrity within the firm, along with the firm's unwillingness to correct its course even after the internal confirmation of misconduct, leading to hefty financial penalties and mandatory corrective actions.

In unpacking this case study, we can clearly see cheating

was not routinely punished by EY's disciplinary matrix and that, when exposed, that disciplinary matrix allowed cheating to turn into organizational lying, omission, and obfuscation at multiple levels of the company. Cheating was therefore being incentivized by the lack of oversight and enforcement. This was clearly a toxic cultural norm, as even when given the opportunity to come clean, the company was incapable of doing so.

By contrast, in 2015, GlaxoSmithKline Pharmaceuticals (GSK) began conducting internal culture audits dubbed "Values Assurance" in the wake of a Chinese bribery scandal that cost the company $500 million in fines,[84] a similar amount in lost business, and significantly more in terms of reputation. This process was designed to highlight understanding, agreement, and alignment with a suite of core values and was conducted across the world by internal audit professionals. Values Assurance has been positively received by both leaders and employees. Leaders appreciate the valuable and honest feedback it provides, and employees appreciate the opportunity to share their own perspectives. This program fills an important gap in traditional audit programs by providing an unbiased perspective on leadership, attitudes, and behaviors that support the internal control framework. It is providing new insights that are improving risk management, strategy, and GSK's reputation.

Impacting the Four P's

Executive influence, in terms of their beliefs, biases, and behaviors, often leads to unstable principles (as these are only as steady and unwavering as are a company's leaders), continuously shifting priorities, unenforced processes, and morphing practices (depending on what the culture is incentivizing and disincentivizing). The good news is that there are several offsets that can be leveraged to convince executives to address their three B's. One is external pressure, which comes in the forms of customers, regulators, competitor performance, societal expectations, and investor sentiment. Organizational culture can be positively shifted by using the correct lever(s) of required change from the external environment—which, after impacting the three B's, can lead to realigned principles, revised priorities, reset processes, and restored practices.

Another, more powerful tool that can be used to impact this shift is the risk mitigation argument we previously discussed in Chapter 4. Effective risk mitigation starts with conducting an organizational risk assessment linked to processes and practices. In this effort, we endeavor to identify processes that are incomplete or are reinforcing poor processes and practices that can cost our reputation, financials, and/or regulatory environment. The outputs of an effective risk assessment will effectively influence the three B's of executives and lead to a reassessment of principles, a realignment of priorities, a resetting of processes, and a restoration of practices.

As you can see, the end result of external pressure and internal risk assessment can be the appropriate shifting of culture emanating from executive beliefs, biases, and behaviors—but one approach (external pressure) is reactive, while the other (risk assessment) is proactive. Proactive measures are far more powerful, but it takes a very mature and open leadership team and culture to lean into this space.

Going back to the GSK example, in addition to the Values Assurance process which provided another layer of insight into the company's alignment between principles and practices, the leaders of the company also instituted far-reaching risk mitigation priorities and processes which eliminated any transfer of value between the company and health care providers (a staple of the pharmaceutical industry). This risk mitigation also eliminated the (well-established) industry practice of compensating sales representatives on prescriptions generated. Starting in January of 2016, the entire company shifted its ways of working and pushed into more innovative methods of gaining the trust of its customers and adding value—and, for a time, there was a singular pharmaceutical entity in the world that had mitigated all risk of undo physician influence and relied on its scientific acumen and product value proposition to generate growth.

Although there was intense skepticism both within the company and within the wider pharmaceutical industry related to GSK's ability to compete with both arms effectively tied behind its back (relative to industry norms), the company grew revenues by $10 billion over the six years after embarking on its trailblazing path. And in the three years post-initiation of the new principles, the company's priorities, processes, and practices delivered $8 billion of that total revenue growth. Unfortunately, the company reinstated payments to health care practitioners and began paying incentives to sales representatives around 2020 and has only delivered $3 billion of incremental revenues since backsliding (this figure has been impacted by the pandemic, as well).

When endeavoring to leverage risk assessment as the primary tool to motivate organizational change, here are a few questions to start with:

- Which business practices have been flagged as high risk?
- What are the SOPs linked to these business practices?
- Who are the business owners accountable for effective implementation of these SOPs?

- Where are the gaps between the SOPs and the actual practices?
- What is the cost of inaction?

Now that we have contended with the headwinds of executive beliefs, biases, and behaviors on the four P's, we can turn to identifying specific objectives and outcomes of our work.

7

ESTABLISHING GOALS, PRIORITIES, AND CAPABILITIES

With a clear why driving our passion and purpose for this work, a novel strategy which informs our approach in the concept of judo, and understanding and alignment with key data and definitions, we have enough background to delve into which combination of the four arguments for change will be most influential on executive beliefs, biases, and behaviors in the context of the alignment (or lack thereof) between company principles, priorities, processes, and practices. In the context of business transformation, we can consider all of these as components of the assessment stage.

A business transformation framework is a structured approach for managing and implementing changes to an organization's processes, systems, and culture to achieve specific goals and objectives. A typical framework may include the following steps:

- **Assessment:** Identifying the need for transformation and evaluating the current state of the organization to understand gaps between the current state and the desired future state.

- **Planning:** Developing a detailed plan for the transformation, including goals, objectives, timelines, and key performance indicators (KPIs).

- **Design:** Crafting the detailed design for the transformation, including the processes, systems, and culture changes required to achieve the goals and objectives.

- **Implementation:** Implementing the changes, including training and communication to ensure that employees understand the changes and their role in the transformation.

- **Monitoring and Control:** Monitoring progress and performance against the KPIs and making adjustments as needed to ensure that the transformation stays on track.

- **Closure:** Conducting a final evaluation, once the transformation is complete, to assess the results and impact of the transformation and to develop an action plan to maintain and sustain the new processes, systems, and culture.

- **Continual improvement:** Regularly evaluating the outcomes of the transformation and making adjustments as required to continuously improve the processes, systems, and culture.

With this clarity, we must now progress from the assessment stage to the planning stage. We do so by establishing Wildly Important Goals, or WIGS.

Wildly Important Goals (WIGs)

According to the *Franklin-Covey Institute:*[85] Wildly Important Goals (WIGs) are a small number of crucial goals that must be achieved in order for other goals to be meaningful. These goals are critical but may be overlooked because of the tendency to focus on urgent matters. To identify WIGs, we must ask, "Which area of our operation, if improved, would have the greatest impact while all other areas remain at their current level of performance?" From there, we gather input and reach a consensus with our teams on these identified goals.

What are our WIGs?

To create a WIG, we must understand our current state, our desired state, and the actions we will take to achieve the desired state within a specific time frame. An example of this structure might be to lose fifty pounds by December 31 by working out at least three times a week and limiting calories to 2,000 per day. In this WIG, we acknowledge that in the current state we are fifty pounds overweight, we wish to be fifty pounds lighter, and we aim to achieve this goal via diet and exercise over the course of a single calendar year. The other great thing about constructing a WIG this way is that our lead and lag measures of success are clearly articulated in the description. The lag measure is the desired state or outcome—in this case, losing fifty pounds. The lead measures will be achieving our exercise frequency and caloric intake targets, which can be adjusted over time to either speed up or slow down our path to goal attainment.

The Four Wildly Important Goals of J.E.D.I. Leadership

Eradicate Injustices   Eliminate Inequities   Expand Diversity   Enhance Inclusion

Now let's turn this thinking to the four macro goals of J.E.D.I. Leadership. We are working to eradicate injustices, eliminate inequities, expand diversity, and enhance inclusion. Because these are the higher-order objectives of our effort, we need to create WIGs that either sit under each letter of our acronym (depth) or cross over all four elements (breadth). A depth WIG, for example, is selecting one specific area (i.e., justice) to dive deeply into for a given period. Rather than working across the spectrum of J.E.D.I., we purposefully select injustice, prioritize areas of focus, define our desired outcomes, articulate lead and lag measures, and then begin tracking our progress as we move into doing the work. Everyone in the organization can then rally around our efforts to eradicate specific injustices, and our communications can be streamlined as such.

Unfortunately, time constraints and pressures often don't allow us to do such focused work, and we must adopt the breadth approach instead. Breadth is going wide versus deep and making sure our efforts contemplate goals across the J.E.D.I. spectrum. In this way, we may have one or two specific outcomes linked to each element of justice, equity, diversity, and inclusion.

Importantly, despite our best intentions, if we bite off more than we can chew, (i.e., attempting to do breadth and depth simultaneously), we will likely burn out—which does no one any good, because our leadership is what is keeping the train on track. It's far better to do fewer things very well and be able to clearly demonstrate impact than to try to tackle all the problems in our organization and end up fixing none of them.

The way we can select between breadth or depth is by considering time, support, and investment. With a clear mandate from senior management to institute needed change, and enough investment and support, we can accomplish quite a bit within a given period, so we should choose breadth and work across the J.E.D.I. WIGs. If this mandate is unclear, it's better to under-promise and overdeliver while deepening our understanding—this indicates depth, and we should choose which element of J.E.D.I. we wish to tackle first, second, third, and fourth.

An illustration of a depth WIG for expanding diversity could be to increase representation of women at the senior executive level of our organization by 50 percent by year-end by enacting a temporary hiring freeze of male senior executives in specific divisions, identifying a pool of talented women to career- accelerate, providing those women with executive coaching support, and having each of them shadow a senior executive mentor. From this WIG, we have identified that in the current state our percentage of women senior executives is lower than desired. We've also clarified that we wish to boost this percentage significantly over the next year and that we will be measuring the identification of the talent pool, ensuring that they are coached and that they gain shadowing opportunities. Should our lead measures be off-target, we can adjust them in number and/or intensity as necessary. The power of depth WIGS, once again, is the focus with which they allow us to imbue our efforts. The story from this year will be about expanding diversity for women within the senior executive ranks.

If breadth is the requirement, however, we still must

prioritize our efforts. One way of doing so is to focus on one aspect of J.E.D.I. at a time via a quarterly cascade. Let's say we decide on the following WIGS across the J.E.D.I. spectrum:

- **Justice:** Minimize the funding to employment practices liability insurance (EPLI) by 75 percent by the end of Q1 while bolstering the use of our speak-up and investigations processes to eliminate bad actors from the system.

- **Equity:** Address the concerns of employees regarding the trade-offs of family planning versus career progression by the end of Q2 by instituting a mandatory paid four-month maternity and paternity leave policy for all full-time employees and conducting regular surveys of this affected population.

- **Diversity:** Increase the number of African American candidates hired in the same period last year by 33 percent by the end of Q3 by building an HBCU talent pipeline for selected functions, identifying a minimum of four HBCU partners, going on quarterly meet and greet and talent identification visits, and offering free seminars for qualified students.

- **Inclusion:** Improve our town halls and all-hands meetings from one-way communications to two-way exchanges by the end of Q4 by leveraging sentiment analysis technology and demographic data to better understand the discrete belonging necessities of different employee constituencies, conducting quarterly focus groups with our employee resource groups, and ensuring a minimum of thirty minutes of Q&A at every collective forum.

Setting Priorities

With clear and aligned J.E.D.I. WIGs, we can set our key priorities linked to each. Importantly, setting priorities must go beyond simply creating a to-do list of imperatives.

As there are any number of areas in which to start, we need to apply some filters to allow us to identify where to focus. We do this by using two different types of prioritization matrices: urgency versus importance, and then effort versus impact.

What is Productivity?

Productivity is defined as the efficiency of manifestation of goods or services expressed by some measure. Depending on the measure, how we see productivity can be positive or negative. For example:

- Getting things done. Many DEI programs look at success this way.

- Getting the right things done. Far fewer DEI programs even know what the right things are.

- Getting the right things done right. This can only occur once we know what the right things are and have created standards for our work.

- Getting the right things done right the first time. We can achieve this level only after repeated attempts and cycles through the overall process to understand the inefficiencies in how we are working so we can ultimately correct and eliminate them.

The discussion of the right things leads to interrogating our list of WIGs.

Justice WIGs

If eradicating injustices is our Wildly Important Goal, what can we achieve this month, this quarter, and this year in relation to it? Well, imagine that we have identified the following risks:

- We don't have a consequence and/or disciplinary matrix in place that minimizes repeat mistakes and offenders (justice).

- Our training doesn't routinely increase understanding, agreement, and alignment (justice).

So, which of these should be prioritized? We must use our filters.

Importance

VI/NU	VI/VU
NI/NU	NI/VU

Urgency

This matrix allows us to prioritize based on importance and urgency. Importance in the context of J.E.D.I. work should always be thought of in terms of our primary stakeholder: employees. Urgency can be thought of in terms of need. Therefore, initiatives that are deemed important and necessary to employees should be placed in the VI/VU or Very Important/Very Urgent box. Initiatives that employees identify as crucial but less necessary in the current context can move into the VI/NU or Very Important/Not Urgent box.

Going back to our justice priorities, then, effective training is arguably more important and urgent than the creation and enforcement of a consequence and/or disciplinary matrix. Therefore, training goes into the VI/VU square, and the consequence matrix goes into the VI/NU square.

Importance

VI/NU	VI/VU
• Increase African Americen candidates hired (D) • Build an HBCU talent pipeline for selected functions (D) • Identify a minimum of 4 HBCU partners (D) • Set up quarterly meet and greets (D) • Create seminar series (D)	• Minimize funding to EPLI (J) • Bolster use of speak up (J) • Enhance investigations process (J) • Institute 4 month maternity leave policy (E) • Rebalance pay and benefits for returning employees (E) • Regularly survey this population (E)
NI/NU	NI/VU

Urgency

THE J.E.D.I. LEADER'S PLAYBOOK

We could certainly stop the prioritization exercise at this point, but taking the next step and filtering initiatives based on Impact and Effort might tilt the scales one way or another toward a given priority. Impact is like importance, in that it relates to measurable positive benefits of an initiative on our primary stakeholder: employees. Effort is an acknowledgement that not all work is created equally and that some lifts—while worthy—may require significantly more effort in terms of hours, investment, alignment, and implementation than others. Taking the time to understand this piece of the puzzle can clarify our starting point, as well as allow us to make necessary trade-offs along the journey.

An example of this kind of matrix looks like:

Impact

HI/LE	HI/HE
• Minimize funding to EPLI (J) • Institute 4 month maternity leave policy (E) • Regularly survey this population (E)	• Bolster use of speak up (J) • Enhance investigations process (J) • Rebalance pay and benefits for returning employees (E)
LI/LE	LI/HE

Effort

We can see here that what we are seeking to understand are the low-hanging fruit initiatives in the HI/LE or High Impact/Low Effort square and the heavier lifts of the HI/HE or High Impact/High Effort square. If something is high-impact, we need to do it; the question is in which order and how quickly. If urgency is paramount, as in the case of enhancing training, then it may supersede the amount of effort required to execute this initiative. If the initiative is less urgent, as in the case of the consequence and disciplinary matrix, but is a lighter lift, we may consider delegating it and getting it done sooner than we would have while looking only at the initial prioritization.

With clarity of goals and priorities, we can finally dig into the true core of our work: driving adoption.

PART II: DEVELOPMENT AND DELIVERY

8

DRIVING ADOPTION

Any successful transformation has three lead measures of success, which we have already touched upon: understanding, agreement, and alignment—or UAA. The UAA framework is essential to achieving our desired objective of broad-based adoption of new incentives, priorities, processes, and—ultimately—practices. With adoption as our guiding light, we need to understand the competencies needed to achieve this outcome sooner rather than later in our organizations. This chapter will describe capabilities from a key discipline that doesn't often get discussed in most DEI circles— marketing— but without which it is impossible to reach our desired state of needed change.

Another Hat

We've previously discussed the broad set of functions a J.E.D.I. leader must serve. Process auditing, rewriting operating procedures, crafting communications, and training are just a few of the hats worn daily by those working within this space. Another of these hats is marketing. Believe it or not, all the good intentions in the world will crumble without an excellent strategic plan, clear positioning, and experiences that lead to broad-based adoption of our initiatives.

The marketing tools most relevant to J.E.D.I. leadership are equally relevant to anyone attempting to drive adoption of any initiative, process, or product—but they are rarely applied in this space, either due to lack of awareness or lack of expertise. As many operating in this realm are either former academics or human resource professionals, this is understandable. The good news is that there is a marketing process that can be easily adapted to our work and dramatically potentialize our efforts.

So, let's try on this marketing hat.

J.E.D.I. SWOT

Strategy is ultimately about choices. Effective strategic planning always begins with the end in mind. Where are we going? Why should we go there? What is the best way to get there? What will be the outcomes we achieve by pursuing this direction? These are the questions top-level strategists obsess over.

Before any strategy can be developed, we need to take stock in where we possess inherent strengths and weaknesses, as well as identify key opportunities (judo) and threats to our success. The SWOT analysis tool was first developed in the 1960s by a management consultant named Albert Humphrey at the Stanford Research Institute.[86] Previously, corporate planning had not met with much success. Fortune 500 companies needed a way to produce long-term planning that was executable and reasonable. Humphrey and his research team proposed the SWOT model to bring accountability and objectivity to the planning process, and it has been popular ever since.

A SWOT analysis is a simple way to discover positive and negative factors in any context. Specifically, it's a four-quadrant diagram that identifies strengths, weaknesses, opportunities, and threats. Creating a SWOT chart forces contributors to critically examine their circumstances and find out which obstacles must be overcome or minimized. A SWOT can also help determine steps that should be taken to achieve short- and long-term success.

The angle here is that we are assessing our work through the lens of progress against the goals of eradicating injustices, eliminating inequities, expanding diversity, and enhancing inclusion; as such, we require four distinct SWOT analyses for each of our four areas of focus. We want to be as specific as possible and move away from generalities.

Leverage the questionnaire below to fill in the blanks. While not an exhaustive list, this assessment will help highlight immediate strengths, gaps, opportunities, and threats. Importantly, any area we answer "no" to on strengths automatically creates a weakness.

Identifying Justice Strengths

- Do we have a strong compliance management monitoring system in place?
- Do we have a strong corrective and preventative actions process in place?
- Do we have a robust consequence and/or disciplinary matrix in place that minimizes repeat mistakes and offenders?
- Do we have excellent training that empirically increases understanding, agreement, and alignment?

Identifying Equity Strengths

- Do we regularly conduct internal pay equity audits across all divisions?

- Do we always collect and use internal data on equity gaps within key demographics?
- Do we systematically work across the organization to eliminate bias from key processes and practices?
- Do we have a paternity leave policy that encourages men to take on the caregiver role after birth?
- Do we have supporting policies that make it easier for women to balance work and family responsibilities?

Identifying Diversity Strengths

- Do we have above-average diversity (gender and ethnic) within executive ranks of the organization?
- Do our managers apply a strengths-based management system to harness the collective power of our organization?
- Do our employees feel empowered to leverage their differences to drive our competitive advantage?
- Do we consistently innovate faster and more successfully than industry peers and competitors?

Identifying Inclusion Strengths

- Do we have evidence that all identities within our organization feel accepted and embraced?
- Do we have systems and practices in place that amplify all voices?
- Do we regularly seek perspectives on key issues from different vantage points?

- Do we highly support different styles of living and being?

As previously mentioned, the no's above become your list of weaknesses so we have already completed the top level of our SWOT:

Strengths
- a strong management monitoring system (justice)
- a strong corrective and preventative actions process (justice)
- above-average diversity (gender and ethnic) within executive ranks (diversity)
- we innovate faster and more successfully than peers and competitors (diversity)
- we regularly seek perspectives on key issues from different vantage points (inclusion)

Weaknesses
- no disciplinary matrix in place that minimizes repeat mistakes and offenders (justice)
- training doesn't routinely increase understanding, agreement, and alignment (justice)
- we don't regularly conduct internal pay equity audits across all divisions (equity)
- we don't always collect and use internal data on equity gaps within key demographics (equity)
- we don't systematically work across the organization to eliminate bias from key processes and practices (equity)
- our managers don't apply a strengths-based management system (diversity)
- our employees don't aways feel empowered to leverage their differences to drive our competitive advantage (diversity)
- we don't have evidence that all identities within our organization feel accepted and embraced (inclusion)
- we don't have systems and practices in place that amplify all voices (inclusion)
- we don't highly support different styles of living and being (inclusion)

Successful J.E.D.I. leaders don't take the strengths side of this analysis for granted. The discussion to be had once these strengths are identified is to understand how to potentialize them even more. J.E.D.I. strengths form the foundation from which all other progress can be achieved, and every organization already possesses strengths in this quadrant. The question is: does everyone understand how these strengths are being leveraged to inform the journey ahead? Often, capitalizing on strengths forms the greatest near-term opportunities.

On the weaknesses side, we need to prioritize, as we can't—nor should we—act on each of these in equal measure. A word of advice is to simply follow the order of our acronym: tackle justice weaknesses, then equity, then diversity, then inclusion. Doing so gives us a systematic approach to our work and makes it easier for others to follow. It is far better to do a few things all the way than to scatter our efforts and see no real impact just because we want to show how many things we are doing.

Moving on to J.E.D.I. opportunities, these are gathered from taking an outside-in look at our organization, benchmarking versus best-in-class operations. An opportunity must be something that your company can and will capitalize on under the right conditions. Here are some questions to ask to fill in this section:

J.E.D.I. Opportunities Analysis

- How can we further capitalize on our strengths to outperform competitors, innovate further, and reduce risk exposure?
- What are trends we are well positioned to leverage based on our strengths?

Finally, we turn to examine key threats. In the context of J.E.D.I. strategy, we must understand our internal environment and external shifts that can increase our risk exposure beyond our degree of comfort. The point of identifying these factors and potential events is to begin the process of contingency and continuity planning that rarely (if ever) happens in this sphere. Weaknesses become threats to the degree that they will obstruct our ability to make progress and/or enhance the likelihood and impact of some negative future outcome.

J.E.D.I. Threats Analysis:

- To what degree have we already identified problem areas in our principles, processes, and/or practices that need to be addressed?
- To what degree does the tone from the top (senior management) not align with the investment and support needed to do the work?
- To what degree is there lack of clarity and agreement on goals throughout the organization?
- To what degree are the right people not in the right jobs and not empowered to act?
- To what extent are efforts to enhance J.E.D.I. work being undermined by conflicting priorities and/or lack of resourcing?

With the exception of the first question, if the answers to any or all of the above questions are "high" to "very high," in terms of the degree away from where we would like to be, then we can perceive them as major threats to our ability to effectively drive our strategy and initiatives. Still, the presence of threats does not automatically disqualify our organizations from making at least some progress toward J.E.D.I. objectives.

Where to Play and How to Win

With clarity on our J.E.D.I. SWOT, we can begin to formulate our strategy. The book *Playing to Win: How Strategy Really Works*,[87] by A.G. Lafley and Roger L. Martin, delves into key concepts related to strategic decision-making, specifically focusing on the framework of "where to play" and "how to win." These concepts provide a systematic approach for organizations to identify the most promising market opportunities and develop winning strategies to capitalize on them. The key concepts are articulated as follows:

- Where to Play: This concept emphasizes the importance of selecting the right markets and customer segments to target. It involves analyzing various dimensions such as customer needs, market size, growth potential, competitive landscape, and the organization's capabilities. By identifying attractive market spaces where the organization has a competitive advantage, it can allocate its resources effectively and focus its efforts on areas that offer the greatest potential for success.

- How to Win: Once the "where to play" decision is made, the next step is to determine "how to win" in those chosen markets. This concept involves formulating a winning strategy that differentiates the organization from its competitors and creates a sustainable competitive advantage. It entails making deliberate choices about value proposition, customer experience, pricing, distribution channels, and other strategic elements to effectively serve the chosen markets.

- Strategic Choice: This concept highlights the need for making strategic choices that align with the organization's strengths, resources, and capabilities. It involves assessing the trade-offs between different strategic options and making conscious decisions about the areas where the organization will focus its efforts. Strategic choices may involve decisions related to product development, geographic expansion, market segmentation, or customer targeting.

- Proximity to the Customer: The book emphasizes the importance of understanding customers deeply and being close to them to develop effective strategies. By gaining insights into customer preferences, needs, and behaviors, organizations can create tailored offerings that resonate with their target audience. Proximity to the customer also enables organizations to anticipate changes in customer preferences and adapt their strategies accordingly.

- Strategic Learning: Lafley and Martin highlight the iterative and adaptive nature of strategy. They emphasize the importance of continuous learning, experimentation, and feedback loops to refine and improve strategies over time. By collecting data, analyzing results, and adjusting approaches based on feedback, organizations can stay agile and responsive in dynamic markets.

- Execution: While strategy formulation is crucial, the book emphasizes that successful execution is equally important. It emphasizes the need for clear communication, effective resource allocation, and strong leadership to translate strategic decisions into tangible results. Effective execution ensures that the chosen strategies are implemented effectively and efficiently, driving the organization toward its desired outcomes.

With this model in mind, let's discuss how to leverage it to increase the success of our J.E.D.I. initiatives.

OMAR L. HARRIS

Eradicating Injustices Strategic Plan

ERADICATING INJUSTICES PRIORITIES	WHERE TO PLAY	HOW TO WIN	STRATEGIC CHOICES	EXECUTION KPI
Strengthening compliance internal control framework				
Strengthing corrective and preventative actions identification and implementation				
Strengthening disciplinary matrix				
Enhancing key policy training				

Create a table with each of the above elements listed as the column headers on top and our J.E.D.I. focus areas as the row headers. As you will recall, it is the guidance of this book to pursue strategic depth, as in completing work under eradicating injustices before moving on to eliminating inequities, expanding diversity, and enhancing inclusion. The example below takes this approach into account.

As you can see, we have taken the priorities from the SWOT example above and plotted each in its own corresponding row. This setup allows us to evaluate different strategic approaches with each priority. With the priorities identified, let's begin completing our strategic plan for eradicating injustices. Where to play, in this instance, will describe the scope of our focus. Are we targeting the entire company? A single function or division? Or perhaps a specific process (e.g., hiring and recruiting that has been identified as a pain point for the organization) as it relates to J.E.D.I.?

Beginning with the end in mind can be quite helpful here, as defining a desired state can often allow us to narrow our focus to deliver the required result. Let's imagine that doing so (beginning with the end in mind), we determine that we want to show progress in our health and wellness efforts by restoring policies to enhance preventative health practices such as vaccination, annual check-ups, paid time off, counseling, maternity/paternity leave, gym memberships, nutrition tips, etc.

This is a good area to examine, because it is well known that policies around health and wellness in organizations can inadvertently perpetuate injustices,[88] leading to unequal outcomes and reinforcing existing disparities such as:

- Access and Affordability: Policies focused on health and wellness initiatives, such as wellness programs or gym memberships, may disproportionately benefit employees with higher incomes. This can create a disparity where employees with lower incomes, who may face financial constraints, are unable to access or afford these programs. As a result, the health and wellness benefits provided by the organization can reinforce existing socioeconomic inequalities.

- Cultural and Individual Differences: Health and wellness policies often assume a one-size-fits-all approach, disregarding the diverse needs and cultural backgrounds of employees. This disregard can lead to a lack of inclusivity, as certain wellness programs or initiatives may not resonate with or be accessible to individuals from different cultural backgrounds. Consequently, these policies may perpetuate disparities and exclusion within the organization.

- Unintended Consequences of Incentives: In some cases, wellness programs that provide incentives for healthy behaviors may inadvertently penalize employees who have pre-existing health conditions or disabilities. These programs can create a punitive environment where individuals with chronic illnesses or disabilities are unable to meet the same health targets as their healthier counterparts. Consequently, the programs can exacerbate health disparities and contribute to a culture of discrimination and unfairness.

- Work-Life Balance and Flexible Policies: While work-life balance and flexible policies are often promoted as part of wellness initiatives, they may inadvertently reinforce gender inequalities. Research indicates that women, particularly those with caregiving responsibilities, may face greater challenges in accessing and benefiting from flexible work arrangements or policies related to family leave. These kinds of challenge can perpetuate gender disparities in career progression and compensation.

- Bias in Health Assessment and Screening: Organizations that incorporate health assessments or screenings as part of their wellness programs may inadvertently introduce biases that disproportionately affect certain employee groups. For example, using only body mass index (BMI) as a measure of health can perpetuate weight bias and discrimination. Similarly, relying solely on certain health metrics may overlook or undervalue other aspects of health and well-being, leading to disparities and injustices.

Understanding these potential outcomes, we have identified where we wish to play—as illustrated here:

Eradicating Injustices Strategic Plan

ERADICATING INJUSTICES PRIORITIES	WHERE TO PLAY	HOW TO WIN	STRATEGIC CHOICES	EXECUTION KPI
Strengthening compliance internal control framework	Health and Wellness Policies			
Strengthening identification and implementation of corrective and preventative actions				
Strengthening disciplinary matrix				
Enhancing key policy training				

Our scope is defined as eradicating potential injustices in our health and wellness policies. Completing the **How to Win** column now becomes a matter of identifying known issues within this set of policies. In order to strengthen our compliance internal control framework, we must invest time and energy into identifying key issues that are driving injustices. This investment may take the form of employee interviews, discussions with policy owners, and/or even leveraging internal audit findings (if they exist). For the purposes of this exercise, let's assume the issue is that health and wellness benefits are linked to rank and title—meaning that the higher up we go within an organization, the better the benefits packages.

OMAR L. HARRIS

Eradicating Injustices Strategic Plan

ERADICATING INJUSTICES PRIORITIES	WHERE TO PLAY	HOW TO WIN	STRATEGIC CHOICES	EXECUTION KPI
Strengthening compliance internal control framework	Health and Wellness Policies	Gym memberships, health screenings, and flexible work		
Strengthening identification and implementation of corrective and preventative actions				
Strengthening disciplinary matrix				
Enhancing key policy training				

This was an issue within various companies I worked with in Brazil, where it is common for executives to receive disproportionate health and wellness benefits versus less-tenured or lower-titled colleagues (as an incentive to keep progressing through the organization). Next to health and wellness policies, we will look to strengthen the internal control framework relative to ensuring all employees receive health and wellness benefits regardless of tenure or title. We will list three policies in particular: gym memberships, health screenings, and flexible work.

Turning to strategic choices, this is where we decide the key levers to pull in order to deliver successful outcomes. In this case, as we are discussing policies that involve some degree of financial impact, we need to decide our budget allocation (including relevant fact-finding and benchmarking efforts). We need to decide which functions will be impacted in which order (as piloting may be preferable to a full-scale implementation in this instance, depending on the size of the organization). Piloting also reduces the financial exposure—but to pilot or not to pilot is a critical strategic choice in and of itself. Finally, we must determine what success looks like for either piloting or rolling out more broadly in terms of clear key performance indicators.

Eradicating Injustices Strategic Plan

ERADICATING INJUSTICES PRIORITIES	WHERE TO PLAY	HOW TO WIN	STRATEGIC CHOICES	EXECUTION KPI
Strengthening compliance internal control framework	Health and Wellness Policies	Gym memberships, health screenings, and flexible work	• Pilot or not? • If yes, which functions/roles? • What is the budget we need? • How will we measure success?	
Strengthening identification and implementation of corrective and preventative actions				
Strengthening disciplinary matrix				
Enhancing key policy training				

Up until now, we have been contemplating efforts relevant to each row header. Execution KPI's, however, should be specific. How do we know that a compliance internal control framework has been strengthened, for instance? Well, just having one in place that is visible is one example. Or it could be measured by the number of corrective and preventative actions it delivers; individuals disciplined due to its reinforcement; or even how well participants understand, agree, and align with its procedures. Still, as we have narrowed our strategic scope enough, it is appropriate in this instance to define a KPI for each row in our plan.

We will agree to strengthen our internal control framework against these specific health and wellness policies by conducting a thorough evaluation of each policy through the lens of our justice objectives. We will create a map of possible corrective and preventative actions for the most common problems that have been identified within a given time frame (e.g., the previous two years). We will specifically refine the disciplinary matrix to incentive the proper utilization of the policy and condemn anti-policy behavior or actions. And we will strike to achieve a measure of understanding, agreement, and alignment from our pilot group (e.g., 85 percent).

You may feel that this approach is too limiting to our far-reaching J.E.D.I. ambitions. Please consider, however, that J.E.D.I. without clear outcomes becomes an empty pursuit. For this reason, practitioners focused on highly visible initiatives such as antibias trainings, difficult conversations, and motivational talks to galvanize their efforts. They misunderstood action for impact; collectively, all of us doing the work have suffered as a result.

Eradicating Injustices Strategic Plan

ERADICATING INJUSTICES PRIORITIES	WHERE TO PLAY	HOW TO WIN	STRATEGIC CHOICES	EXECUTION KPI
Strengthening compliance internal control framework	Health and Wellness Policies	Gym memberships, health screenings, and flexible work	• Pilot or not? • If yes, which functions/roles? • What is the budget we need? • How will we measure success?	Policy reviews completed by end of Q1
Strengthening identification and implementation of corrective and preventative actions				Corrective and preventative actions maps completed by end of Q2
Strengthening disciplinary matrix				Disciplinary matrix redesign finished 1Q post-pilot completion
Enhancing key policy training				85% policy understanding, agreement, and alignment documented

Not that their efforts were for nought; but still, imagine being able to confirm that our efforts have led to a reinvention of our health and wellness policies for all employees—a highly tangible benefit that can be leveraged in recruiting and retention labors—which can be directly correlated to company performance.

This book advocates for the "less is more" approach to doing this work. Prioritizing fewer, but far more strategic and impactful, projects will keep our efforts funded and resources sustained over a longer period.

Selling J.E.D.I.

The disciplines of marketing and sales are intertwined these days, as brilliant strategy with poor execution gets us nowhere closer to our transformational goals. Taking specifically from the online sales world, the J.E.D.I. journey mimics a modern sales funnel—and, as such, requires discrete experiences to drive activation. A sales funnel is a model that represents the customer's journey toward making a purchase, from the initial awareness of a product or service through the development of interest and desire, and finally to taking action or making a purchase. It is visualized as a funnel because it starts with a broad base (many potential customers become aware of the product) and narrows down through each stage (fewer customers remain interested, decide to buy, and eventually complete the purchase). This funnel approach helps businesses understand and optimize their sales process and marketing strategies.

In our case, we want to create a conversion chute versus a sales funnel, as we don't want to lose anyone along the way to adoption.

Chutes Versus Funnels

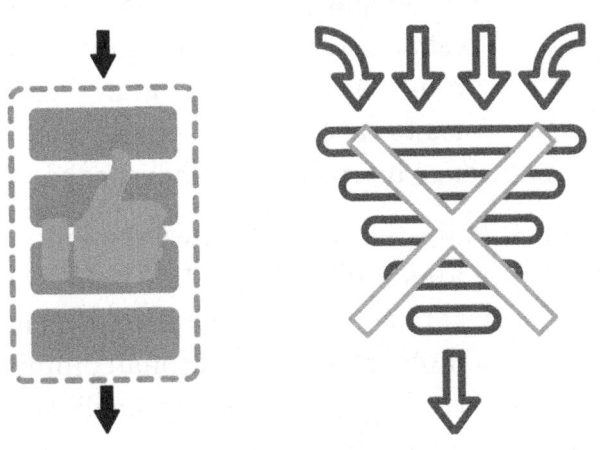

Still, even leveraging our chute analogy, we will need to apply the same principles that guide successful sales funnels—awareness, interest, decision, and action—to our J.E.D.I. initiatives. Here's how it could work:

1. *Awareness:* The first stage of the chute/funnel is awareness, where you aim to create understanding and knowledge about J.E.D.I. initiatives. This involves educational initiatives that inform all stakeholders about our specific approach to J.E.D.I. based on our SWOT and Strategic Plan and how it impacts the workplace and society. It's crucial to communicate the benefits of J.E.D.I. for both individuals and the organization, highlighting its role in fostering creativity, innovation, and productivity.

2. *Interest:* Once awareness is established, the next step is to cultivate interest. Leveraging examples from our health and wellness pilot, for instance, we could engage the organization in deeper dialogues about J.E.D.I., providing resources for further learning. Interactive workshops, discussion forums, and thought leadership content can help spark interest and further conversation. Employee resource groups or diversity committees can be valuable tools to facilitate this phase, and surveys can help gauge interest and gather feedback.

3. *Decision:* At the decision stage, we want individuals and groups to commit to the J.E.D.I. initiatives based on empirical results from our pilots. This involves asking stakeholders to make personal commitments to these principles, whether through signing a

pledge, undergoing training, and/or participating in J.E.D.I.-related activities. It's essential to clearly outline what this commitment entails and how it will be supported by the organization.

4. *Action:* The final stage is action, where the health and wellness New Operating Procedures are ratified, communicated, and trained. This stage involves providing opportunities for employees to take leadership roles in J.E.D.I. initiatives, especially in terms of monitoring compliance and identifying problems and issues. These accountability measures will ensure that the new J.E.D.I. principles are being followed.

5. *Post-implementation (Adoption and Advocacy):* In the context of our chute/funnel, post-implementation stages relate to adherence and advocacy. In the J.E.D.I. context, this involves ensuring the sustained practice of these initiatives and transforming employees into advocates for J.E.D.I. Regular updates about the progress of J.E.D.I. initiatives, continuous training, and forums for sharing experiences and success stories can help maintain momentum.

Remember, each organization's J.E.D.I. chute/funnel will look different depending on its unique context and needs. The key is to ensure the approach is flexible and adaptable to meet the evolving needs of the organization and its stakeholders. It's important to create an environment where feedback is encouraged, and the J.E.D.I. initiatives can be continually refined and improved. This way, the organization can progress toward a more just, equitable, diverse, and inclusive future.

Measuring Adoption

In my previous book *Be a J.E.D.I. Leader, Not a Boss*,[89] I introduced the "Six A's" framework of J.E.D.I. Leadership (awareness, acceptance, appreciation, alignment, activation, and advocacy); this framework is designed to take individuals within an organization from issue-blindness to J.E.D.I. advocacy—which you can see here.

The Six A's

From	To
Issue blindness.	Definition and awareness.
Denial that we may have toxic biases, beliefs, and behaviors.	Acceptance and examples that we do.
Acknowledging the existence of these toxic biases, beliefs, and behaviors.	Appreciating the degree to which they are impacting people, productivity, and profitability.
Disagreement on exactly where and how to act in order to change.	Alignment and clarity on exactly what must be done and how.
Agreement on the need to act.	Taking meaningful action with clear accountabilities and milestones attached.
Being issue-blind with no acceptance, lack of appreciation, little alignment, and low activation.	Making positive change happen and can be a beacon to others seeking to do the same.

Think of the Six A's as a series of gateways people must pass through in order to achieve the enlightened state of mind of J.E.D.I. leaders. Our chute approach is designed to shepherd everyone through these gates. But along the way, we must assess how many people have passed through how many gates—and this is where measuring adoption comes into play. It's important not to lose sight that the goal of J.E.D.I. work is the broad-based adoption and application of a suite of new operating procedures (NOPs) that effectively eradicate injustice, eliminate inequity, expand diversity, and enhance inclusion. Luckily, marketing teaches us how to deliver on this primary objective, as well, by leaning into the adoption curve.[90]

The Adoption Curve

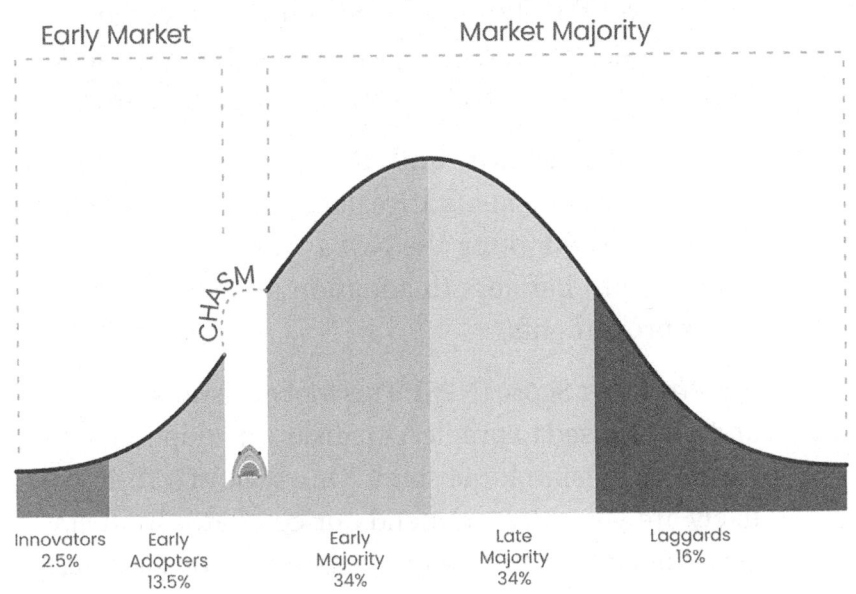

Early Market | Market Majority

CHASM

| Innovators 2.5% | Early Adopters 13.5% | Early Majority 34% | Late Majority 34% | Laggards 16% |

There are five discrete stages of adoption that are linked to percentages of a whole we are seeking to capture. Embarking on J.E.D.I., as with any broad-based change initiative, requires us to confront the brutal fact that not everyone will jump on board right away. In fact, the adoption curve tells us that Innovators (the first to adopt) make up a mere 2.5 percent of a given audience or organization. Early adopters, therefore, represent 13.5 percent. The early majority make up 34 percent, the late majority make up 34%, and finally, the laggards (which are eight times larger than our group of innovators) come in at 16 percent!

There are various tools and techniques marketers use to measure and assess the adoption of a new idea, service, or technology.[91] For our purposes, we will focus on the following:

- **Surveys and Questionnaires:** These are used to directly gauge the level of interest, awareness, and adoption among a target population. They can be conducted online, over the phone, or in person. Sentiment analysis can also be carried out on responses to assess users' attitudes and feelings toward J.E.D.I initiatives.

- **In-depth Interviews and Focus Groups:** These methods provide qualitative data about why people are or aren't adopting the NOPs. They can provide insights into barriers to adoption and suggestions for improvements.

- **Net Promoter Score (NPS):** This tool measures loyalty and can be used to predict expansion of adoption. It's based on one simple question: "On a scale of 0-10, how likely are you to recommend our company/product/service to a friend or colleague based on our justice, equity, diversity, and inclusion stance and progress?"

- **Churn Rate:** Measuring churn rate (how many adopters stop applying the NOPs correctly) can indicate the adoption and satisfaction level among users.

Remember that these tools are more effective when used together, as they can provide a holistic view of the adoption process. Each has its own strengths and weaknesses, so the combination of tools will depend on the specific context of the J.E.D.I. program being implemented.

With a firmer grasp on how to drive adoption of our J.E.D.I. initiatives, we can now turn to the topics of restoration and renewal, which delve into how we can maintain our resilience and high-performance behaviors as we restore our organizations to the sort that can best deliver on the goals of stakeholder capitalism: engaging employees, delighting customers, cultivating communities, protecting environments, and satisfying shareholders.

9

RESTORATION

Our work as J.E.D.I. Leaders comes full circle when we continuously interrogate the following four issues:

1. To what degree are employees living a full and dignified life within this organization? *How do we know this?*

2. To what extent do employees in this organization have access to the same opportunities? *How can we prove this?*

3. To what degree are we valuing and, more importantly, capitalizing on the differences between us? *What do our results show?*

4. To what extent are we centering, valuing, and amplifying the voices, perspectives, and styles of those employees who experience more barriers based on their identities? *What are these employees telling us?*

Through this lens, it becomes clear that we are seeking to enhance knowledge, evidence, results, and sentiment within our respective organizations as it relates to eradicating injustices, eliminating inequities, expanding diversity, and enhancing inclusion. Routine interrogation leads us to rely on solid processes we can return to again and again in our quest for restoration. The term restoration in this context means realigning our companies' practices, processes, and priorities with our stated principles.

> Thus, the underlying assumption of our work is that there is a misalignment between our organization's principles, priorities, processes, and practices as it relates to creating an environment where rules are enforced regardless of position/title, opportunity to participate is more fully realized, difference is a competitive advantage, and everyone's voice matters.

The J.E.D.I. Restoration System™

In the spirit of judo strategy, rather than introduce some newfangled concept without a solid track record of success, the J.E.D.I. Restoration System™ (J.E.D.I.-RS), has been adapted from one of the most successful operational systems in business today: the Internal Control Framework (ICF) from the world of ethics and compliance. The ICF has evolved over time to provide guidelines for ensuring the reliability of financial reporting, compliance with laws and regulations, and effective and efficient operations.

One of the most recognized frameworks is the COSO (Committee of Sponsoring Organizations of the Treadway Commission) Framework.[92] The Treadway Commission was created in 1985 by five private sector organizations—namely, the American Accounting Association, the American Institute of CPAs, Financial Executives International, The Institute of Internal Auditors, and the Institute of Management Accountants. These organizations sponsored the commission with the intent to identify the factors that cause fraudulent financial reporting and to make recommendations to reduce its incidence.

The COSO Internal Control Framework[93] was initially published in 1992 to prevent corporate fraud. It was then updated in 2013 to include more modern concerns such as technology and globalization. This framework is widely accepted as the authority on internal controls and is incorporated into policies, rules, and regulations used to control the behaviors of corporations.

The COSO Framework outlines five integral components vital for robust internal control: Control Environment, Risk Assessment, Control Activities, Information and Communication, and Monitoring Activities. These components are interrelated and are collectively crucial for realizing effective internal control mechanisms within an organization. Within the realm of Ethics and Compliance, this framework offers essential guidance, enabling organizations to proficiently handle and diminish risks related to violations of laws and regulations, instances of unethical conduct, and other challenges that pose a threat to the integrity and repute of an organization. Essentially, it serves as a comprehensive guide to maintaining organizational compliance and ethical standards, ensuring the mitigation of risks and the sustenance of organizational reputation and values.

It promotes the adoption of a culture of ethics and compliance within organizations, the identification and assessment of risks associated with non-compliance or unethical behavior, the implementation of controls to mitigate these risks, effective communication of ethics and compliance information, and ongoing monitoring and improvement of the ethics and compliance program.

It's worth noting that the COSO framework is not the only framework that has influenced Ethics and Compliance functions. Other models, such as the ISO 19600 Compliance Management Systems standard,[94] have also contributed to the development of these functions. Nonetheless, the principles of risk assessment, control activities, information and communication, and ongoing monitoring found in the COSO framework have become a standard part of most Ethics and Compliance programs.

This is judo strategy at its finest—adaptation of an existing standard for a new purpose versus inventing an entire new system for organizations to adopt. An ICF contains the following areas for our J.E.D.I. programs: problem identification and root cause analysis, corrective and preventative actions, a robust disciplinary matrix, J.E.D.I. restoration projects and programs, creation of relevant new operating procedures (NOPs), communication and training on NOPs, and finally, management monitoring.

The J.E.D.I.-RS provides a clear structure for the embedding of J.E.D.I. principles and processes within the organization while also monitoring adherence, identifying and resolving problems, and creating conditions for disciplinary action as necessary. Here is what it looks like:

The J.E.D.I.-Restoration System™

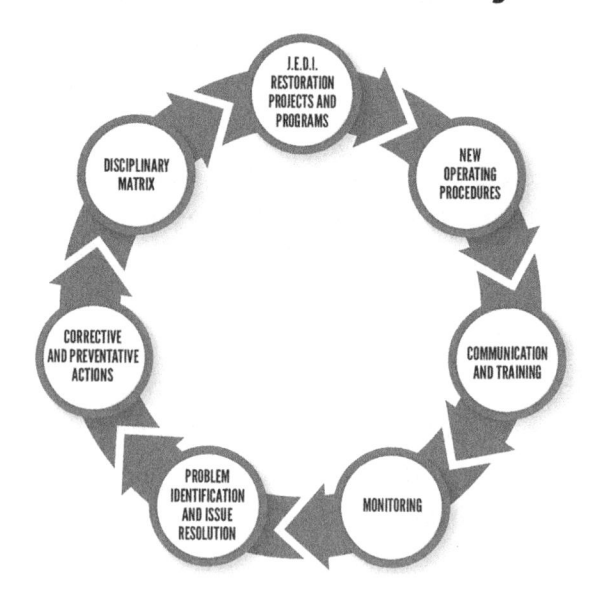

Once everyone is aligned on key definitions and known issues related to injustices, inequities, and gaps within the diversity and inclusion spaces, it will lead to the activation of J.E.D.I. restoration projects and programs.

- This work will require the reconstruction of existing processes into new operating procedures (NOPs).

- These NOPs will then need to be cascaded throughout the organization via repeated communications, campaigns, and training initiatives.

- Once this cascading has been done, monitoring (which should be led by the company's CDO) can commence.

- The point of monitoring is to track adherence to the new standards, while also identifying any problem areas that need to be mitigated and resolved in the form of corrective and/or preventative actions—some of which may include taking disciplinary actions against process violators.

This system will go a long way in driving J.E.D.I. principles into the heart of the organization. Importantly, this system is not all stick and no carrot. It is merely a framework for finding, filtering, and fixing business risks associated with J.E.D.I. issues. Unless you are running a startup and want to get off on the right foot, the J.E.D.I.-RS won't start at the top of the wheel with J.E.D.I. Restoration Projects and Programs. It starts with Problem Identification and Issue Resolution. Only once a few cycles have progressed do we start the wheel at the new projects and programs. Otherwise, we usually start with the problems and issues that need resolution.

To illustrate this, let's use the process of reward and recognition to show how the RS works.

Problem Identification and Issue Resolution

We start with the assumption that there are injustices, inequities, too much uniformity, and lack of inclusion in our reward and recognition systems. We dig for root cause(s) by investigating how traditionally marginalized groups of people are being incentivized, recognized, and promoted in our organization. The five whys approach to root cause diagnosis is a great tool to use in this effort by challenging ourselves to dig beneath the surface and truly find the key source of the issues.[95]

Let's say we identify that the reason our reward and recognition system is disproportionately leading to recognition of a single employee demographic is that we just don't have enough of other groups in our company to impact the overrepresentation of this majority group, something else, or multiple reasons. Once we've identified the problem, it's time to assess the risks this condition may pose to our organization. Importantly, the first time we apply the J.E.D.I.-RS, there will not be any immediate issue resolution; but upon future rotations, issue resolution should occur.

Corrective and Preventative Actions (CAPAs)

The Six A's approach is well aligned to the initial steps to creating a risk-based CAPA process,[96] which starts with inquiry, assessment, and pre-investigation, and then proceeds on to investigation, planning, and execution. In the case of our specific example based on reward and recognition, our inquiry and assessment identifies 1) that we lack quantitative data at a demographic level related to our reward and recognition process; 2) that our one-size-fits-all approach to reward and recognition is actually creating more disenfranchisement of underrepresented employee groups; and 3) that another process—recruiting and hiring—must be addressed, as we need to dramatically reduce bias and increase the diversification of our employee pool. After fully investigating these root causes, we validate them, assess them as major risks to innovation, reputation, and talent attraction and recruiting, and then prioritize our next steps.

Disciplinary Matrix

Prior to our investigation of this process, we never needed to discipline individuals operating in our culture for leveraging the reward and recognition system against minority employee groups. By digging deeper, however, suppose we identify not only bad actors in the system, but also specific teams, functions, and divisions that are creating more risk than others. We need to go beyond statements in our employee handbook and let violators know that there will be repercussions for continuing the status quo beliefs and behaviors related to how, why, when, and who we reward and recognize in our organization. A progressive warning system that potentially results in incentive forfeiture and progresses up to termination for multiple offenses is an example of an effective disciplinary matrix.

J.E.D.I. Restoration Projects and Programs

With clear priorities, we can initiate our efforts to restore our reward and recognition system. We spell out the identified root causes, investigation findings, risk assessment, prioritized actions, disciplinary matrix, and anticipated results. We design programs and projects for restoration, adhering to the processes developed using CAPA. During program and project design, we clarify responsibilities, shared accountabilities, consultations and communications, timeline, and deliverables. Doing so ensures that relevant internal stakeholders fully understand, agree with, and are aligned with the proposed actions, individuals involved, and milestones.

Importantly, here, we also want to define success in the planning process—which should be that we have reformulated our reward and recognition system to ensure that injustices are eradicated, inequities are eliminated, diversity is promoted, and inclusion in the system is enhanced. Now it's time for implementation.

New Operating Procedures (NOPs)

A critical element of the work, the glue that holds everything together, is writing, training, and holding everyone accountable to new operating procedures. In our reward and recognition example, the NOP would specify the requirement to collect and internally report data by demographic group, level, and function. It would outline new processes to individualize the reward and recognition system itself and move away from a uniform approach. It would also address hiring biases and, if necessary, significantly upweight the diversity incoming via our recruitment efforts.

The responsible parties draft the NOPs, revise as necessary based on feedback, and receive approval from the required stakeholders before rolling them out to the company. Then readership, understanding, agreement, and alignment by all relevant employees is certified.

Communication and Training

The communication cascade of NOPs should start at the senior leadership level, with a clear commitment from the executive team to walk the talk and reinforce these new procedures. Leaders should leverage multiple methods of communication, including email, internal social media networks, town halls, department chats, endomarketing, and anonymous feedback lines and/or inboxes to ensure that awareness, readership, comprehension, agreement, and alignment are as high as possible. Repetition is necessary; depending on the culture and its history, among other factors, adoption through to agreement and alignment will likely take some time.

Engagement in the NOPs is then reinforced by a robust training program that starts with on-demand reviews of the NOPs which then progresses to workshops with relevant stakeholders such as managers. Understanding, agreement, and alignment are gauged via pre- and post- training intervention surveys to ensure that the majority of stakeholders understand the new procedures and expected outcomes and are prepared to fully implement them. And for those with more difficulty understanding, repeat training interventions should be implemented.

Monitoring

Once the NOPs have been robustly communicated and trained, it is up to the business process owners—in this case of reward and recognition, HR, hiring managers, and all other managers—to regularly monitor and report on the progress and adherence to these programs. This can be done via interval assessments at designated moments (one month, three months, and six months, for example) post-process rollout to ensure continued high levels of understanding, agreement, and alignment; surveys on process effectiveness; feedback loops from managers to HR on issues in implementing the procedures; and, yes, audits—both internal and external.

If understanding, agreement, and alignment drop below baseline (during the communication and training stage), then it can be a lead measure on the overall implementation. By listening to managers, unanticipated problems related to implementing the procedures can be picked up early in the process lifecycle and demonstrate that senior management is not only committed to improving procedures, but also to supporting those tasked with executing the procedures in the real world. And if there is widespread resistance from managers to the NOPs, it is better to gather this insight and go back into problem identification and issue resolution mode.

The ultimate goal of all this work is to build awareness, understanding, agreement, alignment, and action that is visible and tangible to everyone within the organization.

Adoption of the J.E.D.I.-RS provides what is sorely missing from the work we all do: a systematic and programmatic approach that is easy to understand, follow, and communicate. I personally experienced the power of the ICF when, as a General Manager (GM) in Indonesia with GSK Pharmaceuticals, I was charged with certifying as the designated signatory for my market that my operation was fully in compliance with risk management and oversight, antibribery and corruption, commercial practices, third- party oversight, information protection, scientific engagement, financial controls and reporting, and use of cash focus areas—in a single year! And it wasn't just me. Every GM in the world was held to the same standard of compliance.

The Internal Control Framework approach allowed us to assess as a team our performance in each area and cogently report back on our status. I have endeavored in this book to enforce upon us practitioners that J.E.D.I. work has strong risk management and values adherence components that ultimately link back to the compliance to our processes that impact our journey to eradicate injustices, eliminate inequities, expand diversity, and enhance inclusion. It provided high visibility into areas that most managers took for granted and allowed us to fully inspect what we expected. And it scaled! GSK operates in over a hundred markets and conducts a hundred annual reviews of market compliance. We had no question of what mattered in terms of the linkages between principles, priorities, processes, and practices.

When restoration is literally embedded into the performance management plan for each manager in the organization via the J.E.D.I.-RS, shifting the culture is the inevitable outcome. Still, as must be apparent from this chapter, this work requires heavy lifting; and heavy lifting is dependent on energy and capacity. This is why there can be no significant restoration without an equally focused effort to continuously renew, which is the next area of our exploration in this playbook.

10

RENEWAL

CDO tenures are dwindling,[97] as professionals in this field are experiencing burnout, termination, and roadblocks at an alarming rate. The latest research indicates that the term of service for Chief Diversity Officers (CDOs) at large, publicly traded US firms is significantly decreasing. Surprisingly, from 2018 to 2021, 60 percent of CDOs at companies incorporated in the S&P 500 resigned from their positions. Presently, the average tenure for CDOs in these prominent corporations is less than two years. Even before this recent analysis, it was observed that CDOs held one of the briefest average tenures among the C-suite executives, typically around three years.

Burnout Is Rampant

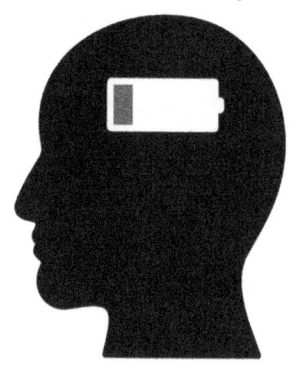

Specialists in diversity and inclusion are not taken aback by this new data. In fact, based on their observations, consultants have noted a mounting sense of dissatisfaction among CDOs. They attribute it to organizations often appointing the incorrect individual to the role or not providing the necessary resources or power for their CDOs to significantly influence the company.

There are many reasons why J.E.D.I. professionals might be experiencing high rates of burnout:[98]

- **Emotional Labor:** J.E.D.I. professionals carry the emotional weight of their work. They often must engage with topics like systemic racism, discrimination, and unfair treatment, which can take a significant emotional toll. As per the research done in various fields like social work and psychology, it is known that this kind of emotional labor can lead to burnout.

- **Under-Resourced:** J.E.D.I. initiatives are often not allocated the necessary resources to effectively execute their plans, causing additional stress. They may have ambitious goals but lack the human or financial resources to accomplish them.

- **Unrealistic Expectations:** The expectation that J.E.D.I. professionals can quickly "fix" deeply ingrained systemic issues can lead to burnout. It often takes time to see the effects of J.E.D.I. initiatives, and the pressure to produce immediate results can be stressful.

- **Resistance to Change:** J.E.D.I. work involves driving cultural changes within an organization, and there can be significant resistance. This constant need to battle against ingrained biases and systemic structures can be exhausting and demotivating.

- **Constant Need to Prove Value:** Despite the increasing awareness about the importance of J.E.D.I., there can be skepticism from senior leadership and employees. This constant need to justify their work and prove its value can be another source of burnout.

Because of the challenges faced by people working in this space, it becomes even more incumbent on them to seek renewal on a regular basis in order to have the power to overcome burnout. This is accomplished by conducting *an Energy Audit®*.[99] This tool was developed by *The Energy Project*—an organization dedicated to helping other organizations create capacity in the face of increasing demands on time, energy, and resilience.[100]

By focusing on four dimensions of energy—physical, mental, emotional, and spiritual—and assessing our strengths and gaps, we can identify opportunities for resetting and renewing that will allow us the capacity to continue fighting the good fight. Once completed, a report is issued that includes scores against the four dimensions, as well as a comprehensive debrief guide with explanations of the results and strategies for improvement.

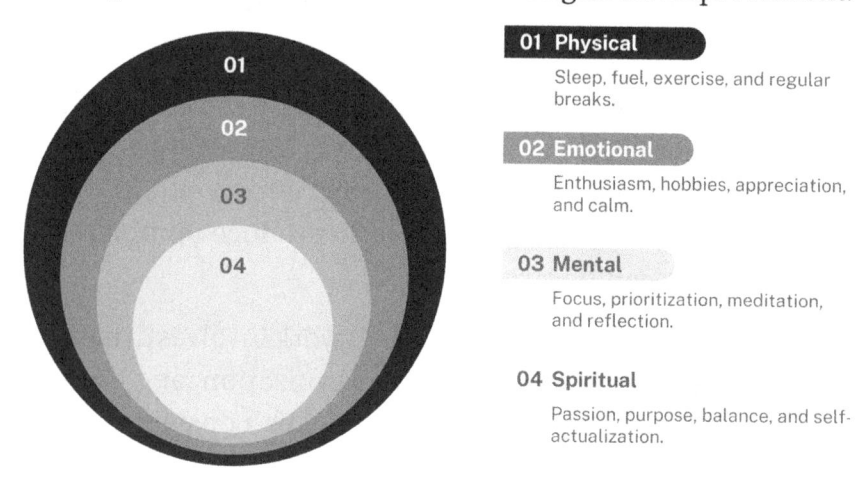

01 Physical
Sleep, fuel, exercise, and regular breaks.

02 Emotional
Enthusiasm, hobbies, appreciation, and calm.

03 Mental
Focus, prioritization, meditation, and reflection.

04 Spiritual
Passion, purpose, balance, and self-actualization.

There are four keys to renewal for J.E.D.I. professionals and allies: sleep (physical renewal), maintaining outside interests (emotional renewal), meditation (mental renewal), and work-life integration (spiritual renewal).

- **Physical Renewal:**[101] Prioritizing physical renewal is crucial for professionals in the J.E.D.I. space due to the demanding nature of their work. Advocacy, addressing systemic inequalities, and supporting marginalized communities can be emotionally and physically draining. Engaging in physical practices such as exercise, proper nutrition, and sufficient rest helps maintain energy levels, manage stress, and prevent physical exhaustion. By taking care of their physical well-being, professionals can sustain their resilience and continue to make a positive impact.

- **Mental Renewal:**[102] The J.E.D.I. space often involves having challenging conversations, confronting systemic biases, and working toward social change. All of this can lead to mental fatigue and overwhelm. Engaging in mental renewal practices, such as mindfulness, meditation, or journaling, allows professionals to cultivate self-awareness, manage stress, and maintain mental clarity. These practices promote mental well-being, enhance focus, and enable professionals to approach their work with a clear and open mind.

- **Emotional Renewal:**[103] Professionals in the J.E.D.I. space frequently navigate emotionally charged situations, empathize with individuals facing injustice, and confront personal biases. This emotional labor can take a toll on their well-being. Prioritizing emotional renewal involves acknowledging and processing emotions, seeking support from peers or mentors, and engaging in activities that bring joy and emotional balance. By honoring their emotional needs, professionals can prevent burnout, resist compassion fatigue, and maintain a healthy emotional well-being.

- *Spiritual Renewal:*[104] Working toward justice, equity, diversity, and inclusion can be deeply rooted in one's values, beliefs, and purpose. Professionals in the J.E.D.I. space often draw inspiration from their spirituality or personal philosophy. Prioritizing spiritual renewal involves engaging in practices that nourish the soul, such as meditation, prayer, or reflection. These practices provide a sense of meaning, connectedness, and resilience, allowing professionals to find inspiration and renewal in their work.

Physical Renewal and the Power of Sleep

Getting enough sleep plays a crucial role in physical stress relief, offering numerous benefits that positively impact our overall well-being. While it may be tempting to sacrifice sleep in the pursuit of productivity, understanding the advantages of adequate rest can inspire us to prioritize it as an essential part of our daily routine.

One of the primary benefits of sufficient sleep is its ability to support the body's natural recovery process. During sleep, our bodies engage in restorative activities such as tissue repair, muscle growth, and hormone regulation. Adequate sleep duration allows these processes to occur optimally, promoting physical recovery from daily wear and tear. This restoration not only helps alleviate physical stress; it also enables the body to function efficiently and maintain optimal performance.

Moreover, sleep plays a significant role in regulating our immune system, which is vital for overall health and resilience. Studies have shown that sleep deprivation can weaken immune function, making individuals more susceptible to illnesses and infections. Conversely, getting enough sleep strengthens the immune system, enabling it to effectively combat pathogens and reduce the risk of various diseases. By bolstering our immune response, sufficient sleep contributes to physical stress relief by promoting a healthier, more robust body.

Additionally, sleep plays a crucial role in managing and reducing inflammation within the body. Chronic inflammation has been linked to various health issues, including cardiovascular disease, diabetes, and certain cancers. Sufficient sleep helps regulate the body's inflammatory responses, contributing to a more balanced state. By doing so, sleep supports physical stress relief by reducing the likelihood of developing inflammation-related conditions and promoting overall well-being.

Sleep has a profound impact on our mental and emotional health—which, in turn, influences our physical state. Inadequate sleep can lead to increased stress levels, anxiety, and mood disturbances. Elevated stress levels can trigger the release of stress hormones, such as cortisol, which, when chronically elevated, can have detrimental effects on the body, including weight gain, high blood pressure, and impaired immune function. Sufficient sleep helps regulate stress hormones, contributing to lower stress levels and improved emotional resilience. By reducing stress and promoting emotional health, sleep serves as a vital tool for physical stress relief.

There are several techniques that can help stressed business professionals sleep better and more restoratively.[105] Here are some effective strategies:

- **Establish a Consistent Sleep Schedule:** Create a sleep routine by going to bed and waking up at the same time every day, even on weekends. This helps regulate your body's internal clock and improves sleep quality.

- **Limit Exposure to Electronics Before Bed:** The blue light emitted by electronic devices can disrupt your sleep-wake cycle. Avoid using screens, such as smartphones, tablets, and laptops, at least one hour before bedtime. Instead, engage in calming activities or read a book.

- **Avoid Stimulants and Heavy Meals:** Limit or avoid the use of stimulants such as caffeine and nicotine, especially close to bedtime. Additionally, avoid heavy meals, spicy foods, and excessive fluid intake before bed, as these can cause discomfort and disrupt sleep.

- **Regular Exercise:** Engaging in physical activity can help reduce stress and promote better sleep. Aim for at least thirty minutes of moderate-intensity exercise most days of the week. However, avoid exercising too close to bedtime, as it can energize your body and make it difficult to fall asleep.

- **Create a Worry Journal:** If your mind is racing with thoughts and worries, consider keeping a journal next to your bed. Write down any concerns or tasks that are occupying your mind before going to bed. This can help offload your thoughts and promote a sense of relaxation.

Remember, it's important to be patient and consistent when implementing these techniques. It may take time for your body to adjust and for sleep quality to improve.

Emotional Renewal and Maintaining Outside Interests

Having hobbies and interests outside of work is extremely important for people in professions that require a lot of emotional effort.[106]

Emotional Effort

These jobs require managing emotions to help others, which can be draining and lead to burnout. Here's a simpler explanation of why having other interests is essential in such jobs:

- People in these careers use a lot of emotional energy to offer support and empathy to others. Having interests outside of work helps them relax and rebuild their emotional strength. Doing things like sports, hobbies, or creative activities offers a break from their job's emotional needs, which helps avoid exhaustion and increases job satisfaction.

- Participating in activities outside of work is also a great way to reduce stress. Jobs involving emotional labor can be stressful, and having hobbies or doing activities like exercising or meditating can help in managing stress and avoiding the buildup of work-related stress.

- Additionally, having interests outside of work helps in mentally disconnecting from job-related stress and responsibilities, allowing individuals to enjoy activities that bring them joy. This disconnection improves work-life balance and promotes better mental well-being.

- Pursuing interests outside of work also leads to the development of new skills. Learning new things, like an instrument or sport, or being part of a book club, can foster personal growth and even improve professional performance and career advancement opportunities.

- Having fulfilling activities outside of work leads to increased job satisfaction and reduces the dependency on work for happiness, preventing the negative effects of a life centered only around work.

Engaging in diverse activities expands professionals' viewpoints, exposing them to new experiences and ideas, and fostering creativity and innovative thinking—which can enhance their performance in their professional roles.

Mental Renewal and the Impact of Meditation

Meditation is a technique that offers substantial benefits related to improving concentration, maintaining productivity, and enhancing endurance.[107] It helps in training the mind to stay in the present moment and focus on the immediate task, which allows individuals to notice distractions without becoming involved in them and results in better efficiency and productivity. For instance, soldiers use mindfulness meditation to stay focused under high-pressure situations, helping them make clear decisions, thus ensuring successful missions. Similarly, in Zen Buddhism, practices like Zazen help in maintaining focused and alert minds, aiding spiritual growth and a deeper understanding of Zen teachings.

Regular meditation supports sustained productivity by improving mental clarity and avoiding burnout. Professionals in demanding jobs can take short meditation breaks to rejuvenate, maintain focus, and prevent mental overload, leading to enhanced work performance. Meditation also builds an individual's resilience and ability to remain calm under pressure, reducing stress and fatigue. Elite military units use techniques like visualization and breath control to increase mental resilience, allowing them to handle rigorous training, lengthy deployments, or challenging missions with more composure and stamina.

In Zen Buddhism, monks participate in lengthy meditation retreats, developing the ability to maintain focus and clarity for extended periods, even amidst physical discomfort. This enduring practice of meditation is beneficial in maintaining mental focus and resilience in various aspects of life, and as a metaphor for enduring challenges in daily life and achieving spiritual growth.

Professionals interested in beginning a meditation journey can take several steps to incorporate this practice into their daily lives, and technology can be a helpful tool in this process. Here's a step-by-step guide on how professionals can start their meditation journey, with the use of technology:[108]

- **Learn the Basics:** Start by learning basic meditation techniques like mindfulness and loving-kindness through books, articles, or reliable websites.

- **Know Why We're Meditating:** Understand why meditation is crucial. It could be for stress reduction, better focus, overall wellness, or inner peace. Knowing your goals keeps you motivated.

- **Make Time & Create a Habit:** Decide how much time to meditate each day. Start small, perhaps with five to ten minutes, and make it a regular part of the schedule, treating it as an important appointment.

- **Start with Some Guidance:** Start with guided meditations available on an app or platform of choice, which can offer support and instructions.

- **Be Mindful All Day:** Apply mindfulness in daily activities, like eating or walking, to extend the benefits of meditation into everyday life.

Remember, consistency is key when starting a meditation journey. Even short daily sessions can yield positive benefits over time. Be patient with and embrace the process, knowing that meditation is a skill that develops over time. With the aid of technology and a commitment to regular practice, professionals can embark on a fulfilling meditation journey that supports their well-being and personal growth.

Spiritual Renewal and Work Life Integration

Work-life integration is about blending personal and professional aspects of life in a balanced and flexible way.[109] It's about combining work duties with personal well-being to find harmony and fulfillment, focusing heavily on spiritual renewal and authenticity in work. In this approach, people are seen as having diverse needs and values beyond their jobs. They're encouraged to merge their personal values and passions with their work, making work a fulfilling part of life, not just a separate obligation. This alignment lets individuals fully express their beliefs and interests in their work roles, giving them more satisfaction and a greater sense of purpose.

This concept is not just about balancing tasks; it's also about integrating aspects like family, hobbies, self-care, and spiritual practices into everyday routines. For example, incorporating meditation or reflection during work breaks can help in maintaining inner peace and improving overall well-being. This holistic approach to life and work helps prevent burnout by promoting the importance of breaks, rest, and self-care.

When people can bring their whole selves to work and integrate their professional and personal lives effectively, they experience a stronger sense of meaning, renewal, and satisfaction in both life domains. By prioritizing well-being and spiritual practices, individuals can find more authenticity and meaning in their work, which leads to a healthier, more balanced life.

Connectedness, a talent theme from positive psychology and CliftonStrengths, is the deep belief in the interrelation of all things. People with this strength intuitively understand the connections between people, events, and ideas, recognizing the world's unity and interdependence. These individuals can see the bigger picture, understanding how actions and decisions impact beyond the immediate context. They approach life with purpose, seeking to create and find connections between different people, ideas, and experiences, and are often drawn to movements or organizations that aim to unify and promote harmony.

Individuals with Connectedness are empathetic and have a heightened awareness of others' emotions, making them excellent collaborators, facilitators, and mediators. They are effective in roles requiring a broad perspective, like strategic planning or team building; they can see patterns and connections, which helps them pinpoint innovative solutions and foresee potential risks and opportunities. In professional settings, those with this strength create a sense of unity and inclusivity, valuing diversity and building relationships. They often serve as mentors, helping others find purpose and make meaningful professional connections.

To harness this strength effectively, individuals can focus on connecting with others, sharing their perspectives, fostering collaboration, and deepening their practices that enhance their sense of interconnectedness and purpose. Professionals aiming for J.E.D.I. can learn from those with the Connectedness strength by embracing a holistic perspective, empathizing with others, and promoting unity and inclusivity. Doing so will allow for a deeper understanding of the world and the opportunity to build more meaningful connections.

Prioritizing renewal practices across the physical, mental, emotional, and spiritual dimensions is crucial for J.E.D.I. professionals. We often face unique challenges and demands in our roles, which can lead to burnout, compassion fatigue, and diminished well-being. Emphasizing these renewal practices across the physical, mental, emotional, and spiritual dimensions can sustain our individual and collective health, effectiveness, and commitment to social change. Renewal practices enable us to navigate challenges, maintain resilience, and avoid the detrimental effects of burnout. Ultimately, prioritizing renewal is a critical investment in our personal and professional longevity.

11

EXTERNALIZING IMPACTS

J.E.D.I. leadership is not a nice-to-have capability. It's not a trend or fad that is going to dissipate in the face of other concerns. Just as leaning into environmental and social governance (ESG) is a requirement the largest investment groups have added to the corporate scorecard, so should an entity's ability to eradicate injustices, eliminate inequities, expand diversity, and enhance inclusion be considered essential. The reason for this prioritization stems from the desire to externalize positive impacts for more stakeholders, including customers, communities, and the environment. But the brutal fact is that this work must be done internally first before any external benefits can be fully realized.

This approach mirrors the first habit of highly effective people,[110] according to Stephen R. Covey, which is to be proactive. Proactivity in this instance is about focusing on what is in our sphere of control and influence and deprioritizing items in our sphere of concern.

Covey states that proactive people recognize they can choose how they will respond to situations. They do not blame circumstances, conditions, or others for their behavior.

This concept is based on the principle that between stimulus and response, there is a space; in that space lies our freedom and power to choose our response.

Applying this habit to the context of a book about J.E.D.I. leadership, we can interpret proactivity as taking the initiative and responsibility to ensure justice, equity, diversity, and inclusion within a team or organization.

J.E.D.I. leaders who practice Covey's principle of proactivity don't merely react to instances of injustice or exclusion; they anticipate them and actively work to prevent them. Furthermore, such leaders do not blame external factors or individuals for any lack of J.E.D.I. in their organizations. Instead, they see it as their responsibility to foster an environment that supports and promotes J.E.D.I. principles. They recognize that they have the power to choose how to respond to any instances of injustice, inequity, exclusion, or lack of diversity—and they do so in a way that aligns with J.E.D.I. principles.

In essence, a J.E.D.I. leader being proactive is about recognizing and taking responsibility for their role in creating a just, equitable, diverse, and inclusive environment, instead of waiting for these conditions to be met or blaming others when they aren't. They understand that their actions, behaviors, and decisions have a direct impact on the culture and norms of their team or organization.

Injustice, inequity, homogenization, and exclusion exist to some degree in every organization. However, allowing them to persist (and even thrive) corrupts everything else we attempt to achieve. This is evident in the numbers—from declining economic indicators of success, to decreases in global happiness, to nose-diving engagement at work, to novel phenomenon of the Great Resignation and the like. If we want our collective work of producing and selling whatever widgets, services, or solutions that drive our bottom line to be sustained, we must be as concerned with fostering environments in which all of us can thrive.

There are five primary areas, therefore, that we must address before turning our attention to the external benefits of our internal work. They are maximizing managerial effectiveness, representing the reality of our customers, elevating the communities where we operate, restoring the environment, and achieving the highest standards of internal governance.

Maximizing Managerial Effectiveness

The primary stakeholders for our internal work are, fundamentally, the people managers within our organizations. They are the translators of organizational principles and priorities, as well as the primary implementers of processes and practices. By centering outcomes on this crucial group of leaders, we can more easily direct our efforts to increase understanding, agreement, and alignment with the new operating procedures linked to our human systems.

Rather than incessant employee pulse surveys and 365-degree assessments that don't truly shift how employees experience management, the focus should be on transforming managers into high-performance coaches. This means shifting the role definition from task orientation to development, engagement, and productivity orientation. This shift requires some degree of training and development for managers utilizing the tools of positive psychology, which incentivize a leader's ability to foster the feeling of importance by inspiring excellence.

2 in 10 U.S. Employees Feel Connected to Their Company's Culture

I feel connected to my organization's culture.

— % Strongly agree

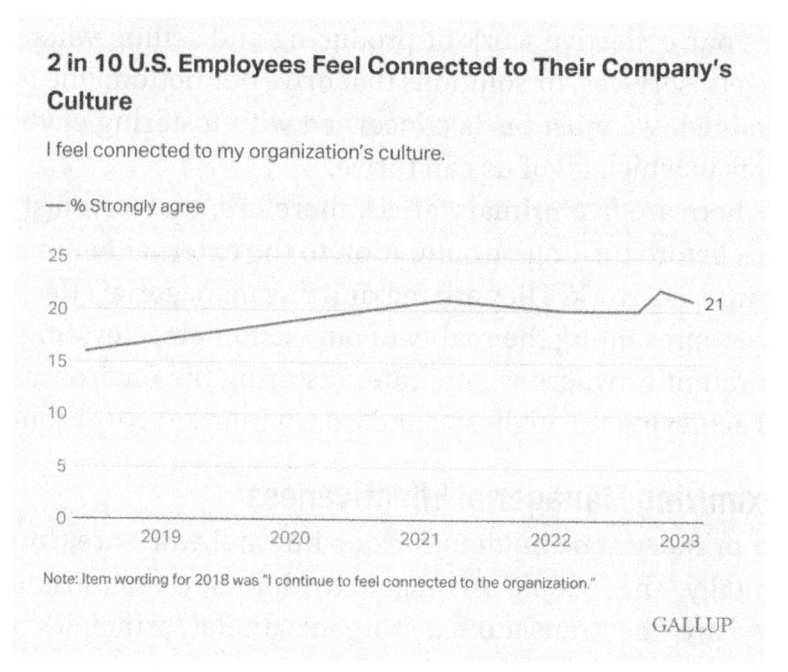

[Line chart showing values from 2019 to 2023, ending at 21 in 2023, with y-axis from 0 to 25]

Note: Item wording for 2018 was "I continue to feel connected to the organization."

GALLUP

Highly skilled individuals prefer to be part of an organization that emphasizes and nurtures individual strengths. It's understood among executive leaders that establishing such a strengths-based culture is a significant advantage in attracting top-tier talent. Furthermore, it fuels performance, allowing each employee to leverage their unique strengths in their role. Within an environment where continuous development of each person's potential is prioritized, there's reported evidence of enhanced outcomes.

Teams have observed improvements such as 23 percent higher employee engagement scores, productivity boosts of between 8 percent and 18 percent, and—notably—20 percent to 73 percent lower attrition rates.[111] Creating this kind of culture isn't an effortless task, though. It requires commitment from the top, with executive leadership and sponsors deciding to make strengths development a key element of the organization's cultural fabric.

Managers play a pivotal role in shaping team engagement, accounting for a staggering 70 percent of its variance.[112] However, only around one in ten are innately adept at managing others. Statistics also reveal that managers are 11 percent less likely to strongly affirm that their job provides them the opportunity to excel in what they are best at. Furthermore, a concerning 36 percent of managers don't fully trust in their skills to accomplish their tasks effectively.

What these figures imply is that there's a significant opportunity for improvement among leaders and managers alike. To enhance their impact on their team members and the organization, most managers need to cultivate self-awareness. This involves investing in self-development and understanding how their unique management style affects others.

Understanding their own strengths and potential blind spots empowers managers to engage and develop each team member more effectively. The most successful managers act like coaches rather than superiors, constantly initiating discussions about performance and development with each team member.

A strengths-based culture offers a common language for managers and their team members, enabling them to discuss project victories, obstacles, and future objectives effectively. Though there are only thirty-four CliftonStrengths themes,[113] the top five themes alone can result in over four million unique combinations. When everyone is aware of their strengths, managers can use this shared language to navigate the intricacies of human nature.

Leveraging strengths-based principles equips both managers and team members for success right from the outset. It provides more precise role expectations than a standard job description, setting the stage for exceptional performance and productivity And this fosters a much deeper connection to an organization's culture.

In essence, an unfavorable workplace culture leads to employee and customer attrition. However, when you establish a strengths-based culture, it offers numerous benefits, such as the ones listed below.

- Drawing more qualified applicants
- Keeping your high-performing employees
- Boosting engagement and productivity
- Promoting employee wellness and safety
- Fostering justice, equity, diversity, and inclusion
- Ensuring optimal customer experience

A well-defined culture serves as a compass for your workforce, directing everyone toward the most significant objectives. When managers become cultural stewards, it ensures unity in action, with everyone working toward the same goals of eradicating injustices, eliminating inequities, expanding diversity, and enhancing inclusion.

Representing the Reality of Customers

Doing the internal work of J.E.D.I. leadership allows an entity to better represent all their customer bases. The best organizations don't take their customer psychographics for granted; they dig deep to build even greater connections to those whom they serve via products, services, and solutions. When leadership is out of touch with customer needs, good decision making is hard to come by. And in this age of information—but also the battle for some semblance of privacy—having people who represent all the customer groups we wish to reach and convert is an invaluable innovation advantage.

This is especially true for senior leaders and for those working in customer value proposition positions, from customer service and sales to digital marketing and supply chain. In 2022, international revenues for McDonald's represented *nearly 60 percent of total sales.*[114] In addition, accessing and delighting younger customer groups is essential to maintaining the company's place in the fast-food market—the core of their *Digital, Delivery, and Drive-Through* strategy. Considering their position in international markets, as well as their drive to keep younger customers connected to the brand, what might the impact be if McDonald's had younger and/or more international leadership representation on their executive team (the current average age of senior executives at McDonald's is 55, and a majority of execs are American)?[115]

Customer representation must be a crucial part of internal talent pipelining, development, promotion, and leadership succession. Because having the right representation in the right forums makes a huge difference on how strategies, tactics, and practices connect with customers. Diversity within an organization can impact performance and growth. Reflecting the customer base provides the following benefits:[116]

- **Improved Customer Insight:** An organization that reflects its diverse customer base will have a broader range of perspectives, which often leads to greater insights into customer needs, preferences, and behaviors. For example, a tech company that has a diverse team of designers and engineers can create products that cater to a more diverse audience.

- **Enhanced Reputation and Brand:** When a company's internal diversity matches its external customer base, it shows that the organization values inclusion and diversity. This perception can boost the company's reputation and make it more attractive to customers who value these same principles.

- **Talent Attraction and Retention:** Companies with diverse workforces often attract and retain the best talent, which can drive innovation, productivity, and business performance. People want to work for organizations that respect and value diversity, where they can see people like themselves represented at all levels.

- **Innovation and Problem-Solving:** Studies have shown that diverse teams are more innovative and better at problem-solving. These teams bring a variety of perspectives to the table, which can lead to more creative solutions and ideas.

- **Greater Market Share:** By reflecting its customer base internally, a company can gain a competitive advantage and capture a larger market share. The company will be better equipped to understand and meet the needs of diverse customers, leading to increased sales and profitability.

Representing the reality of customers therefore requires J.E.D.I. leaders to reinforce servant leadership principles that put the customer, and those employees who are directly involved in customer value creation, at the top of the company's priorities. Everyone else in the system exists to enhance and support this value creation. This inversion effectively "forces" greater customer connection and engagement on everyone operating within the system—especially leadership.

Inverted Hierarchies Serve Customers Better

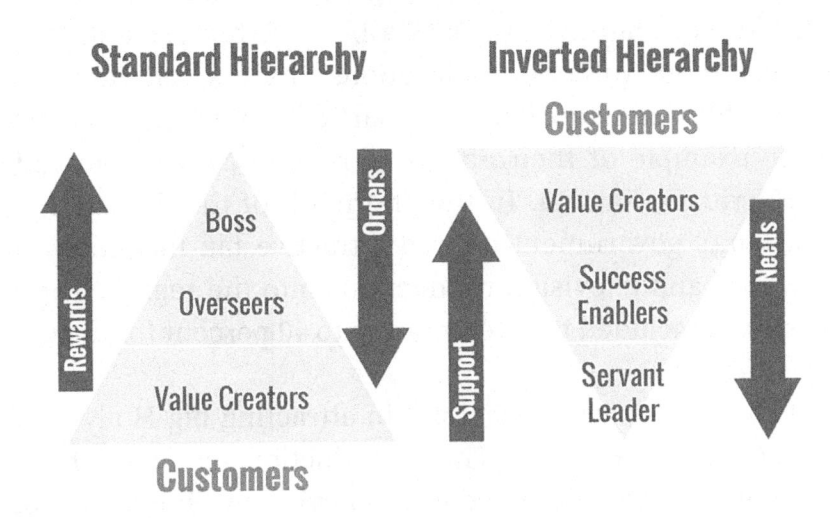

Standard Hierarchy
- Boss
- Overseers
- Value Creators
- Customers

(Rewards ↑ / Orders ↓)

Inverted Hierarchy
- Customers
- Value Creators
- Success Enablers
- Servant Leader

(Support ↑ / Needs ↓)

This transition is as structural as it is philosophical. But it is much easier to grasp when we value, reward, and promote those with a servant leadership mindset and approach rather than those who are seeking to reinforce traditional hierarchies—which are about value for few at the expense of the labor of many. Servant leaders naturally connect with those responsible for creating and enhancing customer value, so designing programs and incentives that reinforce this leadership modality is the work needed to effectively externalize these outcomes.

Elevating the Communities Where We Operate

With the advent of virtual and hybrid work, this third area of externalization becomes more challenging but also creates additional opportunity. An organization that once called itself global, but, in reality, housed 70 percent of its operations in a single municipality (as was the old model), truly was a part of a specific *place*—whether that be a city within a specific state, or a general geographic footprint in a given country. Now, *place* has been replaced with flexible working arrangements, and fewer people are commuting to the office. The way to consider community now is as a broader representation of the customers we serve and locations where we operate.

The film industry does this particularly well, especially in the example of their efforts to rebuild New Orleans after Hurricane Katrina. In the aftermath of the devastation, Louisiana's government offered attractive tax incentives to draw film and television productions into the region. These incentives included tax credits of up to 40 percent for in-state expenditures.[117]

This strategy was successful in attracting big Hollywood productions to the state. These productions created job opportunities for locals, directly supporting livelihoods in the devastated area. In addition, the influx of film and TV crews injected money into the local economy, bolstering a wide range of auxiliary businesses like food services, transportation, and accommodations.

One example of this was the movie The Curious Case of Benjamin Button.[118] Filmed during 2006 and 2007, not long after the hurricane, it became one of the largest movie productions ever in the state. The production provided jobs and stimulated the local economy when it was most needed.

Furthermore, the film industry helped highlight the culture and spirit of New Orleans for a broader audience. Films and television series set in the city, like HBO's Treme,[119] showcased local musicians, cuisine, and unique regional culture, sparking renewed interest in the city's vibrant cultural life. This representation helped to attract tourists back to the city, supporting the hospitality industry that New Orleans is famous for.

In these ways, the film industry played a pivotal role in

THE J.E.D.I. LEADER'S PLAYBOOK

New Orleans's recovery from Hurricane Katrina. The economic impact, combined with a resurgence of interest in the city's unique culture and direct philanthropic efforts, all contributed to rebuilding this iconic city. These examples are inspiring because they demonstrate how individuals and organizations can make positive impacts on communities, and how those communities can also incentivize entities to be more supportive in helping them thrive—a true win-win.

The main questions about creating positive results for the community relate to a company's values, priorities, and ability to create goodwill. A lot of companies have strong programs focused on social responsibility, aiming to give back regularly through activities like blood drives, donations, and more. However, organizing these activities can be huge tasks and often don't involve all employees, since the initiatives usually come from the top down.

Social responsibility programs are more effective when a company is committed internally to fairness, diversity, and inclusion. This means addressing injustices and inequalities within the company. When employees feel fairly treated, and valued for their differences, they are more willing to contribute to the company's efforts to do good in the community.

In short, the success of social responsibility programs is closely linked to employee engagement and well-being. When employees are engaged and feel cared for, they are usually more motivated to contribute to positive changes in society and the environment because they feel part of a fair and inclusive workplace.

An excellent example of this link can be seen in the case of Patagonia, a well-known outdoor clothing and gear company.[120] Patagonia has been a pioneer in promoting employee engagement and well-being. They offer a host of benefits aimed at creating a healthy work-life balance, including onsite childcare, flexible working hours, and a generous time-off policy that allows employees to take paid leave to engage in environmental activism.

These policies have resulted in high levels of employee engagement and well-being. In return, employees are more motivated to contribute to Patagonia's CSR initiatives. For instance, the company's "1% for the Planet" program, where they pledge 1 percent of sales to the preservation and restoration of the natural environment, has seen enthusiastic participation and support from employees.

Similarly, Google is known for its employee-friendly policies and commitment to well-being, providing a variety of perks like free healthy meals, exercise facilities, and a relaxed work environment.[121] Engaged and satisfied employees are more likely to actively participate in Google's CSR initiatives, such as their commitment to become carbon neutral, the Google Green Energy Purchasing Program, and numerous community outreach programs.

In essence, employee engagement and wellbeing lay the groundwork for successful CSR programs. When employees are engaged, feel well, and are happy at work, they are more likely to align themselves with the company's values and objectives, and this includes the company's CSR goals. Moreover, they're more likely to contribute their time, energy, and skills toward these initiatives, creating a virtuous cycle that benefits the company, its employees, and society at large.

The tool J.E.D.I. leaders must learn to employ is Gallup's Q12 assessment.[122] The Gallup Q12 assessment is an employee engagement survey that measures employee engagement based on twelve key workplace elements found to correlate strongly with employee performance. The elements include employees being provided with clear expectations, the right materials and equipment, opportunities to do what they do best, recognition, someone at work who encourages their development, and the feeling that their opinions count.

Gallup's Q12 Assessment

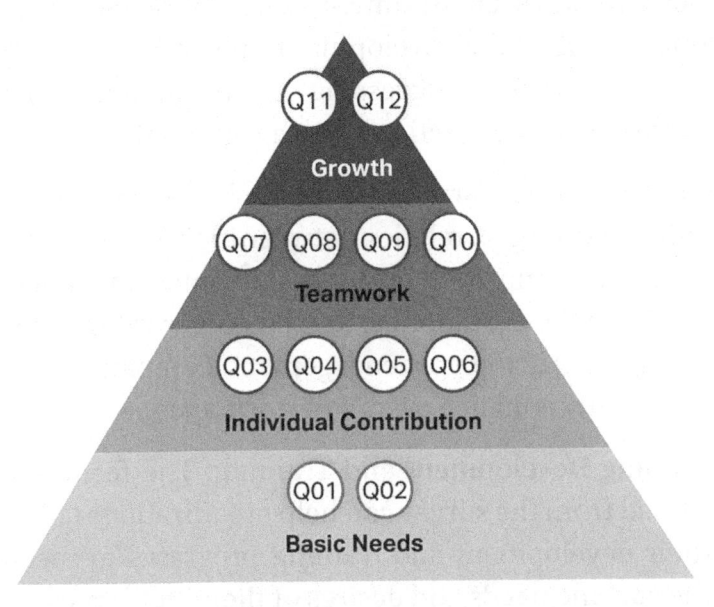

Growth: Q11, Q12
Teamwork: Q07, Q08, Q09, Q10
Individual Contribution: Q03, Q04, Q05, Q06
Basic Needs: Q01, Q02

Implementing the Gallup Q12 assessment offers several benefits that can improve employee engagement:

- **Identifying Strengths and Weaknesses:** The Q12 survey provides valuable feedback about what an organization is doing well and where it may need improvement. These insights can help management make informed decisions about initiatives that could increase engagement.

- **Enhancing Communication:** By asking for employees' thoughts on a range of workplace factors, the Q12 can improve communication between management and staff. This feedback loop can make employees feel better heard and more engaged.

- **Fostering a Positive Work Environment:** The survey focuses on key elements that can contribute to a positive work environment, such as recognition, opportunities for development, and having a best friend at work. Addressing these elements can increase job satisfaction and engagement.

- **Improving Performance:** Gallup's research has shown a strong correlation between high engagement scores and improved business outcomes, including productivity, profitability, and customer ratings. By using the Q12 to boost engagement, companies can potentially enhance overall performance.

- **Guiding Development and Training:** The feedback gained from the survey can help organizations tailor their development and training programs to meet the specific needs and desires of their employees.

- **Retention:** When organizations take steps to improve areas highlighted by the survey, employees can feel more valued and engaged, reducing turnover rates.

Toyota, for instance, has used the Gallup Q12 survey to identify areas of strength and opportunities for improvement in their employee engagement.[123] As a result, they were able to implement changes that increased employee satisfaction and productivity. These changes included measures like greater recognition for good work, more opportunities for growth and development, and efforts to ensure employees had the materials and equipment they needed to do their jobs effectively. Driven by insights from the Q12 survey, the changes helped boost employee engagement and overall business performance.

Clearly, the best tool in our toolbox to externalize positive outcomes for communities is to systematically increase employee engagement and well-being. To the degree that we do this, we can activate far more impactful efforts for the communities within which we serve and operate.

Restoring the Environment

The very act of conducting business has tremendous implications on the environment. The energy we consume connecting via Zoom, the pollution we generate during commutes to and from the office, the waste created by our global supply chains delivering products to customers, the dissolution of oceans due to the plasticization of modern living—everything we do has potentially disastrous impacts on our planet.

Environmental degradation refers to the decline or damage of the natural environment, which includes the exhaustion of vital resources like air, water, and soil. It involves the disruption of ecosystems and the extinction of wildlife species. More specifically, it is any alteration or disturbance to the environment that is harmful or unwelcome. The regenerative movement acknowledges the extent to which we've damaged our planet and asserts that simply halting harmful activities would be insufficient for nature to bounce back. This is why the concept of regeneration includes restoration, aiding nature in regaining its capacity to self-regulate, a process through which life generates conditions favorable to its own proliferation.

The Sixth Assessment by the United Nations unequivocally declares a "Code Red for Humanity."[124, 125] The warning signals are unignorably loud, and the data is undeniable: greenhouse gas emissions from burning fossil fuels and deforestation are suffocating our planet and placing billions of lives in immediate danger. Global warming is impacting every corner of the Earth, with many of the ensuing changes reaching the point of no return. This report should serve as the final alarm for coal and fossil fuels, calling for their end before they lead to the devastation of our planet.

The United Nations established seventeen Sustainable Development Goals (SDGs) as part of the 2030 Agenda for Sustainable Development.[126] Each goal has specific targets to achieve, and they serve as a blueprint for a more sustainable future for all. Unfortunately, the COVID-19 pandemic disrupted and reversed progress made prior to this global reset. Every person should read the 2022 Sustainable Development Goals Report which updates us on the goals and the status of each.[127]

Raising awareness of the SDGs and enhancing the understanding of designing for circularity within our organizations can lead to significantly improved environmental outcomes. The SDGs provide a comprehensive roadmap for sustainable practices, spanning from waste reduction and resource efficiency to responsible consumption and climate action. By embedding these goals into their strategic plans, organizations can consciously address a variety of environmental challenges. They can minimize their carbon footprints, reduce waste, promote recycling, and manage resources more efficiently, thereby aligning their business models with global sustainability objectives.

Meanwhile, understanding and implementing circular design principles can play a crucial role in optimizing environmental outcomes. A circular economy approach aims to eliminate waste and continually use resources, which is a shift from the traditional linear economy of "take, make, dispose." By designing for circularity, organizations can create products and services that are restorative and regenerative by design. This could mean creating products that are durable, reusable, repairable, and recyclable, reducing the demand for resource extraction and minimizing waste.

Integrating these two elements—circular design principles and awareness of the SDGs—can bring about profound changes. For instance, an organization might develop a product following the circular design, which significantly reduces waste (SDG 12: Responsible Consumption and Production) and contributes to climate action (SDG 13: Climate Action) by lowering carbon emissions associated with waste disposal. It might also promote decent work (SDG 8: Decent Work and Economic Growth) by creating new jobs in the recycling and repair sectors.

In this way, organizations can contribute to multiple SDGs simultaneously while benefiting from cost savings, increased customer loyalty, and enhanced resilience against resource price volatility and shortages. Therefore, aligning an organization's strategies with the SDGs and circular design principles not only leads to improved environmental outcomes but also provides a robust path toward sustainable development.

The good news for J.E.D.I. leaders is that the same tool we are leveraging to restore justice, equity, diversity, and inclusion in our organizations—the J.E.D.I. Restoration System™—can be applied to restore and align our principles, priorities, processes, and practices with regards to environmental regeneration, as well. We can leverage the J.E.D.I.-RS™ for internal social gains and external environmental impacts.

Achieving the Highest Standards of Internal Governance

What most investors want, in addition to sustainable and predictable income growth and wealth creation, is to invest in organizations that uphold the highest standards of internal governance. The only thing certain is uncertainty, so when organizations don't proactively manage reputational and regulatory risk on their own, they turn into horrible investments. Unfortunately, systems fail—the hardware of our processes corrodes, and problems arise. This is why ethics, compliance, and alignment with values must live in the heart and mind of each employee.

In his book, *The Four Obsessions of an Extraordinary Executive*,[128] Patrick Lencioni articulated four key principles that executives should target:

- **Clarity:** Extraordinary executives create clarity by clearly articulating the organization's mission, vision, and values. This clarity provides employees with a sense of purpose and direction, which helps to create a more motivated and engaged workforce.

- **Commitment:** Extraordinary executives create commitment by getting everyone in the organization to buy into the organization's mission, vision, and values. This commitment can be achieved through open and honest communication, as well as by providing employees with opportunities to participate in decision-making.

- **Consensus:** Extraordinary executives create consensus by seeking input from all stakeholders before making decisions. This consensus-building process helps to ensure that everyone is on the same page and that decisions are made in the best interests of the organization as a whole.

- **Accountability:** Extraordinary executives create accountability by holding everyone in the organization accountable for their actions. This accountability can be achieved through clear expectations, regular performance reviews, and consequences for non-performance.

In the context of creating a culture of conscience within an organization, these four obsessions are essential. Clarity helps to ensure that everyone in the organization understands the importance of acting with conscience. Commitment helps to ensure that everyone is willing to make the necessary sacrifices to uphold the organization's values. Consensus helps to ensure that decisions are made in a way that is consistent with the organization's values. And accountability helps to ensure that everyone is held to the same high standards of conduct.

By following these four obsessions, extraordinary executives can create a culture of conscience within their organizations. This culture of conscience will help to create a more positive and productive work environment, as well as a more ethical and sustainable business.

Here are some additional tips for creating a culture of conscience within an organization:[129]

- Emphasize the importance of ethics and values. Make it clear that ethics and values are important to the organization and that employees are expected to uphold these values in their work.

- Provide training on ethics and values. Help employees to understand the organization's ethical standards and how to apply them to their work.

- Create a culture of open communication. Encourage employees to raise ethical concerns without fear of retaliation.

- Establish a process for handling ethical complaints. Have a clear process in place for handling ethical complaints so that employees know how to report concerns.

- Take action to address ethical concerns. When an ethical concern is raised, take it seriously and take steps to address the issue.

Still, relative to other parts of the organization, the team responsible for ethics and compliance is miniscule when compared to all other functions combined. For this reason, no amount of SOPs and trainings can force people to stay on the right side of ethics and values. This is where a robust approach toward values-based judgment can be transformative.

Navigating the Gray Zone

Green Zone	Gray Zone	Red Zone
100% lawful	values-based judgement zone	100% unlawful

Values-baed judgment is defined as how people behave in the gray zone between what is 100 percent lawful (the green zone) and what is 100 percent unlawful (the red zone).[130]

Promoting decision-making based on values in a company serves as a guiding principle, aligning everyone's actions with a common understanding of ethics and values. It accomplishes this by building a culture focused on honesty, thereby encouraging good behavior. Having a clear set of values provides a standard for everyone in the company. When the company's values are clear and fully understood, employees know what's expected of them and are more likely to act ethically and consistently.

Leaders play a crucial role in this approach by setting an example with their ethical behavior and decisions, inspiring their teams to do the same. This way, employees are more likely to stay within the organization's ethical boundaries. A culture centered around values creates an atmosphere where open communication is valued. Employees can talk about ethical concerns and report violations without fear, preventing small issues from becoming big problems.

Encouraging values-based decisions lets employees think for themselves rather than just following rules. It helps them make decisions based on values, promoting ethical behavior and moral development. Companies focusing on values-based judgment often reward ethical behavior, showing employees that acting with integrity is appreciated. These rewards motivate employees to continue making ethical choices.

In summary, reinforcing values-based judgment is about creating a work environment in which making ethical decisions is encouraged and comes naturally to everyone.

Harnessing the Toolkit

As the saying goes—if it were easy, they wouldn't need us. This simple statement encapsulates the mission ahead for J.E.D.I. leaders. By focusing on a few proven tools, we can manifest external value for customers, communities, the environment, and shareholders.

- Managerial effectiveness elevates the employee experience via the application of strength-based leadership.

- We represent our customer far better when we implement inverted hierarchies that incentivize servant leadership.

- Employee engagement is the pathway to elevating communities. Leveraging the Gallup Q12 assessment as a systematic pathway to continuously increase engagement will create the capacity for greater corporate social responsibility on a grander scale.

- Regenerating the environment and contributing to the seventeen SDGs can be systematically done by leaning into the J.E.D.I.-Restoration System™.

- Lastly, earning the continued and sustained investment of shareholders is a function of business performance—but also of risk and reputation management—and the primary tool here is values-based judgment.

How J.E.D.I. Leaders Impact Primary Stakeholders

STAKEHOLDER IMPACTED	OUTCOME MANIFESTED	PRIMARY CULTURE TOOLS
EMPLOYEES	MANAGERIAL EFFECTIVENESS	STRENGTHS BASED LEADERSHIP
CUSTOMERS	REPRESENTING THE CUSTOMER	INVERTING THE HIERARCHY
COMMUNITIES	ELEVATING THE COMMUNITY	GALLUP Q12 ASSESSMENT
THE ENVIRONMENT	REGENERATING THE ENVIRONMENT	J.E.D.I.-RESTORATION SYSTEM™
SHAREHOLDERS	MAXIMIZING GOVERNANCE	VALUES-BASED JUDGEMENT

Regardless of our function within our organizations, when we commit to J.E.D.I. leadership, and with the support of resources like this playbook, we can proactively work to influence positive change so that we manifest greater outcomes for multiple stakeholders. This is the ultimate impact we can seek to achieve.

PART III: DISCIPLINE AND DETERMINATION

12

KEEPING SCORE

Measurable progress is the cornerstone of success for any function in an organization. This is especially true for emerging functions, because there may be a lack of clarity in terms of why the role exists in the first place. The other reason why demonstrable results are key is that not everyone within the ecosystem will automatically understand what we do, how we do it, or why it matters. Beginning with the end in mind, we must craft a compelling scoreboard to keep everyone aligned—and abreast of our impact.

The work we are doing is significant, so the story we tell about it should be equally so. Luckily, there is a framework we can adopt that makes this process infinitely easier, whether crafting narrative is our core strength or not. The Franklin-Covey institute innovated a system that creates alignment and visibility into the areas that matter most.

The Franklin-Covey Scoreboard methodology is an approach to performance management that aims to facilitate clear communication, personal accountability, and goal alignment within organizations.[131] The idea is to create a simple, compelling scoreboard that makes it easy for team members to see whether they're winning or losing. It's designed to be easily understood immediately, without the need for interpretation. The methodology is anchored in the belief that when employees know the score, they're more likely to be engaged, motivated, and aligned with the team's objectives.

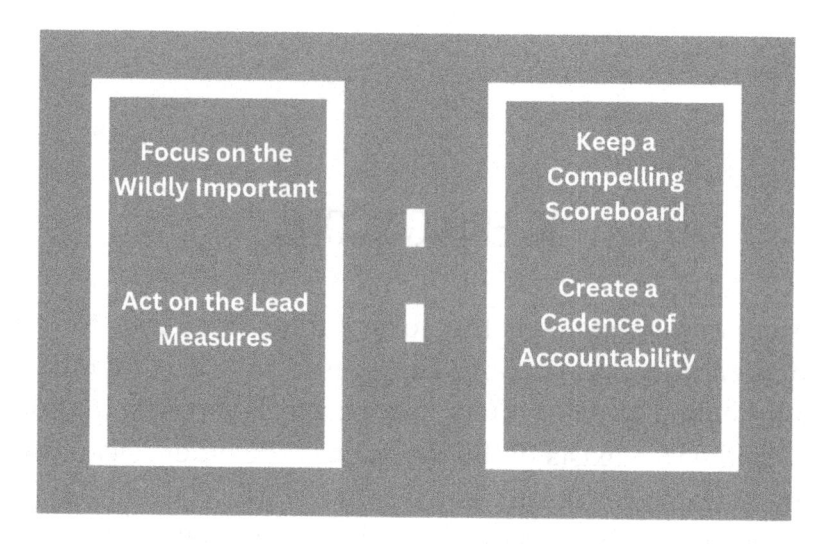

> **Focus on the Wildly Important**
>
> **Act on the Lead Measures**
>
> **Keep a Compelling Scoreboard**
>
> **Create a Cadence of Accountability**

Essentially, the Franklin-Covey Scoreboard serves as a transparent display of key performance indicators (KPIs) that are crucial for achieving the team or organizational objectives. It goes beyond mere numbers; the methodology emphasizes the previously discussed "lag" and "lead" measures. Once more, lag measures are the KPIs that reflect the end result, like annual revenue and lead measures are actionable metrics that influence the lag measures.

Salesforce, a global leader in CRM software, has applied elements of the Franklin-Covey Scoreboard methodology in managing its various teams.[132] By clearly defining lead and lag measures, Salesforce was able to align the sales team's daily activities with broader company objectives. This enhanced clarity and alignment contributed to their continued growth and success in the highly competitive software market.

Similarly, the methodology has been used in healthcare settings. For example, the Cleveland Clinic has been noted for using similar principles to track patient care and satisfaction.[133] By carefully selecting lead measures like patient wait times and staff responsiveness, they were able to positively influence lag measures like overall patient satisfaction and quality of care. As a result, the Cleveland Clinic consistently ranks as one of the top hospitals in the United States.

In the retail sector, companies like Target have employed scoreboard methods to track everything from sales metrics to customer satisfaction.[134] Clear visual representation of these metrics, easily accessible to employees, has been credited with fostering a more engaged and motivated workforce. This, in turn, has led to an improvement in various performance metrics, such as customer satisfaction scores and same-store sales growth.

Elements of a Compelling Scoreboard

To create what Franklin-Covey describes as a winnable game, several components must be in place—the first of which are Wildly Important Goals (WIGs), which we discussed back in Chapter 7. The good news with J.E.D.I. work is that our WIGs are already defined as eradicating injustices, eliminating inequities, expanding diversity, and enhancing inclusion. And as per the chapter on goal setting, our J.E.D.I. scoreboard will allow us to track progress against these four core priorities of our work. Imagine the power of being able to empirically prove to both internal and external stakeholders the exact injustices that have been eliminated, inequities eradicated, diversity expanded, and inclusion enhanced.

But these goals are only lag measures. Lead measures are what we need to track. By acting on the lead, we influence the achievement of the lag. Still, we all need a starting point. With that in mind, here are some initial goals to shoot for and the corresponding lead measures.

Eradicating the Six Most Common Systemic Injustices:

- Bad actors who persist in the organization.
  - ▶ Lead Measure: Employ a robustly enforced disciplinary matrix.
- Corrupt practices and principles.
  - ▶ Lead Measure: Strengthen values-based judgment and internal control framework.
- CEO compensation gap.
  - ▶ Lead Measure: Publish the company's CEO-to-worker pay ratio and set mandatory maximums, with the ratio never to exceed X.
- Favoritism or bias in promotional processes.
  - ▶ Lead Measure: Implement restoration of promotional process to eliminate favoritism and bias.
- Favoring what gets done over how it gets done.
  - ▶ Lead Measure: Implement restoration of incentive policies to value the how as much as the what.
- Disregard for health and wellness.
  - ▶ Lead Measure: Implement restoration of health and wellness policies to enhance preventative practices such as vaccination, annual check-ups, paid time off, counseling, maternity/paternity leave, gym memberships, and nutrition tips.

Eliminating the Five Sins of Inequity:

- Privileged hiring.
  - ▶ Lead Measure: Hire for high-performance behaviors, not pedigree.

- Sink-or-swim onboarding.
  - ▶ Lead Measure: Restore onboarding processes by investing in managerial development and structured onboarding procedures that emphasize trust-building and ninety-day planning.

- Talent whitewashing.
  - ▶ Lead Measure: Identify and develop employee talents into reliable strengths and enforce strengths-based development plans.

- Corrupted compensation.
  - ▶ Lead Measure: Conduct internal equity pay audits across functions to ensure firm and fair guidelines for current employees versus external hires and reduce dependency on external industry benchmarks for compensation-setting.

- Targeted termination.
  - ▶ Lead Measure: Instead of last in, first out (LIFO), early retirement, or other typical termination measures, consider furloughs, salary reductions (especially for executives), and nice-to-have asset sales (unnecessary facilities or perks, like corporate jets).

Expanding Diversity in Five Steps:

- Stagnated talent pipelines.

  - Lead Measure: Commit to expanding the talent pool to unfamiliar sources and working to develop a diverse feeder system.

- Status quo readiness evaluation for senior executive roles.

  - Lead Measure: Reevaluate the definition of readiness for underrepresented groups and accelerate their managerial placement.

- Fixated career pathing.

  - Lead Measure: Customize coaching and development experiences related to underrepresented groups (i.e., overinvest in their capability development for a time).

- Lack of diversity in decision-making forums.

  - Lead Measure: Ensure that underrepresented groups always have representation in promotion and talent development discussions.

- Lack of relevant mentors.

  - Lead Measure: Build an internal and external mentorship network that can support your underrepresented group's matriculation through the organization.

Enhancing Inclusion with Six Actions:

- Inauthentic environments.

- ▸ Lead Measure: Empower underrepresented groups to improve inclusivity within the company environment, from images to messaging to engagement.
- ⊙ Anonymous employee surveys with no demographic drill-down.
  - ▸ Lead Measure: Allow employees to represent their demographic groups when providing crucial feedback so senior leaders can more effectively "hear" their distinct voices outside of majorities.
- ⊙ Corporate culture "brainwashing."
  - ▸ Lead Measure: Avoid building a company of "yes-ers" and instead allow the culture to be a composite of its members versus a top-down definition.
- ⊙ Broken feedback loops.
  - ▸ Lead Measure: Ensure visibility into how the company leverages its speak-up systems, from anonymous reporting to investigations to engagement surveys.
- ⊙ No safe spaces.
  - ▸ Lead Measure: Encourage the creation of single-identity spaces and Employee Resource Groups for underrepresented groups.
- ⊙ Lack of listening, understanding, and empathy.
  - ▸ Lead Measure: Adopt regular application of

"GEMBA" visits, where senior leaders go and see and sit with underrepresented groups and engage with them.

As should be apparent, prioritization of these goals is crucial. Even more so, validation that these are the issues to be prioritized is paramount. Whether you are leveraging these goals, or the process outlined in Chapter 7, the objective is to create a compelling visualization of progress for the functions involved and for senior leadership. Doing so could be the difference between the success and failure of our collective work—the story we tell and the progress we make.

Everything we've discussed thus far culminates in a scoreboard that might look something like this:

Mock J.E.D.I. Scoreboard

WIG 1: Eradicate favoritism or bias in promotional processes.	WIG 2: Eliminate privileged hiring.	WIG 3: Expand career pathing.	WIG 4: Enhance feedback loops.
LM1: Restoration of promotional process to eliminate favoritism and bias.	LM2: Hire for high-performance behaviors, not pedigree.	LM3: Customize coaching and development experiences related to underrepresented groups (i.e., overinvest in their capability development for a time).	LM4: Ensure visibility into how the company leverages it's speak-up systems, from anonymous reporting to investigations to engagement surveys.
Restoration stage: • Disciplinary matrix definition	Restoration stage: • Problem identification	Restoration stage: • NOP training	Restoration stage: • Management monitoring

The top layer of the Scoreboard is represented by the WIGs for each area of our J.E.D.I. objectives. That is then followed by the lead measures defined for each WIG. Lastly, we use the J.E.D.I.-Restoration System to clarify the stage we are in related to the completion of each lead measure. When the restoration stage hits management monitoring, we can report the WIG as green. Please remember the stages of restoration:

- Problem identification and issue resolution
- Corrective and preventative action implementation
- Disciplinary matrix definition
- J.E.D.I. restoration projects and programs
- New operating procedure creation
- Communication and training of the NOP(s)
- Management monitoring

So, by this model, WIG 1 is in stage three of seven, WIG 2 is in stage one of seven, WIG 3 is in stage five of seven, and WIG 4 is in stage seven of seven. This methodology makes it very easy to visualize progress for everyone involved in the work and to report out to key stakeholders on how the work is advancing. More importantly, it allows us to ensure the right cadence of accountability.

The Cadence of Accountability

A scoreboard is only as valuable as those playing the game, and those players need to understand their responsibilities and areas of discrete ownership within the collective process and ecosystem—which is why the Accountability Board lives behind the scoreboard.

An accountability board is comprised of deliverables directly linked to the achievement of lead measures.[135] Deliverables are assigned to a list of responsible individuals with specific deadlines for completion. And there is a regular cadence of reporting out and updating progress, identifying roadblocks, and soliciting support. The only thing that matters is achieving a cadence of achievement that results in completion of lead measures.

Mock Accountability Board

Weekly Plan	Current Week				
Deliverables	M	T	W	T	F
Item 1					John D.
Item 2	Susan				
Item 3			Dave		
Item 4	John D.				
Item 5		Dave			
Item 6					

The way this works in practice is to set a deliverables assignment meeting where the tasks linked to the achievement of lead measures are allocated across the team. In instances where we don't have direct reports, we need to identify individuals cross-functionally with the bandwidth to support our efforts. Once deliverables have been allocated, we set off the cadence of review meetings, usually weekly, where task owners report back on two questions: 1) What progress was made this week? and 2) What support is needed if the desired progress was not achieved? As items are completed, they are crossed off the task list. This cadence continues until every item finished and the lead measure has indeed been secured.

Securing a lead measure is more than just getting tasks off the list; it also involves measuring the effect of the lead measure on the wildly important goal. For instance, in our mock scoreboard above, we are at the final stage of WIG 4 (enhancing feedback loops), which means we have implemented the management monitoring process. Because we've completed all the tasks related to the lead measure—*ensuring visibility into how the company leverages its speak-up systems, from anonymous reporting to investigations to engagement surveys*—we now need a mechanism to demonstrate that we are achieving the desire impact. And as we are ultimately dealing with human sentiment, we must assess the degree to which we have impacted the lag measure (WIG) in the near-, medium-, and long-term.

The best approach is to assess the links between WIG completion and employee productivity, retention, and engagement. The WIG only matters to the extent that achieving it improves the overall employee experience. And employee experience only improves when real, substantive change occurs over a sustained period of time. At the end of the day, the only scores that matters are how employees feel about the place they work, the work they do, and the managers for whom they do it.

With a robust scoreboard in place, we can effectively manage the game. But staying in the game sometimes requires managing trade-offs—which is what we will delve into next.

13

EMBRACING TRADE-OFFS

The last chapter around keeping score is all about possessing the discipline to rigorously march toward necessary achievement and transparently display the results of this effort. But as the Civil Rights protestors marching from Selma to Montgomery learned, discipline is one matter and determination is another. When inevitable obstacles to progress arise, we must also understand how to turn or's into and's (known as paradoxical thinking) and zero-sums into win-wins, and how to influence without authority. These three concepts form the backbone of the science of trading off.

Trading off involves assessing the opportunity costs, benefits, and risks associated with various strategic choices, with the goal of optimizing overall organizational performance.[136] By understanding the interconnected nature of business variables (aka enterprise leadership), managers become able to make informed decisions that balance short-term gains with long-term sustainability, operational efficiency with innovation, and individual goals with collective objectives. The science of trade-offs thereby serves as a cornerstone for effective management, guiding the allocation of limited resources in a way that maximizes value creation for stakeholders.

But before we get into the intricacies of strategic decision-making, we need to also set our clear boundaries—the things we never trade off regardless of the circumstances. We identify these areas by moving away from what's in it for us (such as resources, ideas/credit, privileges, and/or priority) so that we can maintain the areas that matter most to our stakeholders (such as our degree of focus, quality, commitment, and effectiveness). With these areas clearly delineated, we can move into decision-making with greater precision.

Paradoxical Thinking[137]

The essence of great decision-making is not about compromising one value for another; it's about integrating values. For example, integrating short-term gains with long-term sustainability and combining disciplined corporate culture with entrepreneurial spirit leads to better, forward-thinking decisions. Paradoxical thinking is especially crucial in J.E.D.I. leadership, helping navigate organizational change. Some might think focusing on J.E.D.I values might compromise other organizational goals like operational efficiency or profit, but truly innovative leaders see that these concepts are not mutually exclusive and can coexist, benefiting the organization in the long run.

For instance, conventional thought might see increasing workforce diversity and maintaining a merit-based hiring process as conflicting goals. However, a paradoxical perspective understands that a genuine merit-based system acknowledges and works to overcome the historical barriers that some groups have faced, enhancing the overall merit and creating a more dynamic and competitive workforce that is beneficial for both the organization and society.

Furthermore, the concept of "fit" in organizational culture can coexist with diverse thoughts, backgrounds, and perspectives, enriching organizational values rather than diluting them. An inclusive environment brings varied voices that can constructively challenge the existing norms, fostering innovation and contributing to a more adaptive and equitable workplace. J.E.D.I leaders, through paradoxical thinking, navigate beyond traditional dilemmas, recognizing complementarity in apparent contradictions. They align ethical imperatives for justice with the practical needs for organizational success, paving a sustainable and impactful path for enduring change, rather than looking for quick, convenient solutions.

Here are some keys to successfully leveraging paradoxical thinking:

- Embrace "both/and" over "either/or" thinking. By adopting a "both/and" perspective, you open new avenues for solutions that honor multiple facets of a problem or opportunity.

- Practice active inquiry and deep listening. Listening deeply to various perspectives and asking probing questions that challenge our own assumptions as well as those of others expands our understanding of the complexity at hand, enabling more nuanced solutions.

- Redefine success metrics. A paradoxical approach pushes us to redefine what success looks like by integrating conflicting objectives into a cohesive strategy. This could mean devising new KPIs that account for both financial performance and social impact, effectively merging two seemingly opposing goals.

- Cultivate a culture of psychological safety. People will only engage in paradoxical thinking if they feel safe enough to voice unconventional or contradictory opinions. Leaders should create an environment where it's not only okay to challenge the status quo but actively encouraged.

- Apply agile frameworks that allow for iterative learning. Paradoxical thinking is not a "set it and forget it" kind of strategy. It's about continuous adaptation and adjustment. By applying agile methodologies, we can test different approaches, quickly assess their impact, and adjust as we go along, effectively navigating the paradoxes that inevitably arise.

Life is rarely black and white, and the challenges we face are often riddled with nuance and contradiction. Paradoxical thinking equips us with the intellectual flexibility to navigate these complexities—not by simplifying them, but by embracing them in all their messy glory.

Seeking Win-Wins Over Zero-Sums[138]

Now let's talk about one of the most crucial mindsets that differentiate highly effective and intentional leaders from the rest: win-win thinking versus zero-sum thinking. Zero-sum thinking is based on a flawed premise—that there's a finite amount of success, recognition, or resources to go around. If one party wins, then the other loses. It's an antagonistic viewpoint that leads to territorial behavior, office politics, and ultimately stagnation. This mindset diminishes leadership intent, and it corrupts the culture. It is what is at the heart of the karate approach we rejected in Chapter 3.

Having a win-win mindset means realizing that everyone

benefits when we support each other, rather than pushing others down to get ahead ourselves. This is opposite to zero-sum thinking, where it's believed there are limited resources, and if someone gains, another loses. Leadership, fundamentally, is about influencing others positively. Effective leaders know their success is connected to the success of others and focus on enhancing value, serving, and nurturing potential in others, rather than just worrying about protecting what they have.

They understand the strength in "we," rather than "me," and aim to create together rather than get for themselves.

In J.E.D.I. leadership, this win-win mindset is crucial, both morally and ethically. For example, instead of seeing mentorship programs for underrepresented groups as taking resources away from the majority, J.E.D.I. leaders see this as an opportunity to enrich the work environment, benefitting everyone. Implementing specialized mentorship doesn't mean less for the majority; it encourages diversity and innovation, making the organization globally competitive.

The win isn't just for the underserved groups. As diversity grows, the whole organization benefits from varied perspectives and becomes more adaptable, which is a win for the majority and for the organization. It also projects the organization's commitment to diversity, equity, and inclusion, attracting top talents and possibly accessing new markets, thus positively affecting the organizational culture and profits.

In a win-win approach, leaders move past the restrictions of a zero-sum game and build an environment where the progress of one group boosts the success of the whole organization. This approach not only aligns with moral and ethical values but also constitutes wise, lasting business choices that benefit both the internal community of the organization and its external stakeholders. In J.E.D.I. leadership, embracing a win-win mindset is essential; it merges intention, inclusion, and inspiration, fostering a thriving environment for everyone.

Below are the key considerations involved in achieving win-wins over zero-sums:

- Identify common ground. In any situation where conflicting interests seem to dominate, dig deeper to unearth shared goals or values. By highlighting what everyone has in common, we create a platform for cooperative solutions. It's not about compromising; it's about synthesizing diverse needs into an outcome that serves everyone better.

- Adopt a mindset of abundance rather than scarcity. A zero-sum outlook is rooted in the belief that resources are limited, leading to defensive tactics and power struggles. But what if we reframe the situation? What if we consider the possibility that growing the pie could benefit everyone? Shifting our mindset to one of abundance allows us to explore creative solutions that add value to all parties involved.

- Focus on relationship-building. Win-win outcomes are not just transactional events; they are deeply embedded in the relationships between people. By forging trust and understanding, we open doors to long-term collaborations. When we listen actively, empathize, and communicate transparently, we build solid relationships that lay the foundation for future win-wins.

- Leverage the power of co-creation. In a zero-sum world, decisions are often dictated by those with the most power. But in a win-win paradigm, everyone is a contributor. Involve stakeholders in the problem-solving process, encouraging diverse viewpoints and ideas. This shared sense of ownership not only leads to better solutions but also ensures greater commitment to the outcome.

- Be prepared to iterate. Achieving a win-win is often an ongoing process, not a one-time negotiation. Be open to feedback and willing to make adjustments as you move forward. Use metrics and KPIs that reflect the holistic success of the initiative, rather than just individual wins. This ensures that we're not merely ticking boxes but also genuinely creating value for all parties involved.

The shift from zero-sum to win-win thinking is more than a strategy; it's a mindset, an approach to leadership that's deeply rooted in the principles of intentionality, collaboration, and shared value. By applying these strategies, we're not just resolving conflicts or closing deals; we're building a legacy of inclusive success that amplifies the collective potential of our teams, our organizations, and even society at large.

Influence Without Authority[139]

In today's business world, the concept of leadership has significantly changed to focus more on influencing without relying on authoritative power. Leadership is no longer just about positions and titles, but more about building relationships, trust, and collaboration to mobilize people. This kind of leadership starts with the genuine intent to uplift others, rather than self-serving agendas, adopting a servant-leadership approach to attract people to our vision and values.

Influence in leadership is also closely linked to making others feel included and valued, recognizing everyone's unique talents and perspectives. By integrating individual strengths into a collective vision, we allow people not only to "buy in" but also to "thrive in." Inspiration is another crucial aspect; it's about empowering people to align their actions with their values and beliefs, serving as a catalyst for their intrinsic motivation.

The essence of influencing without authority is to serve, include, and inspire, creating an environment driven by purpose where everyone feels they are part of something bigger. This is particularly important in J.E.D.I leadership, where influencing without authority can lead to impactful changes.

For example, a mid-level employee in Human Resources noticing a gap in inclusivity initiatives can act to influence change without having direct decision-making power. By clarifying intent to increase inclusivity and involving colleagues from various departments in addressing the issue, a collective desire for change can be demonstrated. Presenting a well-researched and collective proposal showcases a shared commitment to change. After approval, the spirit of servant leadership continues by coordinating with different departments for implementation, thus leading to a change in company policy and empowering others to recognize their leadership potential, irrespective of their positions.

In the J.E.D.I. leadership realm, influencing without authority means leveraging even small platforms to amplify voices and needs of others, showing that leadership is not about a title but instead about creating spaces in which everyone can contribute their best selves for the collective good. Achieving this makes one not just a J.E.D.I. leader, but also an influential changemaker.

Here are some proven strategies to expand influence without authority:

- Align intentions. This is the backbone of influence. Intent should support with a purpose greater than ourselves—a shared goal or vision that others can rally behind. Once people sense our genuine intent to create win-win outcomes, they are more likely to trust us and be influenced by our ideas.

- Build trust. Influence is a by-product of trust, and trust stems from strong relationships. Spend time understanding people and their pain points, aspirations, and motivations. Go beyond the superficial small talk; delve into what really matters to people. Building these relationships will form the bedrock upon which we can exert influence when it matters most.

- Master storytelling. A well-told story can move mountains. Craft narratives that focus on more than facts and figures and that tap into emotions and universal truths. Make arguments relatable, compelling, and memorable. In doing so, we'll be able to influence more than people's thoughts; we'll also be able to influence their feelings and actions.

- Advocate for inclusion. Leveraging diverse voices both strengthens our influencing strategy and fosters a culture of inclusivity. Include others in the decision-making process, seek out divergent viewpoints, and create a space where everyone feels heard. When people feel included, they're more likely to invest their own influence in our initiatives.

- Offer reciprocation. Be the first to offer help, share information, or acknowledge someone else's contributions. By doing so, we build a reservoir of goodwill that can be drawn upon when we need to influence others. It's not about keeping score; it's about fostering a culture where mutual support is the norm.

Maximizing our influence without authority doesn't happen overnight. It's a journey that requires intent, relationship-building, storytelling, inclusion, and reciprocation. It's a practice in intentional leadership, grounded in the conviction that we don't need a title to make a significant impact. By cultivating these skills and applying these strategies, we position ourselves as leaders who influence outcomes and elevate those around us, creating a ripple effect of positive impact far beyond our immediate reach.

In the complex world of J.E.D.I. leadership, discipline alone can't cut it. The path to real progress is nuanced, and it requires a multi-faceted approach that goes beyond conventional thinking. First, let's talk about embracing trade-offs by leveraging paradoxical thinking. Often, we find ourselves at the crossroads of seemingly conflicting objectives—like fostering individuality while building a unified culture. By embracing paradoxical thinking, we see that these objectives aren't necessarily mutually exclusive. We focus on crafting strategies that sustain the tension between the two, allowing our organization to be both diverse and unified.

Then there's the game-changing mindset of win-win scenarios. Too often, we're stuck in zero-sum games where the advancement of one group is viewed as the setback of another. This is an outdated notion that does nothing but fuel division. By shifting to a win-win mindset, J.E.D.I. leaders create an environment where the success of one individual or group amplifies the collective success of the organization. It's not about taking slices of a limited pie; it's about making the pie bigger and more delicious for everyone involved.

Lastly, we may not always have the positional power to dictate change, but that doesn't mean we're powerless. By fostering relationships built on trust, inclusivity, and inspiration, we can mobilize people at all levels to contribute to our justice, equity, diversity, and inclusion initiatives. It's about leading with intent—and that intent is to serve others in a way that uplifts everyone involved.

Making meaningful progress as J.E.D.I. leaders isn't solely about discipline or policies, or even just awareness. It's about embracing the complexities, the trade-offs, and the paradoxes that come with leading a diverse and inclusive organization. It's about rejecting zero-sum games in favor of win-win outcomes that benefit everyone. And it's about understanding that your ability to influence is not tied to your job title, but to the value you create for others. By skillfully combining these three approaches, we can do so much more than talk about change; we can actually be the change people wish to see—both within their organizations and in the broader world.

14

MAINTAINING MOMENTUM AND COMMITMENT

Discipline creates the rigor and consistency needed to push boulders up mountains. Determination manifests the grit required to make the necessary trade-offs to keep multiple balls in the air. And inspiration is the fuel that keeps the engine of momentum and commitment fully powered on the road to ultimate achievement. This chapter is all about how to maintain inspiration despite the challenges inherent in our work.

This is where we come full circle back to the *why* of the J.E.D.I. leader, which we discussed in Chapter 1. Inspired leaders have a *why* powered by a combination that the authors of *Dare to Inspire* call self-awareness, personal agility, and agency.[140] Each of these qualities on its own can be a significant motivator, but when combined, they put the battery in our backs. Let's discuss each in turn.

Expanding Self-Awareness

When it comes to J.E.D.I. leadership, the work is not just external; it's also internal. It starts with self-awareness, the cornerstone upon which meaningful impact is built. But why is self-awareness so critical for maintaining momentum and commitment in J.E.D.I. initiatives?

Understanding ourselves is the first step in understanding others. If we're unaware of our own biases, triggers, and limitations, we're likely to project them onto others, inadvertently hampering the very objectives we're striving to achieve. Self-awareness allows us to hold up a mirror to ourselves, identifying areas for growth and setting the stage for genuine empathy and understanding toward those we aim to serve.

Next, let's talk about stamina. J.E.D.I. work is not a sprint; it's a marathon. There will be roadblocks, setbacks, and periods of fatigue. Being self-aware helps us recognize when we're running low on mental or emotional energy, enabling us to take necessary breaks or seek support. This isn't a sign of weakness; it's an intentional strategy to recharge and re-enter the fray with renewed vigor.

Self-awareness equips us with the ability to adapt our approach. In the dynamic landscape of J.E.D.I. leadership, one size does not fit all. Being cognizant of our communication style, decision-making patterns, and influence strategies allows us to tailor our approach depending on the situation or the stakeholders involved. Adaptability, rooted in self-awareness, is key to navigating the complexities inherent in our work.

Additionally, self-awareness enhances our credibility. Authenticity is a currency in the realm of influence, especially when leading without authority. People can sense when we're not being genuine, and that undermines our ability to galvanize support for our objectives. Being self-aware empowers us to lead from a place of authenticity, thereby magnifying our influence.

Lastly, let's not forget accountability. Self-awareness is the antidote to the blind spots that can derail even the most well-intentioned J.E.D.I. initiatives. By regularly checking in with ourselves and seeking external feedback, we're better equipped to own our actions, learn from our mistakes, and course-correct as needed.

Self-awareness is not just a personal development tool; it's a strategic asset in the toolkit of every J.E.D.I. leader, as well. It enhances our empathy, stamina, adaptability, credibility, and accountability, acting as a force multiplier in our quest to achieve impactful and sustainable J.E.D.I. outcomes. And when we lead with self-awareness, we're not just impacting the initiatives we spearhead; we're also setting a powerful example for others to follow, thereby amplifying our impact in a way that creates a lasting legacy.

If self-awareness is the bedrock of effective J.E.D.I. leadership, then the million-dollar question is: how do we cultivate it? The journey to enhanced self-awareness is deeply personal; yet there are proven strategies that can serve as our compass.[141] Let's delve into them.

- Introspection. Allocate time regularly to reflect on our thoughts, emotions, and actions. It's easy to get caught up in the hustle and bustle of leadership duties, especially in this space where the work is emotionally taxing and complex. Pausing for introspection allows us to explore our own mental and emotional landscape, shedding light on our motives, biases, and triggers.

- Actively seek feedback. It's often said that feedback is a gift, and rightly so. Yet many of us shy away from it, particularly when it's critical. But remember, the goal is growth, not comfort. Constructive feedback exposes blind spots that we might not be aware of. We should reach out to colleagues, mentors, and even adversaries to gather diverse perspectives on our leadership style and its impact.

- Leverage assessments and tools. Instruments like the Emotional Intelligence assessments, CliftonStrengths, or the Myers-Briggs Type Indicator offer structured ways to understand different facets of our personality and leadership style. While these shouldn't be our sole resource, they offer a starting point for deeper self-exploration.

- Embrace a growth mindset. This concept, pioneered by psychologist Carol Dweck, posits that abilities and intelligence can be developed. When we adopt a growth mindset, we view challenges as opportunities for self-improvement rather than threats to our ego. This shifts our focus from proving ourselves to improving ourselves, which is a potent catalyst for enhancing self-awareness.

- Cultivate mindfulness practices. Whether it's meditation, deep breathing exercises, or simply being present in the moment, mindfulness fosters an acute awareness of our internal state. It creates a mental space where we can observe our thoughts and feelings without judgment, granting us insights into our own reactions and behaviors.

- Maintain a journal. Documenting our experiences, thoughts, and reflections can serve as a powerful tool for self-discovery. Not only does it compel us to articulate our internal state, but it also serves as a record that we can revisit to track our growth and shifts in perspective over time.

- Surround ourselves with a community that fosters self-awareness. Whether it's a formal mentorship program, peer groups, or even online forums dedicated to J.E.D.I. leadership, being part of a community provides us with varied opportunities to learn, share, and grow.

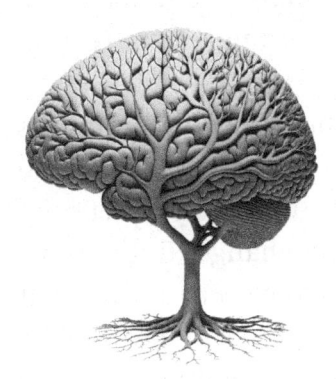

Enhancing self-awareness is an ongoing, ever-evolving process. It's not something we "achieve" and then forget; it's something we continually cultivate. The good news is that every step we take toward greater self-awareness doesn't just serve us; it also enriches our capacity to champion J.E.D.I. causes effectively. So, we dive into this journey with the same fervor and intentionality that we bring to our leadership role, because the rewards are well worth the effort.

Accelerating Personal Agility

In the pursuit of justice, equity, diversity, and inclusion, leaders must recognize that the road ahead is neither straight nor predictable. So, how does one maintain momentum and commitment in this turbulent landscape? The answer lies in personal agility. Accelerating our personal agility isn't just a useful skill; it's a leadership imperative for sustained impact in this space.

J.E.D.I. issues are complex, multifaceted, and interwoven into the fabric of organizational and societal structures. They don't yield to linear thinking or static strategies. An agile J.E.D.I. leader understands this and adapts not just their strategies, but also themselves, by constantly evolving, learning, and pivoting to meet challenges head-on.

Then there's the necessity for resilience. Our work is emotionally taxing; it's work that strikes at the core of human dignity and worth. An agile leader knows how to build resilience through self-awareness, as well as through emotional intelligence, fortifying themselves for the inevitable ups and downs, successes and setbacks. Our agility equips us to bounce back quicker, to maintain momentum, and to recommit to objectives with renewed energy.

Being personally agile enhances collaboration and helps overcome isolated efforts that rarely lead to significant, lasting change. It allows us to work effectively across different areas, forming groups that can make a real difference. Adapting to various working styles, viewpoints, and cultural norms is crucial for the success of such collaborations.

Personal agility is also a remedy for stagnation and loss of focus. In J.E.D.I. leadership, maintaining focus on the mission is crucial, especially when progress is challenging. Agile leaders continually assess themselves, adjust their goals, and are flexible in their approaches, aligning with the changing environments. In problem-solving, being agile helps anticipate challenges before they become obstacles, enabling us to address issues proactively and keep initiatives advancing efficiently and effectively.

To enhance personal agility, it's important to continuously learn, seek feedback, adopt a mindset that welcomes change, and develop the self-awareness to know when adjustments are needed. It's not just about speed and efficiency; it's about improving effectiveness and impact, too. Personal agility is a key skill that boosts all other leadership skills, allowing us to adapt to change and to anticipate it, maintaining momentum and dedication in achieving important goals.

Claiming Agency

Leadership agency is a topic that's often overlooked, but in doing this work, claiming our leadership agency is not a luxury—it's an imperative. Let's dissect why leadership agency is absolutely crucial for J.E.D.I. leaders in maintaining momentum and ensuring long-term commitment to achieving transformative objectives. Agency, in this context, is about staying in the driver's seat in our leadership journeys, making intentional choices rather than being reactive or passive.

It's acknowledging that, yes, the external environment is complex and often discouraging, but we have the agency to affect change within it. We're not spectators; we're catalysts. Now, why is this so important? In our work, we're tackling systemic issues—biases, prejudices, inequalities—that have been embedded for generations. To merely react to the existing landscape is to play an endless game of whack-a-mole. By claiming our leadership agency, we shift from being reactive to being strategic. We start setting the agenda rather than merely responding to it, and that's how we achieve lasting impact.

Taking control and owning our actions empower us to motivate our teams and stakeholders. A leader who acts with agency is inspiring and becomes someone others want to follow. By showing commitment, resilience, and focus on our goals, we encourage others to do the same. This has a multiplying effect, enhancing our impact and creating shared enthusiasm.

Having agency enhances resilience. In J.E.D.I. efforts, challenges and setbacks are common. If we navigate passively, every setback can be detrimental. However, with agency, we turn setbacks into lessons that refine our approach and strengthen our determination, sustaining our and our team's momentum. Embracing our agency allows us to develop leadership skills suited to the unique challenges of J.E.D.I. initiatives— including adaptive leadership to adjust our strategy as required, and transformational leadership to unite those around us toward a shared vision.

These skills are actively developed through a commitment to self-development and the mission. Agency also contributes to personal sustainability, allowing for long-term dedication. It allows us to manage our workload, seek help when needed, delegate tasks, and—importantly—prioritize our well-being, exemplifying justice in our leadership practices.

By owning your leadership agency, you don't just participate in change; you drive it. It's the key to resilience, strategy, sustained momentum, and lasting impact. To my fellow J.E.D.I. leaders: don't just wait for change—be the change. Agency is our power; by embracing and utilizing it, we enhance our impact and maintain our momentum in our crucial work.

15

SUMMARY

Most people who recount the legend of David versus Goliath forget to tell the rest of the story. After David's monumental victory over Goliath, the story became a defining narrative. It wasn't just about the defeat of a menacing giant; it was a triumph of belief, courage, and divine favor. But David's journey to kingship was far from linear—it was rife with trials, tribulations, and valuable lessons in leadership.

Just as a leader in today's volatile, uncertain, complex, and ambiguous (VUCA) world can't rest on the laurels of a single victory, David knew that defeating Goliath was merely the opening act of a career that demanded sustained excellence, intentionality, and a leadership model that incorporated everyone from the general to the gatekeeper.

King Saul, threatened by David's rising popularity, went to significant lengths to thwart David's ascendancy. Yet David responded with patience, kindness, and strategic acumen. He avoided confrontation and possible civil war, displaying a maturity that was well beyond his years.

David understood something critical about leadership: that the journey is a marathon, not a sprint. Saul's reign, mired in ego and pettiness, stood in stark contrast to the emerging philosophy of David. David's actions were motivated by collective well-being and unity, values that every leader should embody. When Saul was finally defeated, David took the reins—not as a usurper, but as a unifier, immediately looking to mend fences and build alliances.

He didn't just assume power; he earned legitimacy.

David's journey from a shepherd to a king is a masterclass in adaptive, inclusive, and intentional leadership. It's not about where you start; it's how you navigate your journey that truly defines your legacy. David's story offers contemporary leaders a roadmap for leadership that is just, equitable, diverse, and inclusive. By putting people first, acting with strategic empathy, and continually adapting to changing circumstances, leaders can not only achieve great things but also create a culture that sustains success long after they're gone.

With that in mind, let's recap all we've learned in this book, chapter by chapter.

What's Your J.E.D.I Why?

Each of us has to determine what we are for in this negotiation for greater justice, equity, diversity, and inclusion. We must reframe the debate from what we are not (racist, ableist, sexist, etc.) through what we are anti (e.g., genderist, classist, ageist) to what we are ultimately for. In this process, we lean into what we are truly fighting for, such as fairness (justice), equal opportunity to fully participate (equity), innovation (diversity), and/or productivity (inclusion).

Being "for" something is about proactive commitment; it's about what you stand to gain rather than what you seek to avoid. On the other hand, being "against" is fundamentally reactive; it's about opposition, and in some ways, it's a posture that keeps you anchored to the very thing you wish to escape or destroy. Consider the energy dynamics.

When you are "for" something, you create an energy that is attractive, magnetic. People want to be part of constructive visions, solutions, and movements. Your focus is on the art of the possible—on creating conditions where excellence becomes the norm, where the collective ambition is inclusive growth, well-being, and shared success. Being "for" something galvanizes people, offering them a shared vision they can contribute to. It's a win-win dynamic that creates a perpetual motion machine of positive energy, effort, and outcomes.

Conversely, when you are "against" or anti- something, your energy repels. It may rally people in the short term based on shared grievances, but it's a zero-sum game. It doesn't create; it obstructs. It doesn't inspire; it triggers. It's not about shared success; it's about shared resistance. And while there's a place for resistance, especially in the face of injustice or oppression, if resistance doesn't evolve into a constructive vision—something people can be "for"—it will ultimately stagnate and become counterproductive.

Being "for" something allows you to tap into the human spirit's aspirational aspects, enabling you to inspire followership, loyalty, and sustained high performance. You're not just solving a problem; you're providing a pathway to a better future. You're not just preventing harm; you're enabling goodness. And you're doing it in a way that includes everyone, not just the loudest or the most privileged.

Additionally, being "for" something is intrinsically aligned with key leadership values like intentionality, empathy, and empowerment. When you're "for" something, you're not just espousing a cause, you're embracing a commitment to serve that cause with everything you've got. It provides you with a north star by which to guide your decisions and actions, and it aids you in articulating compelling stories that enroll others in your journey.

Being "against" or anti- something, on the other hand, often keeps you in a reactive mode. It does not naturally cultivate these leadership attributes, because being "against" is not a strategy; it's a stance. In the grand tapestry of leadership, whether in business or social movements, the leaders who stand the test of time are those who stand "for" something. They are the ones who define their legacies by the positive impact they have made, by the lives they have improved, and by the systems they have transformed for the better.

So, would we rather be magnets or repellents? Would we rather create or obstruct? Would we rather inspire or trigger? The choice is ours, but remember: being "for" is not just a position; it's a direction—a direction that leads to lasting positive change.

Judo Versus Karate

In the spirit of being "for" rather than "against," we embrace the concept of judo versus karate. Judo is about finding what's working, embracing it, and aligning ourselves with it. In our work of J.E.D.I. leadership, the approach we take to gain understanding, agreement, and alignment can make all the difference in our ability to execute effectively and foster a culture of engagement. While both judo and karate are martial arts, their philosophies offer contrasting viewpoints on handling conflict and leveraging opportunities. Judo focuses on using an opponent's force against them, whereas karate is often about meeting force with force. I advocate for a judo approach in leadership because of its emphasis on adaptability, leverage, and strategic empathy.

Let's unpack this a bit.

- **Adaptability:** In judo, the goal is not to resist; it's to adapt and redirect. You use the momentum, the energy of your "opponent"—in the corporate context, this could be a challenge, a market condition, or a skeptical stakeholder—to your advantage. This is analogous to adopting a flexible management style that adjusts based on context and individual team members' needs. In a VUCA (volatile, uncertain, complex, ambiguous) world, this adaptability is not just beneficial; it's crucial.

- **Leverage:** Judo teaches you to leverage your opponent's weight and strength as you seek to gain control. This translates into using available resources, existing systems, or stakeholder influences in the most efficient manner to get to your desired outcomes. Rather than rebuilding the wheel or seeking to overpower existing systems and hierarchies, you leverage them to achieve your aims.

- **Strategic Empathy:** In judo, understanding your opponent's next move is critical to your success. This requires a keen sense of empathy. In leadership, being able to put yourself in others' shoes is a priceless skill. It allows you to understand their motivations, fears, and aspirations, helping you frame your argument or proposal in a way that resonates with them. This "strategic empathy" enables alignment and agreement far more effectively than attempting to simply persuade or overpower your audience.

- **Efficiency of Energy:** Judo is about maximum efficiency with minimal effort. In today's business environment, where resources are often limited, understanding how to do more with less is a valuable skill. The judo approach teaches us not to waste energy on battles that are better won through strategy, influence, and the smart use of available assets.

- **Winning Without Fighting:** One of the most impactful lessons from judo is the art of winning without actual fighting. Sometimes, the mere act of showing understanding and alignment can defuse opposition and gain agreement. We win by turning potential confrontations into collaborations, turning opponents into allies.

Contrast this with the karate approach, which is often about direct confrontation and the use of one's own force to subdue an opponent or obstacle. While there may be times when meeting force with force is necessary, it often expends more energy and creates a zero-sum dynamic that may not be sustainable in the long run.

When it comes to gaining understanding, agreement, and alignment, a Judo approach provides a more nuanced, adaptive, and efficient path. It's not about the sheer exertion of your will or the overpowering of obstacles; it's about the smart utilization of existing dynamics and energies to create a win-win outcome for all involved. And in today's complex world, that kind of strategy is not just smart; it's essential.

Leading Change

A large component of J.E.D.I. leadership deals with change leadership. Ultimately, we are actively resetting the status quo; and when that happens, a certain degree of fallout is to be expected. Still, when we understand how to leverage the four keys of change leadership—context, confidence, construction, and culture—we can more effectively and proactively shift our organizations into the future of modern leadership and stakeholder capitalism.

Context is the intricate web of factors that surrounds and influences the organization, its people, and the change initiative itself. It encompasses the organizational culture, history, industry trends, market dynamics, stakeholder expectations, and even the political and economic landscape. Neglecting to consider context when leading change is like sailing into uncharted waters without a map or compass—it is a recipe for disaster.

Context is crucial to consider when leading change because it can affect the way that people react to the change. For example, if a change is being made in a culture that is resistant to it, that change will be more difficult to implement. Another reason why context is important is that it can affect the way people perceive the change. For example, if a change is being made in an organization that is struggling, people may be more likely to resist.

Remember, VUCA is an acronym that stands for volatility, uncertainty, complexity, and ambiguity. These are the four factors that make the world a more challenging place to lead change. Effective change leaders understand the challenges posed by the VUCA factors and employ specific strategies to navigate them.

Confidence lies at the core of organizational transformation, and it is here that we will learn its importance in shaping change and the methods of instilling it throughout an organization. Confidence is the silent hero in the realm of change management. It's the underlying thread that strengthens the fabric of transformation, and yet it remains in the background, often overshadowed by more visible elements. However, the underestimation of confidence's influence can lead to a massive miscalculation in change management strategies. Confidence, in essence, is the belief in an organization's ability to achieve its vision, the belief in its capacity to overcome the hurdles along the change pathway, and—ultimately—the belief in its success.

The Construction phase is where change leaders engage in the art and science of architecture, designing the approach to the change that will be implemented. It is about making choices on how to maneuver through the intricate and dynamic terrain of change. One of the critical decisions in the construction phase is selecting the appropriate change management model. This is a vital step, because the right model acts as the blueprint for the entire change journey.

Just as we wouldn't begin constructing a building without a detailed architectural plan, we shouldn't initiate a change effort without a clear, strategic framework to guide the process. An inadequate or ill-fitting model may result in a shaky foundation that could doom the entire change movement.

The best change management models consider all aspects of the organization—its culture, resources, capabilities, and structure. They also account for the complexity and type of change, whether it's incremental or transformational, planned or emergent. The selected model should be malleable enough to be adjusted as circumstances shift but robust enough to provide a stable framework.

Before we can facilitate a culture that embraces change, we must first comprehend the existing one. Organizational culture represents the shared values, beliefs, and behaviors within an organization. A culture audit can provide essential insights into the collective consciousness of the organization. Are mistakes allowed and learned from, or are they punished? Is innovation encouraged or suppressed? Are employees competitive or collaborative? The answers to these questions are pointers to the existing culture and the need for its transformation.

Building a change-ready culture involves fostering an environment of trust, open communication, and shared responsibility.

- **Fostering Trust:** A culture of trust is essential for change initiatives. Employees need to trust that the changes are for the best, even if those changes bring short-term challenges. Building trust is a continuous process, but it begins with transparency about why changes are necessary and how they will benefit the organization and individuals.

- **Promoting Open Communication:** Effective communication is key to overcoming resistance and fostering acceptance. It involves clearly articulating the purpose, process, and benefits of the change. Leaders must ensure that communication channels are open and that feedback is encouraged.

- **Encouraging Shared Responsibility:** In a change-ready culture, everyone feels responsible for the success of the change initiative. Leaders must distribute ownership of change initiatives across the organization to foster this sense of shared responsibility.

Three B's and Four P's

Our work is that of influence. But the forces we must confront are some of the most challenging to deal with. Beliefs, whether rational or irrational, create our inherent biases which can manifest in our behavior—good or bad. And in organizations, the beliefs, biases, and behaviors of senior executives have a direct influence over the four P's (principles, priorities, processes, and practices). The advice in this book is, rather than fight (karate) the three B's of our executives, to restore incentives (judo) that realign what we say we value with what actually happens within the system.

There are four key questions in this regard:

1. What desirable behaviors are being incentivized in this culture?

2. What undesirable behaviors are being incentivized in this culture?

3. What is the cost/risk of allowing the undesirable elements to fester and grow?

4. What are some ways to reengineer incentives so undesirable elements cannot survive?

When we talk about reshaping the ethos of an organization, incentives are a fundamental lever of change. Many senior executives may not even realize it, but their beliefs, biases, and behaviors are often a direct response to the incentives they're provided. You perform in the way you're paid to perform. And herein lies both the problem and the opportunity: by rethinking organizational incentives, we can directly influence the actions and attitudes of senior executives. By extension, we can create stronger alignment between organizational principles, priorities, processes, and practices.

In the traditional corporate setup, executives are primarily incentivized based on financial metrics—revenue, profit, stock performance, etc. While these metrics are undeniably important, they can reinforce a belief system that values short-term gains over long-term sustainability. This financial-first focus can lead to biases against initiatives that don't immediately impact the bottom line, like J.E.D.I. efforts or environmental sustainability programs. By diversifying the incentive mix to include non-financial metrics—employee engagement, customer satisfaction, carbon footprint reduction, etc.—we begin nudging senior executives to broaden their belief systems to encompass a more holistic understanding of value and success.

We know that what executives do sets the tone for the entire organization. When the incentives are redesigned to promote customer-centricity, teamwork, and long-term value creation, we'll find executives making more collaborative decisions. They'll be more likely to listen to front-line employees, incorporate customer feedback into strategy, and consider the long-term impact of their decisions on all stakeholders, including the community and environment.

Still, one of the biggest challenges organizations face is the disconnect between what they say they're about (their principles) and what they actually do (their practices). This gap is often the result of misaligned priorities and processes that were designed under an old incentive structure. For example, if an organization claims to value innovation but only rewards cost-cutting, guess what? Innovation is going to take a backseat. By aligning incentives with stated principles, we make those principles actionable. They go from words on a plaque to lived experiences within the organization.

The transformative impact of well-designed incentives can't be overstated. Think of it as resetting the organization's DNA. It affects not only what gets done, but also how it gets done and who gets to participate in the doing. By tying incentives to key performance indicators that truly matter for the well-being of all stakeholders—employees, customers, shareholders, and society—we build a culture in which everyone is a vested participant in collective success.

So, in essence, rethinking organizational incentives is not just an HR task or a financial calculation. It's a strategic imperative for any organization aiming for long-term success and cultural alignment. It's a golden opportunity to align our executives' beliefs, biases, and behaviors with our organizational ethos, leading to an integrated, harmonious, and—most importantly—successful operation.

Risk assessment can also be a powerful motivator. We discussed the following questions to assess risk and gain executive alignment to take action:

- Which business practices have been flagged as high-risk?
- What are the SOPs linked to these business practices?
- Who are the business owners accountable for effective implementation of these SOPs?
- Where are the gaps between the SOPs and the actual practices?
- What is the cost of inaction?

Establishing Goals, Priorities, and Capabilities

The revision of incentives and assessment of organizational risks inherent in misalignments between principles, priorities, processes, and capabilities leads us to establishing wildly important goals (WIGS) that shift our priorities and motivate us to confront the need for certain strategic capabilities. The WIGs of J.E.D.I. work are inherent in the acronym; we are to do the work until we eradicate injustices, eliminate inequities, expand diversity, and enhance inclusion.

We establish priorities under each WIG by making the decision to focus on either depth or breadth of action. Depth is about taking one element of J.E.D.I. at a time and working until we have completely satisfied the key issues in that area. Breadth relates to working across the spectrum of J.E.D.I. and making incremental improvements. The correct choice between the two approaches can best be determined by time, support, and investment. With a clear mandate from senior management to institute needed change, and enough investment and support, we can accomplish quite a bit within a given period; so we should choose breadth and work across the J.E.D.I. WIGS. If this mandate is unclear, it's better to under-promise and overdeliver while deepening our understanding. This approach indicates depth, and we should choose which element of J.E.D.I. we wish to tackle first, second, third, and fourth.

Achieving tangible progress in justice, equity, diversity, and inclusion (J.E.D.I.) is not just a matter of will or intent; it's about strategic execution, as well. One of the most powerful tools you can deploy to this end is effective prioritization. Without it, we can easily become mired in an endless cycle of reactive measures, short-term wins, and well-intentioned but ultimately ineffective actions. Enter the Importance Versus Urgency matrix, followed by the Impact Versus Effort matrix—two vital tools that can reshape our J.E.D.I. journey.

Importance Versus Urgency Matrix

The first step is to list out your J.E.D.I. initiatives and then plot them on an Importance Versus Urgency matrix. Doing so enables us to separate what's pressing from what's peripheral.

- **Important and Urgent:** These are the "fires" we need to put out immediately, like addressing a significant disparity in pay or handling a discrimination case. They require immediate attention and swift action.

- **Important but Not Urgent:** These are our long-term strategic plays—like building out comprehensive DEI training, fostering partnerships with minority-serving educational institutions, or revamping hiring processes. These initiatives are often sacrificed in the daily hustle but are crucial for sustainable change.

- **Urgent but Not Important:** These tasks can often masquerade as critical activities but are usually distractions that don't significantly advance our objectives. They might include surface-level activities like one-off events that look good on social media but don't bring about systemic change.

- **Neither Important nor Urgent:** This is the "busy work" that feels productive but doesn't move the needle—like writing reports nobody reads or attending meetings that have no actionable outcomes.

The goal is to allocate more time and resources to activities that are Important but Not Urgent, without ignoring the Important and Urgent. The latter gets the attention, while the former gets the intention, thoughtful planning, and execution it deserves.

Impact Versus Effort Matrix

Once we've identified what's both Important and either Urgent or Not Urgent, we can then prioritize these initiatives using the Impact Versus Effort matrix. This matrix helps us gauge the ROI of each initiative.

- High Impact, Low Effort: These are the quick wins, like creating an anonymous reporting tool for discrimination or bias.

- High Impact, High Effort: These are the transformative initiatives that may take time and significant resources but will have a substantial effect, like implementing a comprehensive upskilling program for underrepresented groups.

- Low Impact, Low Effort: These may be worth doing if they don't distract from higher-priority items. Think along the lines of a diversity potluck.

- Low Impact, High Effort: These are your resource drains. They require a significant amount of work but provide little in terms of advancing your J.E.D.I. goals.

By applying the Impact Versus Effort matrix to the important initiatives, we can allocate resources more effectively, ensuring that initiatives with the highest impact get the attention and investment they deserve. As we've established, navigating the complexities of J.E.D.I. isn't a sprint; it's a marathon that requires thoughtful prioritization, strategic alignment, and intentional action. Employing the Importance Versus Urgency matrix followed by the Impact Versus Effort matrix allows us to focus our energy where it matters most for sustainable, meaningful change. It turns our good intentions into strategic actions, and it turns our desire for change into a transformative reality.

Driving Adoption

The job of a J.E.D.I. leader is one of many hats, and one such hat is that of marketer. Achieving a competitive edge often involves leveraging proven marketing strategies like SWOT analysis, positioning, and understanding adoption curves. So, why not apply these potent tools to accelerate our progress? Applying a marketer's toolkit to J.E.D.I. initiatives can provide unprecedented clarity, focus, and strategic alignment that could be the game-changer our organization needs.

SWOT Analysis

Let's start with the SWOT analysis—assessing strengths, weaknesses, opportunities, and threats.

- **Strengths:** Recognize our organization's inherent advantages in the J.E.D.I. space. Do we already have a diverse leadership team, for example? If so, we can use that as a beacon to attract diverse talent.

- **Weaknesses:** Being honest about weaknesses enables targeted improvement. If we lack gender diversity, for example, we can't fix it without acknowledging it.

- **Opportunities:** External circumstances can offer chances to advance our initiatives. The increasing societal focus on social justice, for instance, can be an opportunity to champion our organization's commitment to current issues.

- **Threats:** Be aware of external factors that might hinder our agenda, such as emerging legislation or social movements that may not align with our current practices.

Understanding our SWOT landscape guides strategic planning, helping us allocate resources to areas where they'll make the most impact and mitigate potential threats before they become roadblocks.

Positioning

Next, let's talk about positioning. Just as a brand positions itself in a market, our initiatives need to be positioned within our organization and in the broader societal context.

- **Internal Positioning:** How are our initiatives viewed internally? Are they seen as integral to the core mission, or are they nice-to-haves? Effective positioning involves framing these initiatives as business imperatives that drive both culture and performance.

- **External Positioning:** Consider how our organization's commitment to J.E.D.I. is perceived in the marketplace. Our stance on these issues can be a unique selling proposition (USP) that attracts both talent and consumers who share our values.

Adoption Curves

Understanding adoption curves can be especially illuminating. Just like the diffusion of a new product in a market, J.E.D.I. initiatives will face varying rates of adoption within an organization.

- **Innovators and Early Adopters:** These are the champions who will take up the cause eagerly. We can leverage their enthusiasm to gain initial momentum.

- **Early Majority:** Once the pioneers are onboard, focus on this group, showing them the tangible benefits of the initiatives for them and for the organization as a whole.

- **Late Majority and Laggards:** These groups will be the hardest to persuade, often requiring significant evidence of the benefits or institutional mandates to adopt the new norms.

Knowing where different segments of our organization fall on the adoption curve allows for more targeted communication and intervention strategies, thereby accelerating overall adoption. Approaching J.E.D.I. leadership through the lens of tried-and-true marketing frameworks like SWOT, positioning, and adoption curves doesn't just make sense—it's smart strategy. These tools enable us to assess our environment, position our initiatives for maximum impact, and drive adoption across all levels of the organization. It's time we elevate J.E.D.I. from a well-intentioned aspiration to a strategically executed mission—and these marketing tools offer a proven roadmap to get us there.

Restoration

Judo provides the method, incentives create the momentum, and marketing gives us the toolkit. Change leadership underpins everything we do. And what we do is restore our businesses from being houses of shareholder capitalism where few truly benefit to being expansive mansions of stakeholder capitalism where there is room for everyone. The word *restoration* is intentional, as it truly describes the act of taking what we find and modernizing it for today and tomorrow.

We learn from what works and apply it to a new opportunity. And what has worked is the Internal Control Framework (ICF)—a structured method of restoring the foundations of organizations by transforming issues and problems into new operating procedures that will facilitate the eradication of injustices, elimination of inequities, expansion of diversity, and enhancement of inclusion. Rather than multiple (and possibly conflicting) approaches to our work, we can align behind a single proven system that allows us to iterate and scale until we achieve our desired impact.

When it comes to fostering justice, equity, diversity, and inclusion, the ethics and compliance world has a lot to teach us. At its core, both domains aim for a common goal: shaping behaviors and building cultures that are not just law-abiding but also just, equitable, and inclusive. The internal control framework commonly used in ethics and compliance can be a transformative tool, setting the stage not just for incremental improvements, but also for major gains via the following principles:

- **Risk Assessment:** In the ethics and compliance space, risk assessment is paramount. Similarly, J.E.D.I. leaders should identify and evaluate existing or potential areas of risk—whether they be discrimination, unconscious bias, or exclusionary practices—within the organization. They can range from overt actions to subtler, systemic issues, like the lack of diverse candidates in the talent pipeline or imbalances in leadership roles. A thorough risk assessment is the starting point for developing targeted interventions and measures.

- **Control Environment:** The control environment in ethics and compliance encompasses the tone at the top, policies and procedures, and organizational structure. For J.E.D.I. initiatives, this means creating an environment where diversity is celebrated, inclusion is the norm, and equity is a fundamental principle. Leadership plays a crucial role here. From the CEO to middle management, leaders must walk the talk. Codes of conduct, ethical guidelines, and robust policies against discrimination and harassment are non-negotiable elements. They don't just set the boundaries; they define the playing field itself.

- **Control Activities:** In the ethics and compliance universe, control activities include the concrete steps taken to mitigate identified risks. For J.E.D.I. leaders, this could involve a range of activities, such as implementing mentorship programs aimed at underrepresented groups, restructuring hiring processes to minimize bias, or introducing regular diversity training programs. The key is to make these activities consistent, measurable, and subject to ongoing evaluation and refinement.

- **Information and Communication:** Transparency is another cornerstone. The processes, objectives, and outcomes of J.E.D.I. initiatives should be clearly communicated across the organization, just as ethics and compliance directives would be. Whether through town halls, newsletters, or a dashboard that tracks progress on key J.E.D.I. metrics, open and consistent communication fosters accountability and buy-in from all stakeholders.

- **Monitoring:** Just like in the compliance framework, monitoring and evaluation are indispensable. Regular audits and reviews should be conducted to assess the effectiveness of new operating procedures, programs, and activities. Feedback mechanisms, such as employee surveys or third-party audits, offer invaluable insights into what's working and what needs adjustment.

Using the internal control framework borrowed from ethics and compliance not only ensures that J.E.D.I. initiatives are integrated into the very fabric of the organization, but it also helps to make them robust, scalable, and sustainable. We move from tactical, ad-hoc efforts to strategic, long-term transformation. We also create a culture of accountability and continuous improvement, where J.E.D.I. principles are not just espoused but are lived every day, by everyone, at all levels of the organization. And that, my friends, is how we make major gains in the realm of J.E.D.I.

Renewal

Even with the advanced approaches laid out in this book, the work will still be arduous, with fits and starts, good days and bad days, and successes and setbacks. This means that, as with any journey worth undertaking, we must make sure we remain fit for the task at hand. This is where renewal practices such as sleep, meditation, hobbies, and exercise come in to play. Burnout is a real concern for those undertaking this momentous task—but, as with every other section of this playbook, we have practices for this, as well.

Just like athletes in a long-distance race, J.E.D.I. leaders need renewal practices to recharge their batteries, maintain their resilience, and prevent burnout. Remember, the fight for J.E.D.I. is not a sprint; it's an enduring marathon that demands not only intellectual and emotional energy but also a reservoir of physical and spiritual fortitude. There are several factors of consideration when engaged in these valuable efforts:

- **Emotional Resilience:** Leaders engaged in J.E.D.I. work often confront a constant stream of challenges—resistance from different levels within the organization, the need to navigate complex and sensitive issues, and sometimes even personal attacks. Emotional resilience isn't just a luxury; it's a necessity. Renewal practices such as mindfulness, journaling, or even just setting aside time for self-reflection can serve as valuable tools for emotional recharging.

- **Intellectual Vigor:** J.E.D.I. leaders need to be at the top of their game intellectually, capable of understanding complex social issues, designing viable policies, and strategizing for long-term goals. Intellectual vigor can be maintained through renewal practices like continuous learning, engaging in diverse readings outside of the field, or joining discussion groups that challenge our perspectives. This expands our intellectual toolkit, offering new approaches and solutions for the intricate problems we face.

- **Physical Stamina:** Don't underestimate the physical toll that intense, emotionally charged work can take. Physical renewal practices—whether it's regular exercise, sufficient sleep, or proper nutrition—lay the groundwork for enduring stamina. When we're physically fit, we're better equipped to handle the stresses and strains that come with the territory.

- **Spiritual Alignment:** For many, the work of J.E.D.I. is more than a job; it's a calling. Spiritual renewal practices, which could include prayer, meditation, or engaging in a supportive community, can provide a sense of purpose and a reservoir of strength. When our spiritual selves are aligned with our work, the inevitable obstacles and setbacks are easier to navigate.

- **Communities of Support:** Lastly, no one is an island. Building a community or network of like-minded individuals can act as a collective renewal practice. The community provides a platform for sharing experiences, venting frustrations, celebrating wins, and (most importantly) reminding us that we're not alone in this journey.

Being effective J.E.D.I. leaders means recognizing that we, too, need renewing, recharging, and rejuvenating. It's not selfish to focus on renewal practices; it's strategic. The more we renew, the more we can give, and the more resilient we become in the face of challenges. A burnt-out J.E.D.I. leader helps no one; a renewed, resilient J.E.D.I. leader has the potential to inspire an entire organization toward lasting change. So don't just do the work; sustain the work. And to sustain the work, we first need to sustain ourselves.

Externalizing Impacts

The structure of restoration and the practice of regular renewal will enable us to sustain progress for the long term. As per the goals of stakeholder capitalism, once we have restored our internal environments, we can externalize these benefits for customers, communities, the environment, and our shareholders. This is the true goal of our work—to extend the goodwill, collective knowledge, and positive influence of our organizations into tangible good in the real world—whether it's achieved in the form of delighted customers, elevated communities, or regenerated environments. Employee engagement then becomes the ultimate lead measure of the most crucial and wild of all our wildly important goals.

When companies are serious about J.E.D.I., they aren't just improving their internal cultures; they're also generating extraordinary external benefits. And I'm not talking about simply boosting their own public image. I'm talking about tangible positive impacts on customers, communities, the environment, and yes, even the shareholders. Allow me to provide some real-life examples that illustrate this ripple effect.

Customers

- **Target's Inclusive Clothing Line:** Target, for instance, launched a sensory-friendly and adaptive clothing line aimed at kids and adults with disabilities. This isn't just a moral win; it's a win for the business and for customers who have felt overlooked by the fashion industry. Target successfully tapped into an underserved market, improving the lives of thousands of families in the process.
- **Netflix's Accessibility Features:** Netflix has been working diligently to improve the accessibility of its platform. Features like audio descriptions for the visually impaired and better subtitling for the hearing-impaired are direct outcomes of a focus on inclusion.

Communities

- **Salesforce's Philanthropic Model:** Salesforce has a 1-1-1 model of philanthropy, donating 1 percent of their product, 1 percent of their equity, and 1 percent of their employees' time toward community service. Their focus on social justice initiatives and equity enriches the communities they operate in, providing resources and support for underprivileged groups.
- **Ben & Jerry's Activism:** Known for more than just ice cream, Ben & Jerry's has long been committed

to social justice, from supporting Black Lives Matter to campaigning for climate justice. The company's activist stance educates the broader community and elevates important social issues.

Environment

- **Patagonia's Sustainable Practices:** Patagonia's internal commitment to environmental responsibility extends to its product lines, creating a market for sustainable, ethical outdoor clothing and gear. This commitment also includes their Footprint Chronicles, which trace the environmental impact of individual products.

- **Unilever's Sustainable Living Plan:** Unilever aims to halve its environmental footprint by 2030, and they're integrating J.E.D.I. principles into their sustainability efforts. For example, their "Shakti" program empowers rural women in India by providing them opportunities to perform as small-scale distributors.

Shareholders

- **BlackRock's ESG Investment:** BlackRock, the world's largest asset manager, has made it clear that companies with strong profiles in environmental, social, and governance (ESG) factors—which include J.E.D.I. metrics—are more likely to enjoy stronger long-term returns. They are actively directing investments to companies that perform well in these areas, thereby rewarding good practice.

- **Apple's Business Case for Diversity:** Apple believes that diversity drives innovation. The company's increasing focus on J.E.D.I. has made it not only a more inclusive workplace, but also a more profitable one, delighting shareholders with consistent growth and groundbreaking products.

J.E.D.I. work is more than just an internal company effort; it's a strategy for external excellence as well. When we get J.E.D.I. right within the walls of our organizations, the positive effects cascade far beyond, touching customers, communities, our planet, and even those folks fixated on the bottom line. That's the power of genuine commitment to J.E.D.I. principles; and these real-life examples prove that doing well and doing good are not mutually exclusive—they are symbiotically linked.

Keeping Score

Does a tree that falls in the forest make a sound? Not if there isn't anyone there to tell the tale. Many of the misconceptions and misalignments that come with doing this work relate to our inability to craft a compelling narrative about our work. The Scoreboard methodology from Franklin Covey ensures high levels of understanding, agreement, and alignment at all times. And in organizations driven by proof of growth and progress, we must insulate ourselves as well by keeping score.

For those familiar with Stephen Covey's *The 7 Habits of Highly Effective People,* the principle of "keeping score" is crucial for any kind of transformative change. In business, the Franklin-Covey Scoreboard method is a proven tool for performance tracking that provides a visual representation of key performance indicators (KPIs) and the team's engagement with them. For J.E.D.I. leaders, adopting this method offers several critical benefits. Allow me to walk through them.

- **Clarity of Objectives:** The Franklin-Covey Scoreboard shines a light on what really matters. When it comes to J.E.D.I. initiatives, it's easy to get bogged down in an ocean of metrics—hiring percentages, employee satisfaction scores, and so on. But what are our wildly important goals? What are the one or two objectives that, if achieved, would make all the difference? The scoreboard helps us focus on these, providing laser-like attention where it's needed most.

- **Team Engagement:** One of the most potent aspects of the Franklin-Covey Scoreboard is how it galvanizes the team. A well-designed scoreboard turns the pursuit of goals into a "game" that a team can "win," infusing the work with a sense of urgency and competitiveness. Given that our work can often be emotionally and intellectually taxing, the boost in morale and engagement can be a game-changer.

- **Transparency and Accountability:** A public scoreboard cultivates a culture of transparency and accountability. Every team member knows where the organization stands on its J.E.D.I. objectives at any given time. Are we on track to meet our targets for minority representation in leadership roles? Is our mentorship program yielding the expected outcomes? There's nowhere to hide with a visible, constantly updated scoreboard—and in the realm of J.E.D.I., accountability is half the battle.

- **Real-Time Adjustments:** J.E.D.I. initiatives often require agile decision-making. Societal norms evolve, and challenges are ever-changing. The

Franklin-Covey Scoreboard allows us to adapt in real-time. Falling short on a particular metric? The scoreboard provides us with the data and the impetus needed to dig deeper and take corrective action immediately, rather than waiting for quarterly reviews or year-end retrospectives.

- **Celebrating Wins and Learning from Losses:** Finally, the scoreboard is not just a tool for tracking objectives; it's a narrative device. It tells the story of our J.E.D.I. journey, including the peaks and valleys. Celebrating small wins is vital in work that often feels like a steep uphill climb. But equally important is the ability to learn from our losses, to iterate on our strategies and continue to move the needle.

The Franklin-Covey Scoreboard method equips J.E.D.I. leaders with a dynamic tool to clarify goals, boost engagement, and track real-time progress. The scoreboard is much more than a method; it's also a mindset. It turns abstract objectives into tangible targets—and it transforms the noble, expansive, but often elusive ideals of justice, equity, diversity, and inclusion into concrete, achievable wins. This kind of focused, engaged, accountable action is how we move from aspiration to realization in the world of J.E.D.I.

Embracing Trade-Offs

As we negotiate the highs and lows of doing this work, we must understand that once we select judo philosophy, we also need to embrace inevitable trade-offs without sacrificing focus, quality, commitment, or effectiveness. We can't make this work about us, our egos, our trauma, and/or our individual needs; we have to serve the greatest good at all times. With this bar now established, we need to lean into the power of trade-offs by embracing paradoxical thinking, seeking win-wins, and leveraging influence over authority. Here's a quick recap of how each of these approaches can drive progress singularly and collectively.

- **Embracing Paradoxical Thinking:** In the real world, things aren't always black and white, and this is especially true in J.E.D.I. work. Paradoxical thinking allows us to hold two seemingly contradictory ideas at the same time and find a path forward. For example, we can pursue diversity while also pushing for a cohesive organizational culture. It's not one at the expense of the other. When we embrace paradox, we move beyond limiting beliefs and biases, opening up new possibilities for innovative solutions.

- **Seeking Win-Wins:** The idea that for one to win, the other has to lose is an antiquated notion that we must discard, particularly in J.E.D.I. efforts. Win-win scenarios can and should be the norm. When we elevate underrepresented voices, we're not muting others; we're enriching the entire conversation. When we adapt our offices to be more accessible, we're not just benefiting employees with disabilities; we're also creating a more welcoming environment for everyone. Win-wins build collective ownership and investment in J.E.D.I. initiatives, turning them into a shared mission rather than a zero-sum game.

- **Leveraging Influence Over Authority:** Positional authority has its limitations. Just because someone has the title doesn't mean they can effect meaningful change in the attitudes and behaviors of an organization. Influence, on the other hand, is far more potent. Through storytelling, empathy, and demonstrating the tangible benefits of J.E.D.I. initiatives, we can convert skeptics into champions and bystanders into active participants. Influence can cross departmental lines and hierarchical levels, galvanizing a much broader and more committed coalition for change.

When paradoxical thinking frees our minds from traditional either-or choices, win-win scenarios open up new possibilities for collective success, and influence becomes our currency for change, that's when we've got a winning formula for advancing J.E.D.I. When combined, this trio of strategies can create a synergistic force capable of overcoming the most entrenched barriers to progress. This is the art and science of J.E.D.I. leadership: unorthodox, inclusive, and irresistibly impactful.

Maintaining Momentum and Commitment

Inspiration is the perpetual engine that permits us to maintain momentum and commitment for the long haul. And as we discussed within the topic of renewal, we must take care of our own needs in order to steer the ship and coordinate all the collective work we must perform. To both sustain our inspiration and inspire others, we must increase our self-awareness, accelerate our agility, and claim our agency.

- **Increasing Self-Awareness:** Being a J.E.D.I. leader requires a deep understanding of oneself. This isn't navel-gazing; it's mission-critical. We need to know our biases, our strengths and weaknesses, and our triggers. It's like knowing every feature of the vehicle we're planning to drive on a long journey. Are there blind spots? How fast can it go? What kind of terrain can it handle? Self-awareness equips us with the insights to navigate the complex dynamics of organizational culture and social systems. The more self-aware we are, the more effective we become in dealing with others, and the more authentic and impactful our leadership will be. Tools like mindfulness, self-reflection, and feedback loops can enhance self-awareness.

- **Accelerating Personal Agility:** The landscape of J.E.D.I. is dynamic and sometimes even volatile. New challenges arise, situations change, and tactics that worked yesterday may not work tomorrow. Personal agility is our ability to adapt, to pivot when needed, and to embrace change as a constant companion. This is the quality that keeps our leadership fresh and responsive. It enables us to swiftly move around obstacles, adapt our strategies, and find new avenues for achieving our wildly important goals. Agile leaders stay ahead of the curve and can better influence outcomes in fast-moving environments.

- **Claiming Agency:** Agency is about taking ownership and control of our actions and their outcomes. It means we're not merely a spectator or a commentator; we're an active player in the game. Claiming agency empowers us to move from passive concern to active influence. Yes, systemic issues exist—and no, we can't change them overnight. But what we can do is affect the sphere of influence we have, no matter how large or small. Agency is what turns our ideals and visions into tangible actions and results. It gives us the power to inspire change—not just in ourselves, but also in others.

When we combine increased self-awareness, personal agility, and a strong sense of agency, we create a trifecta that sustains our inspiration and momentum. These aren't just qualities we're born with, but skills that can be cultivated and sharpened. With these tools in our leadership arsenal, we sustain our drive and enthusiasm for J.E.D.I. initiatives and also instill that same energy in those around us.

In the end, the work of J.E.D.I. isn't just about making others believe in a better, more equitable world—it's about equipping ourselves to lead them there, sustaining that inspiration and momentum over the long haul. Trust what this book has taught you: it's a marathon, not a sprint. Prepare accordingly.

RESOURCES

As we navigate the critical path of J.E.D.I. leadership, we're going to need an arsenal of tools, frameworks, and resources. The journey ahead requires more than goodwill; it demands a skillful blend of knowledge and execution. Consider this chapter a one-stop shop for instruments that will help convert our leadership aspirations into concrete outcomes.

Books
Knowledge is the first line of defense. Here we'll list seminal works that provide deep dives into subjects like finding purpose, business strategy, stakeholder capitalism, psychology, marketing fundamentals, change leadership, renewal, project management, negotiation, inspiration, leadership, and execution.

Finding Purpose

Garcia, Héctor and Miralles, Francesc. (2017). *Ikigai: The Japanese Secret to a Long and Happy Life*. Penguin Life.

Nafousi, Roxie. (2022). M*anifest: 7 Steps to Living Your Best Life*. Chronicle Prism.

Sinek, Simon. (2017). *Find Your Why: A Practical Guide for Discovering Purpose for You and Your Team*. Portfolio.

Inspiration

Holzer, Allison; Spataro, Sandra; and Grace Baron, Jen. (2019). *Dare to Inspire: Sustain the Fire of Inspiration in Work and Life*. Da Capo Lifelong Books.

Friedman, Ron. (2015). *The Best Place to Work: The Art and Science of Creating an Extraordinary Workplace*. TarcherPerigree.

Howes, Lewis. (2023). *The Greatness Mindset: Unlock the Power of Your Mind and Live Your Best Life Today*. Hay House Inc.

Business Strategy and Culture

Collins, Jim. (2001). *Good to Great: Why Some Companies Make the Leap and Others Don't*. Harper Business.

Collins, Jim. (2011). *Great by Choice: Uncertainty, Chaos, and Luck—Why Some Thrive Despite Them All*. Harper Business.

Sinek, Simon. (2019). *The Infinite Game*. Portfolio.

Semler, Ricardo. (2004). *The Seven-Day Weekend: Changing the Way Work Works*. Portfolio.

Stakeholder Capitalism

Joly, Hubert and Lambert, Caroline. (2021). *The Heart of Business: Leadership Principles for the Next Era of Capitalism*. Harvard Business Review Press.

L. Harris, Omar. (2021). *Be a J.E.D.I. Leader, Not a Boss: Leadership in the Era of Corporate Social Justice, Equity, Diversity, and Inclusion*. Intent Books.

Schwab, Klaus. (2017). *The Fourth Industrial Revolution*. Currency.

Leadership

Lencioni, Patrick. (2000). *The Four Obsessions of an Extraordinary Executive: A Leadership Fable*. Jossey-Bass.

L. Harris, Omar. (2020). *The Servant Leader's Manifesto*. Intent Books.

Brown, Brené. (2018). *Dare to Lead: Brave Work. Tough Conversations. Whole Hearts*. Random House.

Marketing Fundamentals

Godin, Seth. (2018). *This Is Marketing: You Can't Be Seen Until You Learn to See*. Portfolio.

Cialdini, Robert B. (2021). *Influence: The Psychology of Persuasion*. Harper Business.

Berger, Jonah. (2016). *Contagious: Why Things Catch On*. Simon & Schuster.

Psychology

Gladwell, Malcolm. (2002). *The Tipping Point: How Little Things Can Make a Big Difference*. Back Bay Books.

Gladwell, Malcolm. (2005). *Blink: The Power of Thinking Without Thinking*. Little, Brown and Company.

Gladwell, Malcolm. (2013). *David and Goliath: Underdogs, Misfits, and the Art of Battling Giants*. Little, Brown and Company.

Change Leadership

Kotter, John P. (2012). *Leading Change*. Harvard Business Review Press.

L. Harris, Omar. (2023). *Leading Change: The 4 Keys*. Intent Books.

Coyle, Daniel. (2018). *The Culture Code: The Secrets of Highly Successful Groups*. Bantam.

Project Management

Harrin, Elizabeth. (2022). *Managing Multiple Projects: How Project Managers Can Balance Priorities, Manage Expectations and Increase Productivity*. Kogan Page.

Flyvbjerg, Bent and Gardner, Dan. (2023). *How Big Things Get Done: The Surprising Factors That Determine the Fate of Every Project, from Home Renovations to Space Exploration and Everything In Between*. Crown Currency.

Herold, Cameron. (2020). *Vivid Vision: A Remarkable Tool for Aligning Your Business Around a Shared Vision of the Future*. Lioncrest Publishing.

Negotiation and Trade-Offs

Bingham, Christopher and McDonald, Rory. (2022). *Productive Tensions: How Every Leader Can Tackle Innovation's Toughest Trade-Offs (Management on the Cutting Edge)*. The MIT Press.

Kahneman, Daniel. (2013). *Thinking, Fast and Slow*. Farar, Straus and Giroux.

Greene, Robert. (2000). *The 48 Laws of Power*. Penguin Books.

Renewal

Jiminez, Jacinta. (2021). *The Burnout Fix: Overcome Overwhelm, Beat Busy, and Sustain Success in the New World of Work*. McGraw Hill.

Elrod, Hal. (2012). *The Miracle Morning: The Not-So-Obvious Secret Guaranteed to Transform Your Life (Before 8AM)*. Hal Elrod.

Manson, Mark. (2016). *The Subtle Art of Not Giving a F*ck: A Counterintuitive Approach to Living a Good Life*. Harper.

Execution

Covey, Stephen R. (2004). *The 7 Habits of Highly Effective People*. Free Press.

McChesney, Chris. (2022). *The 4 Disciplines of Execution: Revised and Updated: Achieving Your Wildly Important Goals*. Simon & Schuster.

Bossidy, Larry; Charan, Ram; and Burck Charles. (2002). *Execution: The Discipline of Getting Things Done*. Crown Currency.

Crucial Sites

The data in our field is constantly shifting. As such, it is important to draw from the right fonts of information. The following list of sites will be crucial to stay on top of as we do our collective work.

- https://justcapital.com/
- https://aflcio.org/paywatch/company-pay-ratios
- https://www.policylink.org/
- https://opportunity.businessroundtable.org/
- https://news.gallup.com/topic/black-american-experience.aspx
- https://www.mckinsey.com/featured-insights/diversity-and-inclusion

- https://www.mckinsey.com/featured-insights/diversity-and-inclusion/women-in-the-workplace
- https://www.catalyst.org/research/women-ceos-of-the-sp-500/
- https://www.blackentrepreneurprofile.com/collections/black-fortune-500-ceos
- https://nationaldiversitycouncil.org/
- https://data.org/resources/dei-data-standard/
- https://www2.deloitte.com/us/en/pages/about-deloitte/articles/dei/diversity-equity-inclusion-transparency-report.html
- https://www.shrm.org/executive/resources/people-strategy-journal/winter2022/pages/feature-approach-dei-data-morgan-roberts.aspx
- https://hbr.org/2016/07/why-diversity-programs-fail
- https://www.pewresearch.org/social-trends/2023/05/17/diversity-equity-and-inclusion-in-the-workplace/
- https://jedicollaborative.com/
- https://empovia.co/allyship-report/
- https://www.catalyst.org/reports/allyship-curiosity-employees-of-color/
- https://www2.deloitte.com/us/en/insights/topics/value-of-diversity-and-inclusion.html
- https://www.intentconsultants.co/blog

Surveys and Assessment Tools

This entire book is about not recreating the wheel. Leveraging best-in-class surveys and assessment tools can help us gain a leg up on our work. This section will introduce you to surveys and assessment tools designed to measure different J.E.D.I.-related metrics, from inclusion to equity, and offer recommendations for action based on your results.

    https://getreframe.com/

    https://www.qualtrics.com/lp/dei-program

    https://www.surveymonkey.com/toolkit/dei-leader

    https://www.cultureamp.com/platform/features/diversity-inclusion-survey

    https://diversio.com/survey-your-organizations-diversity-inclusion/

Software and Apps

Technology can be a game-changer in managing and tracking our J.E.D.I. initiatives. From platforms that help in diverse hiring to analytics tools that break down pay inequities, this list covers software and apps that can serve as force multipliers in our quest for a more equitable and inclusive environment.

- SeekOut: Helps organizations hire, grow, and retain talent.
- PowerToFly DEIB Business Suite: An all-in-one suite for diversity recruiting, retention, and education.
- DBSquared: Helps companies write unbiased job postings.
- Entelo: Helps businesses automate sourcing, screening, and employee engagement.

- Mathison: Provides employers with a platform to develop, manage, and measure their DEI strategy.
- Manatal: Automatically screens and filters candidates.
- Fetcher: Improves diversity recruitment with AI.
- iCIMS: Transform talent acquisition with the world's leading cloud-based talent acquisition software.
- Greenhouse: The hiring operating system for people-first companies. From sourcing to structured interviewing and onboarding, our all-in-one software gives you the tools to make better, fairer, and more confident hiring decisions.
- Eightfold: Brings to light everything you need to hire and develop people to their highest potential.
- Gem: Get sourcing, CRM, talent marketing, analytics, and an ATS in one scalable platform.
- UserWay: Join over a million websites and millions of users with disabilities who trust UserWay for their digital accessibility needs.
- EquityPulse: Create the burning platform for change by leveraging employee sentiment on J.E.D.I. progress.

Training and Workshops

We don't have to go it alone. There are multiple experts and organizations offering workshops, webinars, and courses aimed at equipping us and our teams with the skills needed to drive change. The most effective ones are listed here, including those we can access right from the comfort of the office.

- https://learning.linkedin.com/cx/diversity-inclusion-training
- https://pointmadelearning.com/programs-and-services/the-american-dream-game/
- https://www.ct3training.com/amplifyyourDEI
- https://store.shrm.org/Corporate-DEI-Training
- https://www.intentconsultants.co

Consultancies and Coaches

Sometimes, the complexity of the challenges you face may require expert guidance. Consultancies and coaches can offer tailored solutions that meet an organization's unique needs. Here are some of the best in the business. These experts approach DEI from the outcomes-based perspective outlined in this playbook.

- Dr. Tiffany Jana is a consultant, speaker, and author focused on equity, diversity, and inclusion.
- Chinyere Ezie is a consultant, speaker, and author focused on diversity, equity, and inclusion.
- Dr. Lori L. Tharps is a consultant, speaker, and author focused on antiracism and equity.
- Dr. Eddie Moore, Jr. is a consultant, speaker, and author focused on diversity, equity, and inclusion.
- Dr. Angela Lee Duckworth is a professor of psychology at the University of Pennsylvania and the author of the book Grit.
- Dr. Carol Dweck is a professor of psychology at Stanford University and the author of the book *Mindset*.

- Dr. Amy Cuddy is a professor of psychology at Harvard University and the author of the book Presence.

- Lily Zheng is a writer for the Harvard Business Review, a LinkedIn Top Voice in DEI, and the author of DEI Deconstructed: Your No-Nonsense Guide to Doing the Work and Doing it Right (November 2022), The Ethical Sellout, and Gender Ambiguity in the Workplace.

- Omar L. Harris is the J.E.D.I. Leader, leadership expert, and author of this playbook, as well as Be a J.E.D.I. Leader, Not a Boss: Leadership in the Era of Corporate Social Justice, Equity, Diversity, and Inclusion.

Networking and Peer Groups

Community is both a resource and a haven. The following list highlights some active forums, online communities, and professional groups where we can connect with like-minded individuals, share challenges and solutions, and stay up to date on the latest in J.E.D.I. best practices.

- Diversity Practitioners Network (DPN): A global network of diversity, equity, and inclusion professionals.

- Society for Human Resource Management (SHRM) DEI Community: A community for SHRM members to learn, share, and connect on all things DEI.

- Association for Talent Development (ATD) DEI Special Interest Group: A community for ATD members to connect with other DEI professionals and share best practices.

- Black HR Professionals (BHRP): A national organization of Black human resource professionals.
- Latinx in HR (LiHR): A national organization of Latinx human resource professionals.
- Asian American Pacific Islanders in Human Resources (AAPIIHR): A national organization of Asian American and Pacific Islander human resource professionals.
- LGBTQ+ in HR (LGBTQ+HR): A national organization of LGBTQ+ human resource professionals.
- Women in HR (WIHR): A national organization of women human resource professionals.
- People of Color in Tech (POC in Tech): A non-profit organization supporting the career development of people of color in the tech industry.
- Women Who Code (WWCode): A global non-profit organization dedicated to inspiring women to learn software development and build careers in tech.
- Lesbians Who Tech (LWT): A global non-profit organization that provides opportunities for lesbians and bisexual women to explore careers in tech.
- National Association of Black Journalists (NABJ): A professional organization for Black journalists.
- National Association of Hispanic Journalists (NAHJ): A professional organization for Hispanic journalists.

Asian American Journalists Association (AAJA): A professional organization for Asian American journalists.

Native American Journalists Association (NAJA): A professional organization for Native American journalists.

Society of Professional Journalists (SPJ): A professional organization for journalists of all backgrounds.

Podcasts and Video Channels

For those who prefer auditory or visual learning, here's a list of podcasts and YouTube channels that offer valuable insights, interviews, and updates on J.E.D.I. topics.

Podcasts:

Inclusion Unfiltered

How Women Lead Podcast

The Culture Code

The HR Happy Hour Podcast

Talent Talks

YouTube Channels:

The Culture Code

The HR Happy Hour

Glennon Doyle

Brené Brown

The Conscious Kid

ACKNOWLEDGEMENTS

I wasn't going to write this playbook, originally. In the two years since *Be a J.E.D.I. Leader, Not a Boss* was published, we've all experienced the intense backlash to our efforts to bring greater inclusivity and civility into our organizations and society as a whole. But I began studying change leadership in 2022 and realized that this playbook is needed now more than ever. Basically, according to change theory, the backlash that was happening was natural—and even to be expected.

We couldn't respond to a known reaction from parties invested in the status quo with shock, dismay, or outrage of our own. We needed to work smarter, not necessarily harder. I decided to call upon my multiple decades of insider experience working for some of the largest corporations in the world across four continents. For a function that has lacked definition, the answers lie in how other emerging functions—such as Digital, ESG, and Ethics and Compliance—have carved out their spaces and transformed organizational cultures for the better.

This playbook is more of a cultural transformation manual than a tome dedicated to the outcomes of eradicating injustices, eliminating inequities, expanding diversity, and enhancing inclusion. I wanted to provide strategies and solutions that the best change leaders apply in instances of functional and outcome ambiguity, internal and external volatility, budget uncertainty, and navigational complexity—the point being that no one needs to be anti-anything to be a strong J.E.D.I. leader, advocate, or ally.

This playbook is dedicated to everyone who is *for* the causes of fairness, opportunity, innovation, and productivity within our organizations. The more fair, accessible, creative, and engaged our organizations become, the more J.E.D.I. principles will have been embedded as core pillars. As such, I must acknowledge all the paradoxical thinkers, win-win masters, and key influencers without authority who find a way to make progress happen despite the daunting circumstances within which they find themselves.

Thinkers like Malcolm Gladwell, Brene Brown, Jim Collins, Simon Sinek, and Ricardo Semler immediately come to mind. Each of these luminaries teaches us that what we perceive may not necessarily be the true reality, and they provide unique approaches to unlock progress when it feels like we've hit a wall. I must also acknowledge my beloved clients who have accepted my somewhat unorthodox approach to this work and have been patient when I have rejected their requests for motivational speaking, antibias training, or other short-term remedial measures of virtue signaling.

Special thanks to my partners at InspireCorps for going on three years of collective success together. Love working with you, Jen, Allison, Sandra, Bevin, Judy, Gaby, Laura, and extended team. Here's to more to come! Another shout-out goes to Melissa Mims, Tejal Vishalpura and Conrod Kelly for being among my biggest advocates—it is a pleasure serving and supporting leaders like yourselves.

Much love to my publishing team: Michael Rehder, cover designer; Gwen Gades, interior designer; and Leslie Wilson, editorial support. You all make me look good!

To those I count as dear friends—Andrew Miles, Federico Barreto, Steve Price, Brad Hershey, Courtney Wagner, JD Capuano, Mike McCann, Stephanie Casher, James W. Lewis, Nekeisha Briggs, Vanessa Vidacs, Julye Williams, Rudy Sharan, Ray Russo, Denise Foy, Alicia Byer, Tatyana Vino, Thomas Halusa, and Anthony R. Howard: thank you for being forces for good in the world and such special souls. I've been lucky to go on this journey with you.

It's been three years since my beloved mother passed away. In that time, I have endeavored to keep her legacy of being a voice for the voiceless and a selfless servant of right and progress alive. Hope you are proud, Mom! I must recognize my small but mighty tribe of family: my father, Samuel; my sister, Sameerah; my brothers John, Patrick, and Kamau; my aunts Janis and Candy; my niece, Kiarra; my nephew, Hamilton; my great nephew, Pharoah and my great-nieces Egypt and Empress for all their continuous love and support.

Finally, I acknowledge every person who picks up this playbook and confronts their own Goliath, as David did, unafraid and fully aware that we have everything we need to make our worlds a better place. Thank you for your steadfast inspiration, optimism, commitment, and drive to never settle for less than a complete transformation of why we do business, from more benefits for the few to exceptional outcomes for employees, customers, communities, the environment, and shareholders.

As is my custom, I'm asking you for two favors. Please, review this book on Amazon.com and pass it on to the J.E.D.I. leaders in your life. I'll see you on the front lines!

Omar L. Harris
September 20, 2023
Charlotte, NC

REFERENCES

1. Gladwell, Malcolm. (2015). *David and Goliath: Underdogs, Misfits, and the Art of Battling Giants.* Back Bay Books.

2. Gladwell, Malcolm. (p. 4).

3. Chen, Sophia. The Equity-Diversity-Inclusion Industrial Complex Gets a Makeover. https://www.wired.com/story/the-equity-diversity-inclusion-industrial-complex-gets-a-makeover/. July 2020.

4. https://metoomvmt.org/get-to-know-us/history-inception/

5. https://blacklivesmatter.com/about/

6. https://stopaapihate.org/our-origins/

7. Lencioni, Patrick. (2000). *The Four Obsessions of an Extraordinary Executive: A Leadership Fable.* Jossey-Bass.

8. L. Harris, Omar. (2021). *Be a J.E.D.I. Leader, Not a Boss: Leadership in the Era of Corporate Social Justice, Equity, Diversity, and Inclusion.* Intent Books.

9. https://www.iii.org/article/what-employment-practices-liability-insurance-epli

10. McGlauflin, Paige. Black CEOs on the Fortune 500 reach new record high in 2023—meet the 8 executives. https://fortune.com/2023/06/05/black-ceos-fortune-500-record-high-2023/. June 2023.

11. https://wbcollaborative.org/women-ceo-report/the-report/2023-executive-summary/

12. https://justcapital.com/

13. https://aflcio.org/paywatch/company-pay-ratios

14. Bolotnyy, Valentin and Emanuel, Natalia. How Unpredictable Schedules Widen the Gender Pay Gap. https://hbr.org/2022/07/how-unpredictable-schedules-widen-the-gender-pay-gap. July 2022.

15. Pinarchick, Cheryl. Follow These 7 Steps to an Effective Pay-Equity Audit. https://hrexecutive.com/follow-these-7-steps-to-an-effective-pay-equity-audit/. February 2019.

16. De Smet, Aaron; Dowling, Bonnie; Hancock, Bryan; and Schaninger, Bill. The Great Attrition is making hiring harder. Are you searching the right talent pools? https://www.mckinsey.com/capabilities/people-and-organizational-performance/our-insights/the-great-attrition-is-making-hiring-harder-are-you-searching-the-right-talent-pools. July 2022.

17. Botros, Alena. What is 'quiet quitting'? Gen Z is ditching hustle culture to avoid burnout. https://fortune.com/2022/08/14/what-is-quiet-quitting-gen-z-tiktok-trend-burnout-great-resignation-quittok-involution-lying-flat/. August 2022.

18. Harter, Jim. Is Quiet Quitting Real? https://www.gallup.com/workplace/398306/quiet-quitting-real.aspx. May 2023.

19. https://www.worldbank.org/en/publication/global-economic-prospects

20. Huang, Georgene. 90% Of Fortune 500 Companies Already Have a Solution to Gender Equality but Aren't Utilizing It. November 2017.

21. https://justcapital.com/reports/2022-corporate-racial-equity-tracker/

22. Kendi, Ibram X. (2019). *How to Be an Antiracist*. One World.

23. Blake, John. Ibram X. Kendi says a backlash has 'crushed' the nation's racial reckoning. But there's one reason he remains hopeful. https://www.cnn.com/2023/03/18/us/ibram-kendi-racial-reckoning-blake-cec/index.html. March 2023.

24. https://justcapital.com/reports/how-business-roundtable-signatories-are-following-through-on-new-corporate-purpose/

25. L. Harris, Omar. *Leader Board: The DNA of High-Performance Teams*. (2019). TPC Books.

26. L. Harris, Omar. *The Servant Leader's Manifesto*. (2020). Intent Books.

27. Zheng, Lily. The Failure of the DEI-Industrial Complex. https://hbr.org/2022/12/the-failure-of-the-dei-industrial-complex. December 2022.

28. https://www.businessroundtable.org/business-roundtable-redefines-the-purpose-of-a-corporation-to-promote-an-economy-that-serves-all-americans

29. Collins, Jim and Hansen, Morten T. (2011). *Great By*

Choice: Uncertainty, Chaos, and Luck—Why Some Thrive Despite Them All. Harper Business.

30. Collins, Jim and Hansen, Morten T. Chapter 3.
31. https://kinginstitute.stanford.edu/selma-montgomery-march
32. Collins, Jim and Hansen, Morten T. Chapter 2 (p. 36).
33. https://www.politico.com/news/2020/03/25/trump-coronavirus-national-security- council-149285
34. Collins, Jim and Hansen, Morten T. Chapter 2 (p. 32).
35. Collins, Jim and Hansen, Morten T. Chapter 2 (p. 93).
36. https://opportunity.businessroundtable.org/ourcommitment/
37. https://justcapital.com/rankings/
38. McLeod, Lisa Earle and Lotardo, Elizabeth. How to Be a Purpose-Driven Leader Without Burning Out. https://hbr.org/2023/07/how-to-be-a-purpose-driven-leader-without-burning-out. July 2023.
39. https://www.jediheart.com/blog-posts/2019/5/1/why-jedi-heart
40. https://jedicollaborative.com/about-us/
41. https://iwpr.org/paying-today-and-tomorrow-report/
42. https://news.gallup.com/poll/1687/race-relations.aspx
43. https://www.mckinsey.com/featured-insights/diversity-and-inclusion/the-economic-state-of-black-america-what-is-and-what-could-be
44. https://leanin.org/women-in-the-workplace

45. https://eeocdata.org/

46. https://www.mckinsey.com/featured-insights/diversity-and-inclusion/diversity-wins-how-inclusion-matters

47. https://womenintheworkplace.com/2018

48. Dobbin, Frank and Kalev, Alexandra. Why Diversity Programs Fail. https://hbr.org/2016/07/why-diversity-programs-fail. July/August 2016.

49. Coffman, Julie; Bax, Bianca; Noether, Alex; and Blair, Brenen. The Fabric of Belonging: How to Weave an Inclusive Culture. https://www.bain.com/insights/the-fabric-of-belonging-how-to-weave-an-inclusive-culture/. 2022.

50. Kendi, Ibram X. (2019). *How to Be an Antiracist*. One World.

51. DiAngelo, Robin. (2018). *White Fragility*. Beacon Press.

52. Livingston, Robert. (2021). *The Conversation: How Seeking and Speaking the Truth About Racism Can Radically Transform Individuals and Organizations*. Crown Currency.

53. McDonald, Kelly. (2021). *It's Time to Talk about Race at Work: Every Leader's Guide to Making Progress on Diversity, Equity, and Inclusion*. Wiley.

54. Collins, Jim. (2001). *Good to Great: Why Some Companies Make the Leap and Others Don't*. Harper Business.

55. Collins, Jim. Chapter 1 (p. 12).

56. Collins, Jim. Chapter 1. (p. 13).

57. Collins, Jim. Chapter 1. (p. 14).

58. Collins, Jim. Chapter 1. (p. 13).

59. Collins, Jim. Chapter 1. (p. 14).

60. Bay, Michael. *Armageddon*. United States: Buena Vista Pictures, 1998.

61. https://www.theatlantic.com/politics/archive/2014/07/population-2043/431130/

62. Lindelof, Damon, and J. J. Abrams. *Lost*. ABC, 2004–2010.

63. Gilligan, Vince. *Breaking Bad*. AMC, 2008–2013.

64. Rowling, J. K. *Harry Potter*. Bloomsbury Publishing, 1997–2007.

65. Martin, George R. R. *A Song of Ice and Fire*. Bantam Spectra, 1996–2011.

66. Kübler-Ross, Elisabeth. (1970). *On Death and Dying: What the Dying Have to Teach Doctors, Nurses, Clergy and Their Own Families*. Collier Books.

67. Kotter, John P. (2012). *Leading Change*. Harvard Business Review Press.

68. Kotter, John P. (2014). *Accelerate*. Harvard Business Review Press.

69. Akala, Adedayo. Cost Of Racism: U.S. Economy Lost $16 Trillion Because Of Discrimination, Bank Says. https://www.npr.org/sections/live-updates-protests-for-racial-justice/2020/09/23/916022472/cost-of-racism-u-s-economy-lost-16-trillion-because-of-discrimination-bank-says. 2020.

70. Roy, Katica. How the gender pay gap cuts through the U.S. economy. https://www.fastcompany.com/90449297/how-the-gender-pay-gap-cuts-through-the-u-s-economy. 2020.

71. Lorenzo, Rocio and Reeves, Martin. How and Where Diversity Drives Financial Performance. https://hbr.org/2018/01/how-and-where-diversity-drives-financial-performance. 2018.

72. https://grow.betterup.com/resources/the-value-of-belonging-at-work-the-business-case-for-investing-in-workplace-inclusion

73. L. Harris, Omar. (2023). *Leading Change: The 4 Keys (Context, Confidence, Construction, and Culture)*. Intent Books.

74. Goldman Sachs. *The Shadow of the Leader*. Goldman Sachs, 2013.

75. Schwarz, Nira. *The Self-Awareness Paradox: Why We Perceive Ourselves More Accurately Than Others Do, but Are Still Biased in Our Self-Perceptions*. Current Directions in Psychological Science 17, no. 1 (2008): pp. 18-22.

76. Luft, J., and Ingham, H. (1955). T*he Johari Window: A graphic model of interpersonal awareness. Proceedings of the Western Training Laboratory in Group Development*. Los Angeles, CA: UCLA.

77. Shermer, Michael. (2012). *The Believing Brain: From Ghosts and Gods to Politics and Conspiracies—How We Construct Beliefs and Reinforce Them as Truths*. St. Martin's Griffin.

78. Gladwell, Malcolm. (2007). *Blink: The Power of Thinking Without Thinking*. Back Bay Books.

79. Gladwell, Malcolm. (2021). *Talking to Strangers: What We Should Know about the People We Don't Know*. Back Bay Books.

80. Bachmann, Hugh; Ligon, Robin; and Skerritt, Dominic. The powerful role financial incentives can play in a transformation. https://www.mckinsey.com/capabilities/transformation/our-insights/the-powerful-role-financial-incentives-can-play-in-a-transformation. January 2022.

81. Sinek, Simon. (2011). *Start with Why: How Great Leaders Inspire Everyone to Take Action*. Portfolio.

82. Lencioni, Patrick. (2000). *The Four Obsessions of an Extraordinary Executive: A Leadership Fable*. Jossey-Bass.

83. SEC Charges Ernst & Young, Three Audit Partners, and Former Public Company CAO with Audit Independence Misconduct. June 28, 2021. https://www.sec.gov/news/press-release/2021-144.

84. https://www.frc.org.uk/directors/corporate-governance/corporate-culture/case-study-gsk-glaxosmithkline

85. McChesney, Chris. (2022). *The 4 Disciplines of Execution: Revised and Updated: Achieving Your Wildly Important Goals*. Simon & Schuster.

86. Humphrey, A. S. (1972). SWOT analysis: A tool for strategic planning. *Management Review*. 61(7), pp. 63–70.

87. Martin, Roger L and Lafley, A.G. (2013). *Playing to Win: How Strategy Really Works*. Harvard Business Review Press.

88. https://www.psychologicalscience.org/news/the-unintended-consequences-of-company-wellness-penalties.html

89. L. Harris, Omar. (2021). *Be a J.E.D.I. Leader, Not a Boss: Leadership in the Era of Corporate Social Justice, Equity, Diversity, and Inclusion.* Intent Books.

90. Rogers, Everett M. (2003). *Diffusion of Innovations.* Free Press.

91. Burkus, David. Get Buy-In for Your Crazy Idea. https://hbr.org/2015/06/how-to-get-buy-in-for-your-crazy-idea. 2015.

92. https://www.coso.org/

93. https://www.coso.org/guidance-on-ic

94. https://www.iso.org/standard/62342.html

95. Taiichi Ohno. (1988). *Toyota Production System: Beyond Large-Scale Production.* Productivity Press.

96. Rodriguez-Perez, Jose. (2022). *Handbook of Investigation and Effective CAPA Systems.* ASQ Quality Press.

97. https://www.kornferry.com/insights/this-week-in-leadership/your-chief-diversity-officer-is-likely-leaving

98. https://inclusionlearninglab.com/dei-leaders-struggle-to-cope-with-burnout-what-you-can-do-to-help/

99. https://theenergyproject.com/solutions/featured-programs/energy-audit-individuals/

100. https://theenergyproject.com/approach/

101. Chamorro-Premuzic, Tomas. How Much Is Bad Sleep Hurting Your Career? https://hbr.org/2020/07/how-

much-is-bad-sleep-hurting-your-career. July 2020.

102. Burns, Stephanie. The Importance Of Cultivating A Passion Outside Of Work. https://www.forbes.com/sites/stephanieburns/2020/03/07/the-importance-of-cultivating-a-passion-outside-of-work/?sh=7e30af35339e. March 2020.

103. Schlefer, Gwen. How Meditation Benefits The Working Brain. https://www.huffpost.com/entry/how-meditation-benefits-the-working-brain_b_57d15638e4b0273330ac36da. September 2016.

104. Hirsch, Arlene. S. From Work/Life Balance to Work/Life Integration. https://www.shrm.org/resourcesandtools/hr-topics/employee-relations/pages/from-worklife-balance-to-worklife-integration. May 2023.

105. Barnes, Christopher M. Sleep Well, Lead Better. https://hbr.org/2018/09/sleep-well-lead-better. Sept/Oct. 2018.

106. Beck, Julie. The Concept Creep of Emotional Labor. https://www.theatlantic.com/family/archive/2018/11/arlie-hochschild-housework-isnt-emotional-labor/576637/. November 2018.

107. Stahl, Ashley. How Meditation Can Boost Your Career. https://www.forbes.com/sites/ashleystahl/2018/10/12/how-meditation-can-boost-your-career/?sh=d6bbabd37017. Oct 2018.

108. Hanh, Thich Nhat. (1996). *The Miracle of Mindfulness: An Introduction to the Practice of Meditation.* Penguin Random House.

109. Kalev, Alexandra and Dobbin, Frank. The Surprising Benefits of Work/Life Support. https://hbr.org/2022/09/

the-surprising-benefits-of-work-life-support. September–October 2022.

110. Covey, Steven R. (2020). *The 7 Habits of Highly Effective People: 30th Anniversary Edition.* Simon & Schuster.

111. Clifton, Jim and Harter, Jim. (2019). *It's the Manager: Moving from Boss to Coach.* Gallup Press. Chapter 8 (p. 36).

112. Suellentrop, Austin and Bauman, E. Beth. How Influential Is a Good Manager? https://www.gallup.com/cliftonstrengths/en/350423/influential-good-manager.aspx. June 2021.

113. https://www.gallup.com/cliftonstrengths/en/home.aspx.

114. https://corporate.mcdonalds.com/corpmcd/investors/financial-information.html

115. https://corporate.mcdonalds.com/corpmcd/our-company/who-we-are/our-leadership.html

116. Hewlett, Sylvia Ann; Marshall, Melinda; and Sherbin, Laura. How Diversity Can Drive Innovation. https://hbr.org/2013/12/how-diversity-can-drive-innovation. December 2013.

117. https://www.louisianaentertainment.gov/film/motion-picture-production-program

118. David Fincher, dir., *The Curious Case of Benjamin Button* (2008).

119. *Treme.* (2010–2013). Created by David Simon and Eric Overmyer. HBO.

120. https://www.patagonia.com/social-responsibility/

121. https://careers.google.com/benefits/

122. https://www.gallup.com/q12/

123. Connelly, Julie. All Together Now. https://news.gallup.com/businessjournal/763/all-together-now.aspx. March 2002.

124. https://www.ipcc.ch/assessment-report/ar6/

125. https://news.un.org/en/story/2021/08/1097362

126. https://www.globalgoals.org/take-action

127. https://www.un.org/development/desa/dspd/2022/07/sdgs-report

128. Lencioni, Patrick. (2000). *The Four Obsessions of an Extraordinary Executive: A Leadership Fable.* Jossey-Bass.

129. Harris, Lori. Conscious Culture: Insights for Customizing Your Company Culture. https://www.forbes.com/sites/forbescoachescouncil/2020/04/23/conscious-culture-insights-for-customizing-your-company-culture/?sh=5e56de097396. Apr 2020.

130. https://www.decadirect.org/articles/the-gray-zone-resources-to-foster-ethical-decision-making-skills

131. McChesney, Chris. (2022). *The 4 Disciplines of Execution: Revised and Updated: Achieving Your Wildly Important Goals.* Simon & Schuster.

132. https://www.simplus.com/case-studies/franklincovey/

133. https://resources.franklincovey.com/all-case-studies

134. Carpi, Raffaele; Douglas, John; and Gascon, Frédéric. Performance management: Why keeping score is so important, and so hard. https://www.mckinsey.com/capabilities/operations/our-insights/performance-management-why-keeping-score-is-so-important-and-so-hard. October 2017.

135. https://intelliven.com/subtools/accountability-boards/

136. https://www.isc.hbs.edu/strategy/creating-a-successful-strategy/Pages/making-strategic-trade-offs.aspx

137. https://www.mbaknol.com/modern-management-concepts/paradoxical-thinking/

138. https://www.indeed.com/career-advice/career-development/win-win-strategy

139. Miller, Kelsey. How To Influence Without Authority in the Workplace. https://online.hbs.edu/blog/post/influence-without-authority. October 2019.

140. Holzer, Allison; Spataro, Sandra; and Baron, Jen Grace. *Dare to Inspire: Sustain the Fire of Inspiration in Work and Life.* (2019). Da Capo Lifelong Books.

141. Raab, Diana. Self-Awareness and Setting Intentions. https://www.psychologytoday.com/us/blog/the-empowerment-diary/202201/self-awareness-and-setting-intentions. January 2022.

ABOUT THE AUTHOR

Omar L. Harris is a former pharmaceutical General Manager (GSK, Allergan), Intent Consulting founder, motivational speaker, executive coach, and best-selling author, with over twenty years of experience building high- performance organizations on four continents. Having managed multibillion dollar brands and led extensive organizations while working in the Middle East, Asia, Latin America, and the US, he innovated blueprints for J.E.D.I. Leadership (leading with justice, equity, diversity, and inclusion), servant leadership, change leadership, and Twenty Team Performance Acceleration Principles (TPAPs) that can be applied by leaders at all levels of professional experience.

He is the author of eight titles: *One Blood* (under pseudonym Qwantu Amaru); *From Authors to Entrepreneurs* (with co-authors Stephanie Casher and James W. Lewis); *Leader Board: The DNA of High-Performance Teams*; *The Servant Leader's Manifesto*; *Be a J.E.D.I. Leader, Not a Boss: Leadership in the Era of Corporate Social Justice, Equity, Diversity, and Inclusion*; *Hire the Right W.H.O.M.*; *Leading Change: The 4 Keys*; and *The J.E.D.I. Leader's Playbook: The Insider's Guide to Eradicating*

Injustices, Eliminating Inequities, Expanding Diversity, and Enhancing Inclusion.

Omar is passionate about helping people live their best lives via the adoption of servant leadership principles. He feels that to accomplish this mission, leadership must evolve beyond the top-down hierarchical status quo into inverted hierarchies that embrace inclusion and diversity while eradicating injustices and eliminating inequities. Omar feels that shifting to this kind of structure is needed to achieve the higher-order goals of more outcomes for more stakeholders—including employees, customers, communities, the environment, and shareholders.

Omar resides in Charlotte, North Carolina with his family. In his spare time, he loves traveling the world, connecting with and experiencing diverse cultures and people, and reading for inspiration and pleasure—all while staying in close touch with his closest friends and family.

www.omarlharris.com
www.intentconsultants.co
www.jedileader.com
LinkedIn: omarlharris/
Facebook: @authorleadercoach
X (Twitter): @strengthsleader
Instagram: omarl.harris

EXCERPT FROM *LEADING CHANGE: THE 4 KEYS*

Embracing the Power of Change

Change is an undeniable force that shapes our personal lives, our communities, and the organizations we belong to. In today's dynamic and ever-evolving business landscape, the ability to effectively lead and navigate change has become a critical skill for leaders at all levels. This chapter will explore the importance of change leadership, the need for adaptability, and the key elements for setting the stage for successful organizational change.

The Importance of Change Leadership

Change leadership is not just a buzzword or a passing trend. It is a fundamental competency that can determine the success or failure of an organization. In an era of rapid technological advancements, shifting customer expectations, and global competition, organizations must be agile, flexible, and capable of adapting to change. Change leadership provides the guidance and direction necessary to navigate these turbulent waters and turn change into a strategic advantage.

As a change leader, you play a pivotal role in inspiring and guiding your team and organization through the complexities of change. You are the catalyst who ignites the transformational journey—the one who sets the vision, aligns stakeholders, and empowers individuals to embrace change. Your ability to effectively communicate, engage, and motivate others during times of change can have a profound impact on the success of the organization and the well-being of its employees.

The Need for Adaptability in Today's Business Landscape

The business landscape of today is characterized by constant disruption and uncertainty. Markets shift, technologies evolve, and customer preferences change at an unprecedented pace. Organizations that fail to adapt are left behind, while those that embrace change with open arms thrive and lead the way. Adaptability has become a key competitive advantage, allowing organizations to respond swiftly to emerging trends, seize new opportunities, and stay ahead of the curve.

As a leader, your willingness to embrace change and cultivate adaptability within your organization is paramount. You must create a culture that encourages experimentation, learning from failures, and continuous improvement. By fostering an environment that values agility and embraces change as a natural part of the business, you position your organization for long-term success in a constantly evolving landscape.

Setting the Stage for Successful Organizational Change

To embark on a successful change journey, it is crucial to set the stage effectively. Setting the stage involves laying a solid foundation, aligning stakeholders, and establishing a clear direction for change. The following key elements contribute to setting the stage for successful organizational change:

- **Anticipation and Planning:** Anticipating change allows leaders to respond proactively rather than reactively. By recognizing emerging trends, shifts in the industry, or potential challenges, change leaders can take preemptive measures to prepare their organization for what lies ahead. This proactive approach enables them to stay ahead of the curve and seize opportunities for growth and innovation.

- **Vision and Purpose:** A compelling vision serves as a guiding light, providing a clear direction and purpose for change. It inspires and motivates employees, helping them understand the why behind the change—and the benefits it brings about.

- **Change Readiness:** Assessing the organization's readiness for change is crucial. This involves understanding the current state, identifying potential barriers, and gauging the organization's capacity to embrace and implement change successfully.

- **Leadership Alignment:** Change initiatives require strong leadership alignment. Leaders must be united in their commitment to change, ensuring consistency and coherence in messaging, decision-making, and actions throughout the organization.

- **Stakeholder Engagement:** Engaging stakeholders at all levels is essential for change success. By involving key stakeholders early on, actively listening to their perspectives, and addressing their concerns, you build a sense of ownership and collective responsibility for the change process.

Embracing the power of change is not merely an option; it is an imperative for leaders in today's dynamic business landscape. By recognizing the importance of change leadership, fostering adaptability, and setting the stage for successful organizational change, you lay the groundwork for a transformational journey that can propel your organization to new heights.

In the chapters ahead, we will delve deeper into the intricacies of change leadership, exploring practical strategies, tools, and insights to guide you through the complexities of leading organizational change.

Thank you for reading this book! Please post a review on Amazon.com at your earliest convenience!

Made in the USA
Columbia, SC
23 December 2023